Playing for Time

War on an Asiatic Fleet Destroyer

Lodwick H. Alford

MILITARY MONOGRAPH 93
BENNINGTON, VERMONT
2012

First published in 2006 by the Merriam Press

Third Edition (2012)

Copyright © 2006 by Lodwick H. Alford
Book design by Ray Merriam
Additional material copyright of named contributors.

All rights reserved.
No part of this book may be used or reproduced in any manner whatsoever without written permission, except in the case of brief quotations embodied in critical articles or reviews.

WARNING
The unauthorized reproduction or distribution of this copyrighted work is illegal. Criminal copyright infringement, including infringement without monetary gain, is investigated by the FBI and is punishable by up to five years in federal prison and a fine of $250,000.

The views expressed are solely those of the author.

ISBN:9781475020496
Merriam Press #MM93-P

This work was designed, produced, and published in
the United States of America by the

Merriam Press
133 Elm Street Suite 3R
Bennington VT 05201

E-mail: ray@merriam-press.com
Web site: merriam-press.com

The Merriam Press is always interested in publishing new manuscripts on military history, as well as reprinting previous works, such as reports, documents, manuals, articles and other material on military history topics.

Contents

Acknowledgments 5

Chapter 1: Pearl Harbor Attacked 7
Chapter 2: The Asiatic Fleet: USS *Stewart* (DD-224) 15
Chapter 3: War! 33
Chapter 4: Playing for Time 47
Chapter 5: Saga of the USS *Peary* (DD-226) 55
Chapter 6: Japanese Juggernaut Rolls South 63
Chapter 7: Destroyers Win One 73
Chapter 8: Impending Disaster 83
Chapter 9: The Beginning of the End 97
Chapter 10: Baptism of Fire: USS *Stewart* 105
Chapter 11: Abandon Ship! 145
Chapter 12: Allied Defeat! 155
Chapter 13: The Enemy Mops Up 167
Chapter 14: Escape From the Java Sea 175
Chapter 15: Ordeal of *Edsall* and *Whipple* 179
Chapter 16: *Isabel* Runs Gauntlet 187
Chapter 17: "Titivate Ship" 195
Chapter 18: Born Again—Under the Rising Sun 207
Chapter 19: Homeward Bound 217
Chapter 21: Remaining Destroyers and Other Ships 223

Appendix 1: Personae 227

Appendix 2: Recognitions, Decorations and Awards 231

Appendix 3: Ship's Company Personnel of USS *Stewart* (DD-224) at Time of Battle of Badoeng Strait, 20 February, and Abandonment, 22 February 1942 233

Bibliography 239

Brief Biography of Lodwick H. Alford 243

Photographs 115

Acknowledgements

I am deeply indebted to Command Master Chief Signalman William E. Kale for allowing me the use of his personal log of the time *Stewart* was at war to her abandonment. He was also very helpful in making suggestions for the book and for giving me insights on what was going on in crew's quarters of *Stewart*.

I also want to thank very much Mr. John W. Klar and Warship International for permission to use his masterful study of the "Operational History of the USS *Stewart* (DD-224) and the follow-up piece "USS DD-224 (ex-*Stewart*): The Voyage Home."

A debt of gratitude is also owed to Mr. George Saqqal for granting me permission to use material he developed about the service of ex-*Stewart* in the Japanese Navy.

I also wish to thank my wife Frances DuPriest Park Alford for encouragement, patience and forbearance in enduring late hours and a husband lost in history made over fifty years ago.

It is also hoped that this book will furnish some basis for bragging rights of my children and grandchildren when they ask that old question, "What did you do in the war, Granddaddy?"

Chapter 1

Pearl Harbor Attacked

IT was 2 o'clock early on the morning of 8 December, 1941 on board the old four-stack destroyer USS *Stewart* (DD-224) then peacefully anchored in the harbor of Tarakan on the northeast coast of the island of Borneo, Netherlands East Indies. The petty officer of the watch was eagerly looking forward to about 3:30 am when he would awaken his relief to assume the watch from 4 am to 8 am. It had been a long and uneventful time since he came on watch at midnight—the universally dreaded midwatch or graveyard shift as some sailors called it.

But at that moment it was 7 am on the Sunday morning of 7 December, 1941 at Pearl Harbor, the Hawaiian Islands, where the bulk of the U.S. Pacific Fleet was anchored or moored to Ford Island. For them a terrible calamity was impending. Japanese planes from aircraft carriers were airborne approaching Pearl Harbor from the north loaded with bombs and torpedoes. Most experienced travelers will recognize the difference in dates because of the international dateline in mid-Pacific Ocean where one adds a day to the calendar when crossing the 180th meridian from west to east longitude.

The attack at Pearl Harbor came at 7:53 am on 7th of December. It was then 2:53 am the 8th on board *Stewart* but word on the start of the war did not reach the ship until 0325.[1] It came by radio as an urgent message from the Commander-in-Chief, Asiatic Fleet to the Asiatic Fleet, "Japan started hostilities, govern yourselves accordingly." But we on board *Stewart* knew nothing about how the war started. We in the Asiatic Fleet had always assumed that if and when the war started, we would be the first ones hit by the Japanese Fleet. Little did we know.

The radioman on watch upon receiving the message quickly rushed down to the captain's quarters and showed it to our skipper, Lieutenant Commander Harold Page Smith, Class of 1924 at the Naval Academy. And as quickly he awakened the commodore in his cabin

---

[1] Navy time runs on 24 hour clocks. Thus 0325 is 3:25 a.m., 1525 is 3:25 p.m., 2159 is 9:59 p.m., 2359 is 1159 p.m. and so on. It is not necessary to write a.m. or p.m. nor to use the word "hours."

adjacent to the radio room. The Commodore, Commander Thomas Howell Binford, Class of 1920, who was Commander Destroyer Division 58, of which *Stewart* was his flagship, briefly conferred with Captain Smith while still in their bathrobes. They quickly got dressed as General Quarters sounded.

It was 0345 in what seemed the middle of the night when the crew of the *Stewart* were awakened by those chilling words "Man your battle stations, we are at war." The petty officer of the watch no longer needed to worry whether his relief was awake. It was an eerie feeling to be startled out of a sound sleep when the alarm was sounded and to learn quickly that the war had started. I shuddered as a cold shiver went up my spine. I pulled on something hurriedly and climbed the three ladders from my cabin just forward of the wardroom to my battle station on the director platform above the piloting and navigation bridge. From this station, Lieutenant(jg) Lodwick Alford, gunnery officer (yours truly), controlled the main battery of four 4-inch/.50 caliber guns using the gunfire control director. By telephone I also controlled our .50 cal. machine guns on the galley[2] deck house and our one anti-aircraft gun, 3-inch/.23 cal. located on the fantail. The word was promptly put out to make all preparations for war. We already had some ready ammunition for the guns but now we filled all ready ammunition boxes. Torpedo warheads were installed. Airflasks were charged. Depth charges were armed. Recoil cylinders were topped off. Darken ship measures were perfected and unnecessary lights doused. In the darkness before dawn I made my way down to the main deck and commenced checking the gun crews at their guns as preparations were being made.

First I went to the No. 1 four-inch gun on the forecastle[3] forward of the bridge superstructure. It was soon apparent that tension was high among the men and emotions seemed to run the gamut from apprehension to exhilaration that the war was now on and lets get on with it. Some wanted to talk while others seemed to be lost in their private thoughts. Maybe it was my imagination but my presence seemed to have a reassuring and calming effect.

---

[2] The galley is where food is cooked and prepared for the crew.
[3] In old sailing ships such as in Columbus' day the forward parts of the ships were built up above the main deck somewhat resembling a castle and designated the forecastle. The word was mostly pronounced as "fo'c's'le" with two syllables. On these ships there were no structures above the main deck on the bow and the word just indicated the forward part of the ship.

Proceeding aft through the superstructure on to the quarterdeck,[4] past number one stack, I reached the midship deckhouse where the galley is located between number two and three stacks. Climbing the ladder leading to the top, I reached numbers 2 and 3 four-inch guns and our two .50 cal. machine guns. The mood and demeanor of the gun crews there seemed to be about the same as those on the forecastle with perhaps a bit more confidence. Descending again to the main deck still in darkness I proceeded aft on the portside past number four stack. The quadruple stacks of these small destroyers were their most distinguishing characteristic recognizable from great distances. The ships were nearly always lovingly referred to as "four stackers" or sometimes as "four-pipers" Next on the portside were two triple tube torpedo mounts where the torpedomen in low voices with small flashlights were busy arming and setting running depths for the deadly "fish."[5] Walking along the main deck of *Stewart* I was aware of the 315 ft length and narrow 31-foot beam of these 1200-ton ships. The shallow draft of 11 to 12 feet further gave me a sense of the slimness and fragility of the ship.

Now reaching the after deckhouse on top of which No. 4 four-inch gun was mounted, I tried to speak some words of encouragement to the gun crew as well as those manning the 6-inch/.23 cal. anti-aircraft gun on the fantail.[6] Noting that men were busy checking the settings of the depth charges in their racks at the stern of the ship, I also noted that dawn was beginning to break. Hurriedly I made my way forward up the starboard side past two more triple tube mounts, across the quarterdeck and climbed back to my battle station as word was passed to make preparations for getting underway. As soon as it was daylight enough to see well we commenced stripping unnecessary wood and other flammables from the ship. We went about these tasks with a will and as we did so I could not help but think-how has it come to pass that this small ship in this place has perhaps reached her destiny? Will we and our sisterships be sunk by the superior Japanese Fleet?

---

[4] The quarterdeck is a place usually on the main deck designated for official functions or ceremonies such as rendering honors to visiting flag officers or other dignitaries.
[5] In these ships torpedoes were always referred to as "fish."
[6] The fantail is the area of the main deck farthest aft on the ship-the stern. Looking down on the ship with the propeller guards protruding from the extreme stern there is sort of a resemblance to a lobster or shrimp with tails flared out.

Then my whole life began to parade through my mind as they say happens when one is suddenly thrust into a life or death situation. Where was I born? Where did I come from? Has my life and a promising career been destined to come to naught? Was my adorable and adoring young wife never destined for fulfillment? How did I get here or more to the point what the hell is Lodwick Houston Alford doing here at this time in this place?

In one sense it is a long story of 27 years from my 1914 birth in Sylvester, Georgia to the remote island of Borneo at a place hardly anyone ever heard of. In another sense it seems like yesterday. As a small boy at the end of World War I, I became aware that one of my uncles had served in the Navy and in the early 1920's one of my half brothers enlisted in the Navy. I was fascinated when he came home on leave and told us about Navy ships. In grade school when I learned about the U.S. Naval Academy I knew instantly that I wanted to go there and single-mindedly set graduation as my goal. I sought a congressional appointment to the Academy but none were available.

Upon learning that the Secretary of the Navy could make up to 100 appointments each year from enlisted men of the fleet, I determined to go that route. Enlisting in the Navy in August 1932 and completing boot camp later that year, I was assigned to the battleship *Mississippi* for a year before being sent to the Naval Academy Prep Class at the Naval Base, Norfolk, Virginia. This was a school run by the Navy for the noble purpose of preparing ambitious young enlisted men to pass the Naval Academy entrance examinations. In the tests of April 1934 I passed and late that summer was transferred to Annapolis where I was discharged from enlisted status and sworn in as a midshipman.

The four years at the Academy were exciting and memorable. With over two years enlisted service, the marching, drills and discipline part of it were a piece of cake and I managed to get through plebe year without a single demerit. But academics were another matter. The high school in Georgia, while excellent, had not adequately prepared me for the fast-paced, "book of the month club" advanced math courses at the Academy. It was a difficult academic struggle at first but got better as the four years went by. On Christmas leave in 1935 I paid the first social call on my future bride Katherine Kirkland. At the end of the four years came June Week and graduation. My fiancée could not come but my mother came and my was she proud! She had worked so hard to educate her children. President Franklin D. Roosevelt gave the graduation address and delivered our diplomas with a firm handshake.

A few moments later on 2 June 1938 I was commissioned Ensign, U.S. Navy and assigned to the new construction light cruiser USS *Phoenix* (CL-46) for my first duty as an officer.

Phoenix was at that time building in a commercial shipyard in Camden, New Jersey across the Delaware River from the Naval Shipyard, Philadelphia. Late in the summer of 1938 she was moved over to the shipyard, fitted out and commissioned. This was followed by a great shakedown cruise on the east coast of South America. In early 1939 *Phoenix* transited the Panama Canal and was assigned to the Pacific Fleet then homeported at Long Beach, California. With the coming of the war in Europe and the rising tensions in the Far East, the fateful decision was made to move the Fleet, including *Phoenix*, to Pearl Harbor.

It was a great two years on board USS *Phoenix*. I spent several months in navigation, communications, engineering and gunnery qualifying in each department. And I achieved perhaps the most sought after qualification of a young aspiring officer, that of Officer-of-the-Deck Underway. Finally I was permanently assigned to the gunnery department as Turret 4 Officer. *Phoenix* had five turrets each of which had three rapid-fire 6-inch guns firing semi-fixed ammunition. In this capacity my reputation and expertise in gunnery steadily increased. We won the coveted "E" for excellence in gunnery and I received a nice letter of commendation signed by none other than the future Commander of the Pacific Fleet, Admiral Husband E. Kimmel.

Towards the end of my two years on board *Phoenix*, the ship was again ordered to visit South America but this time on a goodwill cruise down the west coast. We felt the ship was picked for this tour because of the good impression *Phoenix* had made on our shakedown cruise. The west coast also was a great cruise and at Valparaiso, Chile, my detachment orders were received. The captain allowed me to leave at Panama when the ship put in there on her return voyage to Pearl Harbor. So it was August 1940 when I finally said goodbye to my two-year shipmates of *Phoenix*. During the war I would see the ship again in unusual, fearsome and dangerous circumstances. We were both lucky to have survived. Proceeding by Pan American clipper from Panama to Miami, thence by train to my hometown Sylvester, I was married to my fiancée on 10 August 1940. After a brief and abortive interlude at flight training in Pensacola, Florida I received orders to proceed by first available transportation to Manila, The Philippines, and report to the Commander-in-Chief, Asiatic Fleet for further assignment. Subsequent orders were received to sail on the SS *President Pierce* from San

Francisco, California in early December. A request for my bride to travel with me to the Far East was denied. Tensions were already high out there and rising all the time. No more dependents were allowed to travel to Manila and those already out there were being sent home.

Arriving in San Francisco on 5th December I reported in to the Commandant, 12th Naval District and was given further orders from the Commander, Asiatic Fleet assigning me to the four-stack destroyer USS *Alden* (DD-211) upon my arrival in Manila. That was fine with me and I began to look forward to it remembering how I had grown to like these little warships. *President Pierce* sailed at 1500 on 6 December and as we passed under the Golden Gate Bridge I said a prayer and made a note in my journal, "Goodbye to USA. Hope to be back." Much to my surprise and delight I found two of my classmates also on board as well as several other officers en route to the Asiatic Fleet. The classmates were Howard P. Fischer and F. Bruce Garrett, great friends and shipmates.

The ship made just one brief call at Honolulu and then set course for Yokohama, Japan. On the long haul from Hawaii to Japan I began to think more and more about serving on board four stack destroyers. I had learned to like these sleek, fast ships when I had observed them in the Norfolk Naval Shipyard back in 1933 and 1934. Then at the Academy my class spent second class summer cruising up and down the east coast on the old four-stackers. I was assigned to the *Babbitt* (DD-128) and was quartered way down below in the forward crew compartment with pipe bunks and horizontal clothes lockers. To find an item you stirred with a locker stick. Little did I think that I would ever be assigned to an old four-piper, and much less riding one of them into battle.

On Sunday, 15 December 1940 the *President Pierce* crossed the 180th meridian from west to east longitude[7] and at the next minute it was the next day Monday 16th. It was mind-boggling at first and required a bit of getting used to. Some ships have elaborate ceremonies on crossing the 180th meridian similar to those on crossing the equator. We did not have a ceremony but were given fancy nautical language certificates attesting to the fact. But more important was the fact

---

[7] Longitude is the meridian of any spot on earth measured east or west up to 180 degrees from zero degree at Greenwich, England. In this case we were at the international dateline which is 180 degrees and exactly on the other side of the world from Greenwich. Sailing west one day had to be added to the calendar.

that we had "chopped." That is, we had passed out of the domain of the Commander, Pacific Fleet to that of the Commander, Asiatic Fleet. Now we officers on board *President Pierce* had a new boss, Admiral[8] Thomas C. Hart, CINCAF.

Now as the *President Pierce* approached the Empire of Japan we officers on board seemed to experience thoughts and emotions ranging from curiosity to apprehension. It was not exactly fear but was a healthy respect for the formidable armed forces of the Empire. We had seen those photos and silhouettes of wicked looking Japanese battleships with tall pagoda masts. We had experienced the anger over the ruthlessness of Japan in dealing with any nation that got in her way such as the U.S. river gunboats on Chinese rivers. And we were well aware of the rising tension between the United States and Japan. In retrospect it is perhaps significant that we had not seen photos and were not aware of the new aircraft carriers, heavy cruisers and destroyers Japan had added to their fleets. We did not know of their lethal torpedoes.

President Pierce arrived in Yokohama on Friday 20 December and we classmates promptly took shore leave and caught a train for Tokyo. We just had the afternoon and barely had time to see the Emperor's Palace grounds, a bit of downtown Tokyo and the old Imperial Hotel built by Frank Lloyd Wright which had withstood the terrible earthquake of 1923. This was our first trip to the Orient and we were fascinated by the sights, sounds and smells. The women were especially interesting in their kimonos and obis. The war was less than eleven months away but we could not detect the slightest evidence of the rising tension between our two nations. However, perhaps my most lasting impression of Japan was the high number of Japanese Army officers with clanking swords at their sides swaggering about the streets everywhere we looked.

The next day we sailed for a short overnight trip to Kobe, Japan. This was a brief port of call at a commercial port and *President Pierce* again sailed on 23 December en route to fabulous Hong Kong, British Crown Colony. The ship had also been scheduled to call at the port of Shanghai, China but this was cancelled. I could never find out why but there were rumors the Japanese were causing trouble. It was a three day voyage from Kobe to Hong Kong and we were at sea on Christmas Day. We made the best of it and had a good dinner with Christ-

---

[8] Admiral rank with no prefix has four stars on his flag and is senior to vice admiral with three or rear admiral with two stars.

mas music and decorations but a minimum of gifts to be opened. My thoughts were with my family back home in Sylvester.

The day after Christmas the ship arrived in storied, exotic Hong Kong. Howard Fischer, Bruce Garrett and I went on shore leave and visited the city proper on Victoria Island and Kowloon, also a part of the Crown Colony. There we savored the Victorian delights of the famous old Peninsula Hotel. Hong Kong was and is one of the most fascinating places on earth. One can only hope that the takeover of Hong Kong by Communist China in 1997 will eventually soften the hard-line Red Regime.

The next day, Friday, the 27th, *President Pierce* sailed from Hong Kong and arrived in Manila Bay late on the 28th. Shortly a staff officer from Asiatic Fleet Headquarters came on board with some changes to orders. Mine were modified to divert me from the USS *Alden* (DD-211) to the USS *Stewart* (DD-224). In those days Bureau of Naval Personnel (BUPERS) normally did not order officers to specific ships by name out there. In effect Commander-in-Chief Pacific Fleet had his own little BUPERS in the Far East.

Chapter 2

The Asiatic Fleet

USS *Stewart* (DD-224)

A ND so at 1900 on Saturday, 28 December 1940, I reported aboard the old four-stack destroyer USS *Stewart* for duty. Thus did I join the wonderful wacky world of the Asiatic Fleet. Immediately upon climbing the ladder to the quarterdeck and saluting the flag I was promptly introduced to one of the oldest traditions in the Fleet. The duty officer who was the only officer on board, gave me the duty on the spot, granted himself shore leave and went ashore. There I was within five minutes of reporting aboard, the only officer on the ship, not knowing anyone and with the responsibility of the ship and safety of the crew on my hands. It was a sobering thought as well as a heady one. Here I was a young ensign just two and a half years out of the Academy and abruptly handed the buck. I made myself known to the senior petty officers of the watch very quickly.

The action of the duty officer in going ashore after I relieved him was understandable. This was between Christmas and New Years Day and the ship had been on holiday routine for some time. There were parties and family gatherings ashore. But more importantly dependent wives and families were being sent home because of the rising tension in the Far East. Indeed some of the wives of the officers and men of the *Stewart* departed on the *President Pierce* which sailed from Manila on her return voyage stateside a few days after we disembarked. I did not even get to meet the departing ladies including the wives of the captain[9] and the commodore[10] of the Destroyer Division Fifty-Eight.

---

[9] The captain of a Navy ship is always spoken of orally and sometimes in casual writing as "Captain" although he may be of any rank such as lieutenant commander.

[10] The commander of two or a group of ships is always spoken of orally and sometimes in casual writing as "Commodore" although he too may be of any rank such as captain. There is an exception—if the commander of a group of ships is in any of the ranks of admiral, he is addressed that way. In

continued...

The next day was Sunday and continuing holiday routine so I had an opportunity to bone up[11] on the history of the ship. USS *Stewart* was built at the William Cramp & Sons Ship & Engine Building Co. Philadelphia, Pennsylvania. Her keel was laid 9 September 1919 and she was launched 4 March, 1920. Her sponsor was Mrs. Margaretta Stewart Stevens, granddaughter of Rear Admiral Charles Stewart of War of 1812 fame, for whom the ship was named. She cost $1.5 million and was first commissioned on 15 September 1920. Her designed speed was 35 knots but on her trials she made 35.76 knots.

The old adage "Join the Navy and See the World" was certainly true for any sailor who might have stayed on board during the entire career of *Stewart*. From her commissioning through 1921 she was engaged in fitting out, shakedown, overhauls, training and exercises off the East Coast. In early 1922 she visited ports in the Caribbean Sea and on 20 June 1922 she sailed from Newport, Rhode Island across the Atlantic on a cruise that would eventually take her around the world. She cruised through the Mediterranean Sea with ports of call Gibraltar, Algiers, Malta and Ismalia. She transited the Suez Canal, the Red Sea and the Indian Ocean with calls at Aden, Colombo and Singapore. In August 1922 *Stewart* joined the Asiatic Fleet and soon after visited the first Chinese port of many which were to follow for more than eighteen years. Among these were Shanghai, Hong Kong, Chefoo, Tsingtao, Hankow, Tangku, Amoy and Swatow. There were others.

The following year *Stewart* steamed up to Yokohama, Japan to lend humanitarian assistance to the victims of the great devastating Japanese earthquake of 1923. In 1925 she took a detachment of marines to Shanghai and in 1927 she escorted a convoy of merchant vessels up the Yangtze River as far as Hankow past hostile warlords who peppered the ship with small arms fire. From 1927 to 1932 there was continued fighting between the Nationalist government and warlords and amongst each other with U.S. ships including *Stewart* assisting in the protection of United States citizens. There were more voyages up the Yangtze all the while adhering to the general pattern of Chinese ports

---

...*continued*
    the old Navy there was the rank of commodore but it was not used in the years between the World Wars. It was revived later in World War II, then discontinued and revived again upon the so-called unification of the services. The corresponding rank in the Army and Air Force is brigadier general.

[11] "Bone up" is a midshipman slang term meaning to study.

in summer and Manila or southern ports in winter. Interspersed with these were Cavite shipyard overhauls, dry-docking and tender repairs.

From 1932 to 1936 there were increasing incidents of Japanese aggression in Chinese ports and encroachments on Chinese sovereignty. Again U.S. warships were busy protecting U.S. interests. Meanwhile there were opportunities for shore leave and sightseeing. This letter home from *Stewart* crewman Lloyd C. McKenzie is an example of the glamour side of travel with the Navy to see the world:

> July 27, 1936
> Peking, China
>
> Dear Mother and Dad,
> I'm on leave until the 31st of July, here in Peking. The ship came up to Tangku, and anyone desiring to go to the Great Wall of China was allowed six days leave, so I took the leave and went. We took some pictures and walked along the top of the wall for a long way, where I pulled out a small piece of brick to show you when I come home. I never thought I'd ever get to the Great Wall, but joining the Navy has let me travel more than anyone I know. This morning, the same two guys and I went to The Forbidden City, where centuries ago the emperor lived, away from the rest of the world. Though weeds have been allowed to grow and dirt to gather, it is very pretty and must have cost an enormous amount of money, as there are six marble bridges, solid bronze statues, and Buddhas, some of which stand 15 feet high. This afternoon we're going to the summer palace. When I get home, I'll have a lot of pictures to show you.
> I went up for Seaman 1st Class last week, and I'm pretty sure I made it, but I won't know for about a month and a half. If I did make it, I'll receive 18 dollars more a month. Then when I qualify on the rangefinder, it will be five more dollars a month, making my base pay $59 a month, instead of $36. I have marks this quarter of 4.0, the highest you can get, so there is nothing to stop me there. I'll close for now but will write more often if I've made Seaman 1st Class because I won't have so much studying to do.
>
> Love, Lloyd

In 1937 came the massive invasion of China by Japanese forces and an increased level of tension between the United States and Japan. Later that year the Japanese bombed and sank our river gunboat *Panay*, almost a *casus belli* right there. Tension continued to rise. Another letter home by crewman Lloyd C. McKenzie seems to capture the atmosphere in China at the time:

> Tsingtao, Northern China
> August 17, 1937
>
> Dear Mother, Dad and Dorothy,
>
> I guess I'd better write and let you know I'm O.K., as we're where part of the war is going on, but right now it's quiet. All liberty in Chefoo was cancelled Saturday night, and we headed for Tsingtao—just us and the *Bulmer*. We're now doing patrol duty. We're all set to land if trouble breaks out. We'll have to pick up the American people and take them, probably, to Hong Kong. We received a message to break out all service ammunition. That means warheads on the torpedoes, 500 lbs. of TNT apiece. That's a lot of explosive. I don't believe we'll use them, but we're ready, in case. I think after this trouble, I'll be a veteran of foreign wars and rate a service bar, because the guys got them in '32, when they had trouble up the Yangtze. I hope what I wrote doesn't worry you, because as far as I can see, there is nothing to worry about. Dorothy, I'm having your kimono made, but I don't know when you'll receive it, because I don't know when we'll be going back to Chefoo, if we go back this year, but you'll get it. I sent a tea set to you, but I can't get ashore to send a money order for paying the duty, because there is no liberty.
>
> Love, Lloyd

In 1938 *Stewart* made the usual trek to China, visited French Indochina and searched for a downed Pan American plane east of the Philippines. In 1939 she was at Tsingtao when the war started in Europe and the Asiatic Fleet was ordered back to Manila Bay. In 1940 time in China was cut short and on 9 October *Stewart* left China for the last time for Manila Bay where I found her on Saturday, 28 December 1940. I also had the opportunity on Sunday 29th to look around the ship and started to get acquainted with some of the officers and more of the crew.

The ship was then anchored off the Army-Navy Club in Manila where the officers landing dock was located. The club was the center of social activities for officers of the fleet and featured a famous long bar where women were not allowed. But it was not until Monday, 30 December, that I got to meet the captain, Lieutenant Commander Harold Page Smith, class of 1924, the commodore and the other officers. The commodore at that time was Commander Charles E. Coney, class of 1919 who was a true southern gentleman from Georgia. But he was a short timer and was soon relieved by Commander Thomas H. Binford, class of 1920, as Commander Destroyer Division Fifty-Eight.

The executive officer[12] was Lieutenant John M. Bermingham, class of 1929 who was also the navigator. The gunnery officer was Lieutenant E.C. Long but he too was a short timer and soon left the ship being relieved by Lieutenant junior grade James C. Shaw, class of 1936. The communications and torpedo officer was Lieutenant junior grade Archibald Stone, Jr., class of 1934. The engineering officer was Lieutenant junior grade Edwin L. Kyte, also class of 1936. I had known Lieutenant Shaw and Lieutenant Kyte back at the Naval Academy when we were midshipmen. I did not study Spanish but I knew that Captain Smith had been a Spanish instructor in the Language Department at the Academy. It seemed like a pleasant and congenial wardroom. I was warmly welcomed.

My assigned job on the ships roster of officers was as first lieutenant and being the newest and most junior officer on board I was "George." He is the one who gets the dirty jobs, who is the boat officer if needed, shore patrol officer, commissary officer, ship's stores officer, wardroom mess treasurer and possibly many other jobs depending on how the captain wants to run the ship. When the ship is at sea the most junior officer gets most of the dreaded mid-watches, that is from midnight to 0400. But my primary duty was as first lieutenant and as such I was responsible for maintenance, cleanliness, neatness and general appearance of the sides of the ship, the topsides, the boats, the ground tackle,[13] life rafts, lifelines and all manner of gear on decks. For this I was in charge of the deck force consisting of boatswain's mates, coxswains and seamen. For getting underway from an anchorage or

---

[12] The executive officer of a Navy ship is the next senior in rank to the captain and may be of any rank. If he is of rank below that of commander he is spoken to and of as "Mister." If he is in the rank of commander he is addressed that way. In casual writing and conversation the executive officer may be referred to as "the exec" or simply as "the X.O."

[13] Ground tackle is a general term for the anchors, chain and other associated gear used in anchoring the ship.

dropping the hook[14] on entering port I was in charge on the forecastle in handling the ground tackle, the anchors, chains and associated gear. Or for handling the mooring lines if the ship was tied to a pier. I relished the job and had a great time doing it.

The deck force was a great bunch of sailors. The petty officers were competent, experienced and very knowledgeable about the ship, their shipmates and what it took to get along in the Asiatic Fleet. Some of them were "old China hands" who were much respected and listened to by the younger men. They knew how to scrounge in the shipyard, finagle spare parts and bargain with cumshaw, a term denoting free goods and services.[15] Soon I learned that the ship was affectionately spoken of as the "Stew Maru." Our men were intensely proud of the ship.

It was not long after I reported on board that I began to be regaled with tales of the antics, practical jokes and odd behavior of some of the officers who had preceded me on board *Stewart*. And also of some who were attached to other destroyers in the fleet. There were stories of some who as midshipmen back at the Academy were on the swimming or water polo teams and as officers of the Asiatic Fleet when returning from shore leave late at night at the Army-Navy Club boat landing and finding no boats, would not hesitate to plunge into the water and swim out to their ships at anchor. Sometimes a petty officer of the watch on the quarterdeck was startled by this apparition appearing at the top of the ladder dripping wet and saluting smartly.

Sometimes when an officer was believed to be or suspected of being somewhat prudish, some of his wardroom[16] officer shipmates late at night would sneak aboard a prostitute and have her crawl into the bunk with the target of the prank. And how the embarrassed victim by some strange feat of levitation would move up and over the whore out of the bunk without ever touching her. Uproar and gales of laughter! The captains of the ships had to keep a tight rein on this sort of thing which had the potential for terrible trouble and disciplinary action. For one thing, it might involve a boat crew in sneaking a woman

---

[14] The hook is a slang term for the anchor.
[15] Cumshaw is U.S. sailors pronunciation of a Chinese term "kam sia" meaning a tip, gratuity or bonus and widely used in the Asiatic Fleet and the Far East.
[16] The wardroom on these ships is sort of a combination lounge and dining room for officers.

on board. But by and large the pranks were mostly harmless and made for camaraderie and cohesive wardrooms.

This was the Asiatic Fleet and the officers and men serving in it were or seemed to be a special breed. When one joined the Asiatic Fleet or soon after, it was more than a geographical thing of having gone to serve on a ship in the Far East. When it was said that one had gone "Asiatic," it meant that he was now a free-spirit, a man of the world, perhaps an old China hand prone to walk on the wild side. While this was not true in all cases, nevertheless there was a special aura of dash, panache, air of worldliness and a bit of nuttiness of those in the fleet.

I remember when as an apprentice seaman in boot camp back at the Naval Training Station, Norfolk, I would occasionally go down to the waterfront at the Naval Base and watch Navy ships come and go. Among these was the old transport ship *Chaumont* returning to the states from the Far East with a shipload of sailors who had completed their time in the Asiatic Fleet. Talk about a salty looking bunch, they were the epitome of sea dogs. There were luxuriant beards, handlebar mustaches, swaggering sea legs in tight bell-bottomed trousers and what seemed to be a wild look in their eyes. Gone "Asiatic" meant offbeat appearance, swagger and attitude. Did this include morality? Some said yes, some said no. To say one had gone "Asiatic" could be a compliment or an epithet.

It was commonly said that practically everyone in the Asiatic Fleet was crazy. And that either you were crazy before and that is why you were sent out there or you went crazy after you got out there. Oh, there were good-natured arguments as to which category you were in or when you moved from one category to another. But there seemed to be no doubt that now every one wacko in one way or another. While this is an exaggeration we can with confidence say that the officers and men of the Asiatic Fleet if not unique were certainly a different breed. As long as the wives and families of some of the men of the fleet were still out in the Far East, they acted as an ameliorating influence on behavior. And this included men who were shacked up with native women whether in Manila, China or wherever. Indeed the term "to shack up" came from the Asiatic Fleet where it was true that most of the men who were in such co-habitation with native women lived in nipa shacks. These were small buildings with roofs and sides thatched with nipa, an Asian palm with feathery fronds. Our shacked up men were usually quite loyal to their, in effect, common-law wives who smoothed out their behavior.

But as the wives and families of the officers and men of the Asiatic Fleet were being sent back stateside[17] about the time of my arrival in the Far East and with tension rising steadily, there came the realization in the Fleet that war was inevitable and we had damn well better get ready for it. No longer could service in the Asiatic Fleet be considered nice, relaxed duty in far off exotic places where one could live cheaply with amahs,[18] servants and yardboys—all on a little bit of cumshaw.

Now we turned our attention to such mundane matters as ammunition. Did we have enough of it? Was it any good or had it deteriorated in the magazines? Were our torpedoes really any good? For the first time in about twenty years fleet routine was changed. For many years the fleet spent the winter in Manila and the Philippines and in the summers went up to various ports in China, mostly the northern areas. But no more. As the new year 1941 broke the Fleet Commander scheduled more time at sea in individual ship exercises, division, squadron and fleet exercises in and around the Philippines. Later in the year exercises were expanded south into the Dutch East Indies. At the same time fleet material maintenance and readiness were emphasized.

As the individual ships readiness and training increased, the fighting spirit and morale of the crew increased. The absence of wives and dependents and the influence of other womenfolk did not result in any increase in bad behavior. Neither was there any relaxation of standards or marked changes in attitudes. What little there was manifested itself in growing beards, mustaches and an occasional swear word. But there was a noticeable increase in ship's pride, ship's spirit and what I can best describe as a go for broke, hell for leather attitude. We put to sea in early January and commenced intensive training and exercises.

But then in late January, 1941 we went into the Cavite Naval Shipyard for repairs, drydocking and cleaning of the ship's bottom. In Philippine waters fouling of ship's bottom by barnacles and other marine growth was virulent and reduced ship's speed markedly. Frequent cleaning and application of anti-fouling paint was necessary. At one point the ship was put in a floating drydock up in Subic Bay north of Manila Bay. Later on the ship was hauled on an ancient marine railway

---

[17] Stateside is a Chinese term for the United States which was used in Chinese ports, picked up by U.S. sailors and widely used in the Far East.
[18] Amah, another term picked up in China ports, is a female servant for looking after a baby or small child.

whose machinery creaked and groaned like it was about to expire. The ship looked so precarious sitting high and dry on the marine railway seemingly with no visible signs of support. We were almost afraid to breathe for fear it would topple over and even worried about the wind blowing the ship off her keel blocks. The marine railway was owned and operated under contract to the Navy by an old Scotsman who, according to rumors circulating among the crew was really a spy for the Japanese. We never heard what happened to him after the war started and the enemy forces occupied the Philippines.

Always after a period at sea or in the shipyard there were days at anchor off the Army-Navy Club in Manila Bay. And I was not unmindful of a sense of history in these waters. It was precisely here where we were anchored that the Battle of Manila Bay was fought in 1898, in which Admiral George Dewey defeated the Spanish Fleet, resulting in the Philippines becoming a U.S. possession. Indeed one could occasionally see portions of sunken and wrecked Spanish warships sticking out of the water.

Later in March the ship went south into the central Philippines visiting the port of Cebu on the island of the same name and Iloilo on the island of Panay. I had always had a keen interest in geography and I was fascinated by the hundreds of islands—to mention only a few of the larger ones—Luzon, Mindanao, Negros, Leyte, Mindoro, Samar and Palawan in addition to those already mentioned. Equally fascinating were the passageways and seas among the islands. There was the Sulu Sea, the Sibuyan Sea, the Visayan Sea, the Samar Sea, the Mindanao Sea, the Celebes Sea and numerous straits, gulfs and bays. But where was my beloved blue sea? No where to be seen. The sea was greenish in these waters with flotsam and jetsam everywhere. Whole coconut trees as well as coconuts, kelp and marsh grass were seen floating. Some of these seas are quite deep but still were green.

At the end of March 1941 the ship moved on down into the southern Philippines and the first port of call was Zamboanga, famed in song and story as the real jumping off place to nowhere. The sailors joked that if it were ever decided to give the world an enema, this is where they would insert the tube. The port is on the western tip of the big island of Mindanao and there we moored alongside the destroyer tender *Black Hawk* for overhaul. This repair ship was specially designed for repair of destroyers in forward areas away from shipyards. In addition the ship carried spare parts, torpedoes, depth charges, ammunition and all kinds of stores for destroyers. And most important she carried medical and dental officers and facilities for attending to the health needs of the destroyer men. The destroyers did not normally have medical officers on board nor paymasters. There was a great need for doctors in the fleet to combat malaria, other tropical diseases as well as heat rash and sunburn. And when it was time go on liberty, the paymaster was a popular fellow.

But talk about an exotic place to visit, this was it. In any boat returning sailors or officers from the town to their ships, there was certain to be a burst of singing that old traditional song of the Asiatic Fleet—"Oh, the monkeys have no tails in Zamboanga." There were many verses to the song and many ships added new verses. Another song was the Armored Cruiser Squadron.

During this time a new young officer reported on board. He was Ensign John Thomas Brinkley, Naval Reserve, hometown Memphis, Tennessee and was assigned to share my stateroom. At last I had someone on board junior to me and he immediately became "George". But the Captain was reluctant to allow me to pass on to him some of the collateral duties I had pending Mr. Brinkley proving himself able to cut the mustard. After all officers of the destroyers had been one hundred per cent Naval Academy graduates and the idea of a reserve officer coming on board was somewhat viewed with disdain. Moreover some of us sort of looked on reserve officers as freaks who would never be able to carry the load. I had observed some of them aboard the *President Pierce* on our passage from San Francisco to Manila and was not impressed. But Ensign Brinkley quickly proved affable, eager to learn and quite competent. Ultimately he proved himself to be a wonderful roommate and a great shipmate.

Now our stay in the southern islands was extended six weeks partly for the purpose of familiarization and establishment of forward bases when and if war came. Briefly we visited the port of Davao, on the southern coast of Mindanao then a more extended stop at the port of Parang also on the south coast in the Moro Gulf, an arm of the Celebes Sea. From Parang several of us took buses to the inland city of Cotabato and to Lake Lanao, high in the 9000-plus-foot mountains and about 100 miles in the interior. The cool in the mountains was a welcome respite from the heat on the coast. But most of all this trip was educational. The natives of Mindanao are mostly Moros, Filipinos all right but with a big difference from those in the islands to the north. The Moros are adherents of the Muslim religion whereas those of the northern islands are overwhelmingly Catholic Christian. Not many of us knew that the stars and stripes flew over Muslim lands where polygamy was practiced. It was quite a sight to see a native chieftain walking through the mountains with his wives lined up behind him in order of seniority. The number of wives varied from two to several but was usually about four.

From Parang the ship moved on down the Sulu Archipelago stopping at Tutu Bay, Jolo Island and Tawitawi Island the last in the chain with the great island of Borneo in sight and just across the Sibutu Passage. Each of these places would qualify as among the most wild and exotic places in the world and would give Zamboanga a close race as to the jumping off place of the earth. The waters around Tawitawi were infested with sea snakes, recognized as perhaps the most poisonous in the world. At Jolo Island the local bigwig was the Sultan of Jolo with many wives and life or death power over his subjects. He and his Moro kinsmen on the big island of Mindanao brooked no interference in their customs and traditions by those hated infidels—the Christians of Manila and the north. Every year there were instances where Moros had gone "juramentado", that is, had run amuck killing as many Christians as possible before being killed themselves and thus assuring a place in paradise. In the early days of the U.S. taking over the Philippines after the turn of the century these incidents were quite frequent. A favorite setting for running amuck seemed to be an army post commanders garden party on a peaceful Sunday afternoon with the officers in immaculate white uniforms, the ladies in their finery and Moro servants circulating among the guests with tea and cookies. A Moro bent on "juramentado" would tightly wrap himself with bamboo thongs so that knives and swords would not penetrate. Then when he was ready would suddenly whip out his *kris*, a sharp pointed knife with wavy cutting edges, and wreak great slaughter before he could be brought down. Indeed, U.S. Army pistols of that day would not stop them and the .45 caliber pistol was specifically designed for the purpose of countering Moros running amuck. When nothing else would stop them, the .45 caliber would knock them down by sheer force. Needless to say we of the *Stewart* were quite wary when in the presence of Moros.

Towards the end of May the ship returned to Manila Bay and in June we rode out a typhoon[19] at anchor with all hands on board. And in June the Gunnery Officer, Lt. (jg) James C. Shaw completed his 30 months duty in the Asiatic Fleet and was detached. I was slated to relieve him as Gunnery Officer and welcomed the new job in gunnery,

---

[19] The typhoons of the Pacific are the same weather phenomenon as the hurricanes of the Atlantic Ocean.

my first love. Jim Shaw was a true friend and I hated to lose a great shipmate but I was glad he was going back stateside to rejoin his family. Mr. Brinkley took over as first lieutenant. I had hoped my promotion to Lt. (jg) would come through on 2 June 1941, the third anniversary of graduation from the Naval Academy, but the delay in the mails, the ship being down south away from Manila, all prevented the completion of necessary papers.

An unusual incident occurred on one of our sea training cruises. A young fireman living in the cramped compartment of the engineering department where the bunks are stacked and very close together, had initiated a homosexual contact. Uproar! Several of the men told me they would kill him if he as much as touched them. On orders of the captain we cleared out the little ship's store in the after deckhouse and confined him there under armed guard. This was for his own safety until we returned to port where he was transferred to the brig ashore. This was duly reported by the captain to Admiral Hart who in a later conference of all commanding officers said to them this little gem: "Gentlemen, we have a cocksucker in our midst. Now, my staff chaplain and staff legal officer tell me there is new thinking on this subject and that maybe they can't help it—maybe they are born that way. But I say the hell with all that." And with that the Admiral banged his fist on the conference table and in a firm, clear voice said "GENERAL COURT MARTIAL!" Captain Smith told the wardroom officers of *Stewart* that these were almost the exact words of the Admiral.

In July the ship had to return to the Cavite Naval Shipyard for repairs but this time because of the stifling heat the officers and crew were moved ashore to cooler quarters. Moreover the officers took turns of a few days at Camp John Hay, a resort at Baguio, high in the mountains about 100 miles north of Manila. It was cool up there and those pine trees reminded me of Georgia. Meanwhile tension between Japan and the U.S. was steadily increasing. War seemed inevitable. There was debate as to which side was most responsible for the rising tensions. Certainly there was plenty of blame to go round. Japan had for years been following an aggressive policy of aggrandizement. But the U.S. seemed to be following a policy of pushing Japan into a corner where to them there was no alternative but to fight. This was especially true in regard to cutting off Japan from access to oil. Japan had no oil wells. Sometimes it seemed that the U.S. was trying to provoke a war with Japan.[20] But these matters were not for us to decide. We in the Asiatic Fleet had to do our part to carry out the policies of the U.S. whatever they might be.

The increased exercises at sea greatly reduced the times I could visit the city of Manila. But sometimes I went ashore. A night on the town might include a steak dinner at the A/N Club followed by a visit to the Jai Alai Club. Or we might start out at Jai Alai and try some small stakes gambling on the players. On a few of these occasions I met some of the upper crust Filipinos who were very interesting indeed. This was true also of a few old line Spanish families who fiercely clung to the customs and traditions of the old country. They seemed to be on top of the heap socially followed by the educated Filipinos, the *mestizos* and the natives. The latter came from many tribes, some of whom in the mountains were fearsome head-hunters.

I rarely got to see one of my classmates in the Asiatic Fleet but sometimes would run across one of them at the Army-Navy Club. Bruce Garrett and Howard Fischer who had arrived in the Far East with me on the *President Pierce* went to *John D. Edwards* (DD-216) and *Pillsbury* (DD-227) respectively. When we arrived out there we found two others in destroyers, Bill Spears in *Pope* (DD-225) and Obie Parker in *Parrott* (DD-218). I got to see Obie more than the others because our ships were in the same division. There were three divisions of destroyers of four ships each plus the flagship *Paul Jones* (DD-230) comprising Destroyer Squadron 29. All three divisions were in different training and overhaul cycles and rarely operated or were in port together. Later in the spring another classmate Edmundo Gandia came out and went to *Pillsbury* along with Howard Fischer. Edmundo was that rare bird who on graduation from the Academy had grey hair and looked middle-aged. There were two classmates in submarines out there, Bob Fletcher in *S-38* and Guy Gugliotta in *S-39*. Also Marion Buaas and Hal Hamlin were on board *Houston*. But I don't recall running across any of them until after the war started.

Now the crisis was deepening. Manila Bay had been mined starting back in July. Destroyers were patrolling the entrance to Manila Bay and PBYs of Patrol Wing Ten were making reconnaissance flights in the South China Sea and waters to the north and east of the Philippines. Submarines likewise were patrolling these waters. I remember one occasion when *Stewart* was patrolling off Manila Bay with ship

---

[20] Robert B. Stinnett, *Day of Deceit: The Truth About FDR and Pearl Harbor*, The Free Press, New York, p. 5.

darkened and I was officer of the deck on the midwatch and barely averted a grounding. On the northern leg of the patrol as the ship approached the Bataan Peninsula I made a navigation error but fortunately discovered my mistake in time to change course to deep water. It was there that I began to suspect that I might have a guardian angel.

On into November 1941 the tension between the United States and Japan became white hot. Admiral Hart had intelligence the Japanese Fleet was at sea but no one knew where. It was always assumed that they would hit the Asiatic Fleet first. There was no time to lose. All ships that could move were ordered out of Manila Bay and to head south. Those that could not move were ordered to get ready for sea as soon as possible and then sail. On Tuesday, 25 November 1941, USS *Stewart* sailed from Manila Bay but before departure the executive officer Lieutenant John M. Bermingham was detached to await transportation back to the states. Our new executive officer was Lieutenant Clare B. Smiley.

As *Stewart* exited Manila Bay she turned south and formed screen on the light cruiser USS *Marblehead* (CL-12)[21] and the destroyer tender USS *Black Hawk* (AD-9). Other destroyers in the screen were *Paul Jones* and Destroyer Division 57 consisting of *Alden*, *Barker*, *John D. Edwards* and *Whipple* plus *Edsall* and *Parrott* of Destroyer Division 58 of which *Stewart* was flagship. For some reason unknown to us *Bulmer* of our division remained in Manila Bay as did Destroyer Division 59. *Peary* and *Pillsbury* were in the Cavite Naval Shipyard while *John D. Ford* and *Pope* were patrolling the entrance to the bay. Soon the formation passed through the Mindoro Strait and headed south across the Sulu Sea. Around the decks and in the wardroom there was much discussion going on and there was pretty much the opinion that Admiral Hart was very wise in getting as many ships out of Manila Bay as quickly as he could. It was obvious that war was very close and no one in the Asiatic Fleet wanted to chance being trapped in the bay by the greatly superior Japanese Fleet. It was quite a remarkable turnaround in the esteem of which Admiral Hart was held in the Fleet.

In late 1940 and early 1941 the Admiral had been perhaps the most unpopular officer in the Fleet. This was largely because he had decreed

---

[21] USS *Marblehead* (CL-12) was a 7,000-ton light cruiser of the *Omaha* class (ten ships) built soon after World War I and was both lightly armed and armored. She had four stacks and was frequently mistook for a four stack destroyer and vice versa.

that wives and dependents of Fleet personnel then living in the Far East must be sent home. While the order for evacuation of families had not named just exactly who had originated the order, it was worded in such a way as seeming to imply it might have been the U.S. State Department. Indeed that was exactly my impression when I was ordered to the Asiatic Fleet but my wife was denied travel with me.

But it gradually became known that the Admiral himself had originated the order. This might have been deduced from the fact that that evacuation of Army families was not ordered for some months later. In fairness to the Admiral let it be said that he sent his wife and daughter home with the other evacuees. He suffered the pain of separation from his family and experienced loneliness as did the rest of us. But sending families home was not the only reason he was unpopular in the Far East.

The Admiral on arrival out there and taking command of the Asiatic Fleet had laid about him with a "cat-o-nine tails".[22] He found the ships of the laid back Asiatic Fleet to be in deplorable readiness condition, the shore establishment and logistics very inadequate. He chewed out many officers, sent some home, read the riot act to others and drove a few senior officers nuts. I mean literally. But he got results. By mid-year 1941 the ships of the Fleet were showing marked improvement in readiness.

As it became known about the travail Admiral Hart was having in trying to deal with the ego of General Douglas MacArthur,[23] the esteem of the Admiral began to grow. His part in sending families home began to be forgiven and even praised while the General was moving from the amusement and derision category to low esteem or downright contempt by officers and men of the fleet. In the fall of 1941 as the situation worsened the wisdom of the Admiral in improving the readiness of the Fleet and sending families home out of harms way became more and more apparent.

Meanwhile rumors were flying that the Asiatic Fleet would be augmented by additional combat ships. These were sparked by vague

---

[22] An abbreviated version of the term "cat of nine tails" which was a whip with several strands at the end used to flog miscreant sailors in old sailing ship days. Here the term is meant to convey that Admiral Hart took stern measures, sometimes disciplinary action to improve readiness in the Asiatic Fleet.

[23] James Leutze, *Biography of Admiral Thomas C. Hart,* Naval Institute Press, Annapolis, 1981 p. 212.

hints or half-promises in Navy Department dispatches and by the occasional appearance in Manila Bay of cruisers on escort duty from the Pacific Fleet. But before the war these cruisers always returned to the Pacific Fleet and there were no assignments of additional surface ships to our fleet.[24]

On the 26th and 27th of November our formation continued south across the Sulu Sea with destination we knew not where. Around the decks, below decks in the living compartments and in the wardroom there were intense discussions among the officers and men as to where we were headed. We continued intense training. On the morning of Friday, 28 November 1941, *Stewart* and the other ships of the formation left Philippine waters and passed through the Sibutu Passage, with Tawi Tawi Island at the western end of the Sulu Archipelago on our portside and the large island of Borneo in sight on our starboard side.

In the afternoon soon after entering the Celebes Sea the *Black Hawk*, *Alden*, *Edsall*, *John D. Edwards* and *Whipple* left the formation and set course for Balikpapan on the southeastern coast of the island of Borneo, Netherlands East Indies. *Marblehead* with *Stewart* and the remainder of the ships headed for the port of Tarakan on the northeast coast of Borneo. Once again with war imminent the wisdom of Admiral Hart in splitting up the ships to several ports was apparent—much to the plaudits of men of the *Stewart*. The next day, 29 November, our group of ships arrived at Tarakan and anchored in the harbor.

The captain of the *Marblehead* was the senior officer present afloat and there followed a series of official courtesy calls among our ships, Dutch officials on shore, and small Dutch Navy units in the harbor.[25] During the week beginning Monday, the 1st of December, the destroyers took turns topping off from the fuel piers, patrolling off the harbor entrance and conducting various kinds of drills. In addition to general quarters, there were gun drills, fire and rescue, fire, emergency landing force and repel boarders drills. We stayed busy but there was some limited shore leave granted to the officers and crew. There wasn't much to see or do over in the town of Tarakan except to satisfy our curiosity about the place. There were always the age old questions of sailors in far away exotic ports—"Are the natives friendly? Is it safe to

---

[24] Robert B. Stinnett, op.cit., p. 8.
[25] The senior officer present afloat (SOPA) regardless of the nationality of ships always controlled the routine of the harbor.

drink the water?" Strangely there were few natives to be seen. But there was a plethora of jokes about the "Wild Man From Borneo." The few times I went ashore I spent most of the time at the Dutch Navy Officers Club listening to the skippers of the K class submarines tell wild stories while they drank oceans of Bols gin. They were a laid back bunch but appeared to be competent and determined to fight hard if war came. I liked them but decided early on there was no way we could keep up with them in the consumption of Bols.

Meanwhile rumors were flying thick and fast. One rumor was that two divisions of American destroyers would be sent to Singapore to join the task force of British Admiral Sir Tom Philips who had among other ships, the recently arrived battleship *Prince of Wales* and the battle cruiser *Repulse*. Indeed the *Prince of Wales* had been in the British task force in the Atlantic in early 1941 including the magnificent battlecruiser *Hood* which was blown up and sunk with nearly all hands by the equally magnificent German battleship *Bismarck*. Let it be said to the everlasting credit of the British—that when the situation in the Far East worsened and war seemed imminent, they sent ships and reinforcements, not just promises. But our Navy Department under Secretary of the Navy Frank Knox and Chief of Naval Operations Admiral Harold R. Stark kept hinting at or making promises of help on the way for the Asiatic Fleet which never materialized.[26] Gradually we officers and men of the Asiatic Fleet began to suspect there was never any intention of sending more ships out to help us. In our Fleet this translated into dismay and some bitterness. But not to worry. If we of the Asiatic Fleet could survive the initial attack of the Japanese Fleets, and fight a delaying action as we retreated south, the mighty Pacific Fleet would eventually come to the rescue and save us. While this line of reasoning may have been a bit naive, it had a good deal of common sense in it and everyone knew that it roughly approximated war plans in existence at the time.

Thus did the early days of December 1941 pass in a sort of suspended animation for *Stewart* and other U.S. Navy ships in Tarakan Harbor. December 7th was a quiet day in the Far East. We wondered how it was on that same day which was December 6th back in Pearl Harbor and the States.

---

[26] James Leutze, op.cit., p. 187.

Chapter 3

War!

BACK on board *Stewart* in Tarakan harbor after word that hostilities had commenced, the ship had been at General Quarters since 0345 on 8th of December and completing preparations for a shooting war. Now as dawn was approaching preparations were made for getting underway and at 0531 it was "Anchors Aweigh" for the first time for war at sea. It was both scary and exciting. For all we knew the whole damned Japanese Fleet might be just outside the harbor entrance ready to blow us to kingdom come. Or it might be just submarines. With our rather old sonar, modern submarines could be expected to have a field day with our old World War I ships. Or it might be airplanes—we certainly did not want to be caught in the harbor with little or no maneuvering room to dodge bombs or plane-launched torpedoes. On the other hand there was a feeling that the war was inevitable and now that it was here, lets get with it and get it over with. Among men of the *Stewart* there was a noticeable spirit of "Let me at 'em."

Soon we formed column astern the *Marblehead* with *Barker*, *Parrott* and *Paul Jones* following us headed out the channel through the minefields to sea. Soon the *Barker* and *Paul Jones* were detached to rendezvous with *Boise* and *Houston* coming down from the north. *Boise* was a new light cruiser the same class as *Phoenix* and had escorted a convoy to Manila when war broke out. She was immediately chopped from the Pacific Fleet to the Asiatic Fleet and was most welcome indeed. The rest of us headed off in a southeast direction for Makassar Strait at various speeds and zigzagging.[27] At 1400 we rounded Cape Mangkalihat and turned southwest towards Balikpapan. It was somewhat of a relief that we were not hit immediately upon sticking our nose out of the harbor and our confidence began to grow. All day on the 8th and 9th as we steamed south bits and pieces of messages coming out of the radio shack began to reveal to some extent the damage to the

---

[27] Zigzagging is an anti-submarine defense tactic by which surface ships steer random courses to prevent submarines getting accurate solutions for aiming torpedoes.

Pacific Fleet at Pearl Harbor. But no one out there could possibly imagine the awful truth. Although the Asiatic Fleet had escaped disaster the first two days of the war, we felt that when the Japanese did come after us, we were not going to get much help from the Pacific Fleet and what we did get would be late coming. Many of us felt the enemy would not be long in going after oil in the Netherlands East Indies.

On the afternoon of the 8th we crossed the equator but there was no ceremony. Steaming darkened all night we went to General Quarters at dawn on the morning of the 9th. This was standard practice when we were at sea in wartime. About 0900 our three ships formed column and went through the minefield to the anchorage in Balikpapan Harbor. In the harbor was a varied assortment of Dutch small craft, some U.S. and Allied merchant ships. We soon learned that Destroyer Division 57 had sailed even before hostilities to join the big British capital ships off Singapore. All day on the 9th we continued to get some news of Japanese attacks in the Philippines from our radiomen and from commercial radio in Manila. Many were wild rumors as well as flat out falsehoods. But what was not false was that General MacArthur's Army Air Force at Iba and Clark Air Fields had been almost destroyed on the ground eight hours after he had news of the attack on Pearl Harbor. How could this be! This was inexcusable and somebody should be court-martialed.

On the 10th of December we remained at anchor all day while the bad news continued to pour in. The British battleship *Prince of Wales* and the battle cruiser *Repulse* ventured to sea from Singapore without air cover and were promptly sunk by Japanese land-based naval aircraft. Our U.S. Destroyer Division 57 arrived just in time to help rescue the survivors. But alas, British Admiral Sir Tom Phillips was not among them. This was a severe blow to whatever poor chances we allies had for survival in the Far East and for delaying the inexorable Japanese advance into the East Indies for access to oil. With those ships we might have held them off for several months until we got some assistance.

The next bad news was the bombing of the Cavite Naval Shipyard on 10 December with severe damage to shops, and to the destroyers *Peary*, *Pillsbury* and two submarines. The *Peary* received a direct bomb hit on the foremast which rained shrapnel all over her bridge, decks and the *Pillsbury* moored just across the pier. Both ships suffered severe casualties. There were seven dead on the *Peary* including the executive officer Lieutenant Gates. Fourteen of her crew were missing or killed on shore while carrying wounded to the dispensary. Another eighteen wounded were transferred to the hospital. Among these were the captain, Lt. Commander H.H. Keith and my classmate Lieutenant junior grade Don Hamilton. The *Pillsbury* had two dead on board, ten missing or killed on shore and sixteen wounded. Among these was my fine classmate Howard Fischer who had traveled to the Far East with me. Fortunately his wounds were minor and he stayed on board. While enemy planes were busy bombing Cavite, *John D. Ford* and *Pope* spent a nervous day underway in Manila Bay dodging our submerged submarines and alert to dodge enemy bombs. But no runs were made on the two destroyers and late in the day Admiral Hart released them to escort *Holland*, *Otus* and *Isabel*[28] out of Manila Bay and south to the Netherlands East Indies. *Bulmer* remained patrolling the entrance to Manila Bay.

Back in Balikpapan, on Thursday am 11 December a report of unidentified warships about 50 miles up the coast came in and *Stewart* along with *Parrott* and *Marblehead* got underway and proceeded out the minefields to investigate. The cruiser launched search planes but found nothing. All ships returned to the anchorage about mid-afternoon. The next day Captain Smith gave the crew a pep talk on the forecastle and at about noon we got underway with *Parrott* and *Marblehead* heading north to meet the convoy coming down from Manila. The *Marblehead* turned back during the night but we pressed on and made rendezvous soon after dawn on the 13th. We joined the screen and headed off on a southerly course towards Balikpapan. In the formation were *Holland*, *Otus*, *Isabel*, *Boise*, *Houston* and sisterships *John D. Ford* and *Pope*. The cruisers were convoying in the Sulu Sea and joined the *Holland* formation on the 12th. We were glad to join the big cruisers.

By noon the on the 14th the formation arrived at Balikpapan and all ships fueled to capacity from oilers *Pecos* and *Trinity*. Other ships in the harbor included the *Langley* (AV-3), *Marblehead*, *Paul Jones*, *Barker* and various allied merchant ships. Later in the day the supply ship USS *Gold Star* entered the harbor and created quite a stir when it was rumored she had several thousand cases of beer on board. Actually it was

---

[28] *Holland* and *Otus* were submarine tender repair and re-supply ships. *Isabel* was a patrol yacht modified and fitted out as an alternate flagship of the Asiatic Fleet with quarters suitable for a four-star admiral and adequate for ceremonial occasions and entertaining of high-ranking foreign and domestic dignitaries.

1500 cases but this was not just any old beer. This was good San Miguel beer from Manila and thirsty mouths began to water.

This was the first concentration of forces of the Asiatic Fleet and except for the destroyer tender *Black Hawk* and several of our four-stack destroyers, it was just about all of our surface forces. This was Task Force 5 and Rear Admiral W.A. Glassford was the commander, flying his flag[29] in the *Houston*. In the evening of the 14th of December, Captain Smith and Commodore Binford attended a conference with Admiral Glassford of over two hours duration. The officers and men of the *Stewart* were not briefed on what went on at the conference. But at meals in the wardroom with the captain at the head of the one table and the commodore on his right, I was able to pick up snatches of the conversations. Being next to the most junior officer on board I was at the other end of the table and could not hear everything. As near as I could tell the conference with Admiral Glassford went something like this, "well boys, what do we do next? We are certainly in a hell of a situation. Do we stand here and fight or do we keep moving south? If we move south, do we turn left at the island chain and fight a delaying retreat on down to Australia? Or do we turn to starboard, go on to Java, join up with the Netherlands Navy and make a stand there?"

It was obvious the decision had not yet been made and when it was made it would have to be by Admiral Hart. There was much speculation around the decks, down below and in the wardroom as to when the decision would be made and several different opinions on what the decision should be. But these were put forth only when there was a break in discussions of Topic A. No, it was not about what you think. Our wives and sweethearts were safely back at home, there was an enemy to fight and a war to be won.

Topic A was about food. Commodore Binford considered himself a gourmet and an expert on beef. We were treated to long dissertations on the care and feeding of beef cattle, the slaughtering, butchering and hanging of beef—especially the ageing process. He frequently made inquiries to me as commissary officer as to whether we had some good tenderloin on board and if not when would we get some. But he was always courteous and in good humor-seeming to chuckle when he spoke to me. Like a lot of Mississippians and other southerners he

---

[29] If a flag officer (rear admiral and above) is on board a Navy ship his personal flag is broken and flown from the mainmast.

seemed to have trouble with his g's, his l's and his r's. His "Good Morning, Mr. Alford" came out as something like "Mawnin, Affud."

I never quite figured him out but most of us considered him as charming but sort of a Col. Blimp. He had the figure for it-middle aged, balding with quite a paunch and a broad bottom. And when the Commodore came on deck the perception was of an apple on two toothpicks. Captain Smith never told me what he thought of the Commodore which he was careful to conceal even into his very old age and I never dared ask him.

Captain Smith was also a southerner from Mobile, Alabama, soft-spoken, courteous equally to his officers and men with barely a trace of a southern drawl. But underneath he was hard steel, smart, competent and demanding—just the way a captain should be. At the head of the wardroom mess table he presided at all meals and was the mess president as well as the mess treasurer. He approved the menus prepared by the officers steward and no one dared grouse to him about the food. The meals were normally very good if the steward could get fresh food items.

But now some three weeks after the ship had departed Manila, many items of food were becoming scarce and re-supply was rarely possible. Inevitably the meals began to deteriorate as we turned more and more to canned meats and vegetables. One time in the wardroom we had pickled pigs feet as the main dish much to the delight of the southerners and stunned silence of the northerners who had trouble staying at the table. I had no idea why the pinkish color of the pigs feet seemed to bother them. It was not hard to guess to whom the scowls of disapproval and frosty stares were directed—to me, the commissary officer.

Our new executive officer, Lieutenant Clare B. Smiley always sat at the captain's left across from the commodore and was quite an affable messmate. Like the captain, he too was an Alabamian with hardly a trace of drawl. He had been divorced and had at one time had duty up in China, Chefoo, Tsingtao, Shanghai and other ports where he considered himself a connoisseur of fine White Russian women. We felt that he had truly gone "Asiatic" and listened to his stories with our mouths open with disbelief. To some junior officers he was the suave, laid back, mustachioed man of the world some of us may have aspired to be.

On the commodore's right sat Lieutenant Archibald Stone, Jr., the communications officer. He was from upstate New York and was a great bear of a man with a neatly trimmed mustache kind of like the modern day movie star Tom Selleck. We sort of considered him as a playful, boisterous, overgrown puppy. But he seemed to be quite competent in his job and was a most congenial shipmate. But he like most of us had occasional lapses of judgment. One time a man in his division glared at him in a disrespectful manner whereupon the man got a swift kick in the rear. Striking another person in the naval service is serious business. To his credit Mr. Stone apologized.

On the left of the executive officer and across from Mr. Stone sat the engineer officer Lieutenant junior grade Edwin L. Kyte. He was a native of New Jersey and a most peculiar fellow. He was likable in a lot of ways but was a hypochondriac about food. Every meal in the wardroom with him was an adventure. Someone in his family history had a terrible experience with trichinosis and he would not eat pork in any form. When a messboy with a platter reached him he would anxiously inquire of the messboy what was in it. Or if there was a meat pie or other dish with a crust on top, he would pry up the crust and peep under to make sure there was no pork hiding under there. The captain's face would turn red with anger but only rarely did he admonish Mr. Kyte at table. What was done privately I can only imagine. The captain did seem particularly demanding of Mr. Kyte as engineer officer. The captain had come to command of *Stewart* from his previous job as chief engineer of the *Marblehead* and I am sure he knew more about the engineering plant on our ship than Mr. Kyte ever would. Ed used to complain to me that no matter what he did, he just could not please the captain.

Sitting next to Lieutenant Stone was the torpedo officer Lieutenant junior grade Francis E. Clark, class of 1937 and the most recent officer to come on board. He came to us from the *Isabel* in August 1941 and was a most welcome addition to the watch list. I could not comment as to his competency in his job but he was very pleasant in demeanor and a good shipmate.

Opposite Mr. Clark on the other side of the table I sat alongside Mr. Kyte and had first hand knowledge of his determination that no disguised pork would escape his discovery. And of course our most junior officer, Ensign Tom Brinkley sat at the foot of the table opposite the captain. Mr. Brinkley and I rarely said anything at table but we tried to listen very carefully. Tom's eyes seemed to get bigger and bigger at the stories of this collection of personalities.

On balance, with the exception of an occasional rise in tension from Mr. Kyte's aversion to pork, it was a most congenial and cohesive wardroom. Uniform of the day for officers out there in the Philippines and the Netherlands East Indies was white short sleeve shirts with open collar, white shorts, white shoes and white ankle length socks—comfortable but not very good looking. It was rather amusing the way both officers and men came to recognize officers by their legs and knees. Final and conclusive identification of various officers was agreed when it was mentioned, "you know, the one with the knobby knees," or you know, the bow-legged one," or the one with knock-knees, skinny legs or piano legs.

Rank was shown by a small metal insignia pinned on the shirt collar and was not readily recognizable except when close up. The Australian, British and Dutch naval officers out there had a much more practical and semi-dressy uniform. It was simply wearing knee length socks along with short sleeve white shirts and shorts plus black gold-braided shoulder boards showing rank.

Meanwhile the crew of *Stewart* had an opportunity to swap stories with the men of the *John D. Ford* which was nested with us alongside *Pecos* during fueling operations on the 14th. *John D. Ford* having been in Manila Bay on the 10th of December during the bombing of the Cavite Naval Shipyard in which *Peary* and *Pillsbury* suffered heavy damage and casualties, her crew had some wild tales to tell our men. Now the war was becoming real and personal as our men learned of former shipmates or friends on these ships who were killed or wounded. In my discussions with members of our crew, morale continued to be high and there seemed to be renewed determination to get our licks in towards defeating the enemy. The men wanted in on the action. Always there was friendly rivalry and razzing going on among the crews of the ships as to which were veterans of enemy action and which were not. Our crew had yet to see a live enemy.

There seemed to be varying degrees of realization among the crew of the mortal danger we were in. I was reluctant to discuss with crew members the overwhelming odds I felt were against us for fear of damaging morale. But I had long been an avid student of Japanese naval history and the modern Imperial Navy. I felt that in the Far East they would sooner or later overwhelm us. With the disaster at Pearl Harbor, the full extent of which we did not know, it seemed doubtful whether any help would arrive in time for our survival.

But there was no doubt that we should train as much as possible in order to do as much damage to the enemy as we could before going down fighting if that was to be our fate. Man, did we train! In my gunnery department we drilled and drilled some more during morning and evening general quarters and at every other opportunity. Every man knew his job and we practiced all possible emergency situations. We exercised director fire control of the four 4-inch/.50 cal. guns with the pointer and trainer at the guns matching pointers with the director. We trained at local control with the gun captain at each gun firing his weapon independently of the director. But we all kept in mind that the main battery of the ship was the twelve torpedoes we carried. Our guns were secondary and besides we could only bring three of them to bear on each side. I knew we were no match for the large new Japanese destroyers. But we hoped our guns could finish off any enemy we hit with our torpedoes. We trained until every job was second nature. And the training bred confidence and morale.

Early on Monday morning the 15th of December the *Houston*, *Boise*, several of the auxiliary ships and three of our destroyers left the harbor of Balikpapan. Undoubtedly Admiral Glassford realized the danger of such a group of ships remaining too long in one place. We had no idea where those ships were headed. *Marblehead*, *Langley*, the two oilers, supply ships, seaplane tenders, various minecraft and three destroyers—*Barker*, *Paul Jones* and *Stewart* remained behind. In the forenoon the commodore and the captain went to another conference with Captain Robinson of the *Marblehead*, but when they returned there was no hint of what was discussed.

The next day, the 16th most of the remaining ships got underway in the afternoon and left the harbor of Balikpapan. Soon we learned we were headed for Makassar, the Celebes, Netherlands East Indies. It was the last we would see of the island of Borneo and we hoped it was the last of the lame jokes about the "wild man from Borneo" which mercifully had already subsided. Some of the crew had hoped we were headed for Surabaya, Java and some much needed liberty on shore. There was some indication that the men were getting on edge and each other's nerves. In the wardroom there was continued speculation whether the big decisions had been made and if so we wondered if we would go east, south or west. Generally it was a pattern that our destination or next port of call would not be announced before getting underway to preclude any inadvertent disclosure of ship movements to potential spies. A rumor that we were headed for Surabaya was probably wishful thinking.

All day on the 17th our course was generally southeast across the Makassar Straits towards the port of the same name on the large island of Celebes. During the day there were reports of unidentified ships and planes. Sometimes there were false reports of periscopes sighted. Each report had to be investigated by the ships in the screen but on this voyage we were assisted by the *William B. Preston* (AVD-7), a four-stacker converted into a seaplane tender. *Paul Jones* destroyed a floating mine by gunfire.

On the previous day two of our ships had actually fired on a Dutch plane approaching the formation in a menacing manner. It was hard convincing the aviators it was not only how they looked but how they behaved when approaching our ships. Besides we joked that we did not want either enemy or friendly bombs to hit and sink our supply ship *Gold Star* with that beer on board. There seemed to be a special solicitude for that beer cargo. It was clear that officers and men needed some relaxation ashore. But there was none in sight.

At about noon on the 18th we arrived off the harbor of Makassar. Before proceeding to our anchorage we fueled alongside *Pecos*. In the harbor we found nearly all the ships which had departed Balikpapan the day before we sailed except the *Houston*. Rumor had it that she had proceeded independently to Surabaya. On the 19th it was a happy event when *Bulmer* (DD-222) entered the harbor. She had just arrived from Manila Bay and there were fears she would not make it. *Bulmer* was one of the four destroyers in our Destroyer Division 58 and our crew had many friends on board. During the day on the 19th, various destroyers including *Stewart* patrolled off the harbor entrance but returned to the anchorage in the afternoon.

The other happy event on the 19th was taking on food and stores. As commissary officer it was my job and late in the afternoon I took off in the motor whaleboat with a long requisition in hand for the items we needed. We were anchored in the outer harbor and it was a long boat ride to the supply ship. We did not get all the items we wanted but we got a lot and loaded the boat to the gunwales. Meanwhile it got dark and foggy and all ships were darkened. Complicating matters, in the outer harbor were some small islets with palm trees which loomed like ships. But we made it back to *Stewart*. I do not know who deserves the credit, the captain or the executive officer, but it was a shrewd move to make the unloading of food and stores an all hands evolution. It was a break in the routine for the crew and they could see good food coming on board. There was a noticeable relaxation of tension and return to light-hearted banter.

During the next two days the fleet remained at Makassar but there was much coming and going of ships, shifting of berths and anchorages, destroyers patrolling to seaward of the harbor and arrival of additional ships. The old river gunboats of the China Station, some minecraft and a submarine came in the harbor. Again there was growing concern among the officers and men about the fleet staying so long in one port. Instinctively we knew the enemy bombers would soon be after us followed by the enemy cruisers and destroyers. On the morning of 21st December the *Boise* and two destroyers sailed for we knew not where.

On Monday the 22nd general quarters was at 0230 and we knew something was up. By 0600 all ships had cleared the harbor and we soon learned that our destination was Surabaya, Java, the main island of the Netherlands East Indies. We also learned that the *Boise* and the two destroyers had proceeded to Balikpapan to escort some merchant ships to Surabaya. Aha! We guessed that the big decision had been made that the U.S. Asiatic Fleet would join up with the Royal Netherlands Navy and make a stand in Java and the chain of islands to the east and to the west.

How had it come to pass that the war had been going on for two weeks before decisions were made as to how the Asiatic Fleet would be employed in the war, whether we would operate with the Netherlands Navy and what kind of command structure would be set up? It was an almost unbelievable tale of high level folly in Washington and the Far East, especially the difficulty Admiral Hart was having in dealing with General Douglas MacArthur.

From my arrival in Manila Bay in late December 1940 I was acutely aware of the presence of General MacArthur by a constant stream of radio and newspaper stories. He appeared to be an avid publicity hound and always seemed surrounded by sycophants and bootlickers. Occasionally I got a glimpse of him at social functions in the Army-Navy Club. Officially he had been retired from the U.S. Army for many years and was then hired at a very high salary to head up the Philippine Army. There he was ensconced with his family in the penthouse suite on the top floor of the Manila Hotel and lord of all he surveyed. He and President Manuel Quezon had cooked up for him a fancy title and uniform—he was Field Marshal Douglas MacArthur of the Philippines. In the Asiatic Fleet he was the object of some derision and amusement because he inspired images of a pompous comic opera general.

But in July, 1941 we quit laughing. General Mac was recalled to active duty and given command of Army Forces, Far East. But alas, he was recalled as a lieutenant general—only three (gasp) stars. Admiral Hart had four stars. In retrospect it appears the general began right then a campaign of denigrating Admiral Hart, the Asiatic Fleet and the Navy in general.[30] Some historians have written that in this he was aided and abetted by Secretary of War Henry L. Stimson.[31] For decades both the Army and Navy had agreed that the Philippines could not be defended for very long against a determined attack by the formidable Japanese war machine. At best it was hoped and plans were made to fight a delaying action down into the southern Philippines and the Dutch East Indies to give time for the mighty U.S. Pacific Fleet to come to the rescue.

Immediately upon being recalled to active duty General MacArthur began telling his staff, Admiral Hart and Washington that he would not be bound by any war plans. Moreover by fooling himself about the capabilities of the Philippine Defense Forces and if he could get reinforcements in troops, bombers and fighter planes, he could and would defend the Philippines. To this end he began hounding the War Department for reinforcements and supplies. But he made little or no effort to coordinate his ideas and thoughts with Admiral Hart and at one point he declared I have my plans, the Navy has their plans, implying there was no need for coordination. Admiral Hart had to take the initiative in proposing joint plans and operations. These were steadily and haughtily rejected by the general.

By mid-September General MacArthur had 130 fighter planes, a promise of a squadron of B-17 bombers and was exuding confidence all over the place. Some of this may have been infectious for Admiral Hart and since the Asiatic Fleet had been augmented by another squadron of submarines, he began to rethink the idea that the Philippines might be defended after all. Despite the insults and patronizing by MacArthur, Admiral Hart felt an obligation to support the U.S. Army in the Philippines as much and as long as he could. In his desire to please and to cooperate, he leaned over backward to make a decision about mid-October, against his better judgment he would later admit. The decision was, if war came, to fight the Asiatic Fleet from Manila Bay. It was indeed a momentous and earth-shaking decision and it was 27 October 1941 before he could bring himself to inform the Navy Department. But he did not inform the fleet of his decision and began to sweat out approval or thumbs down on the plan from the Chief of Naval Operations Admiral Harold R. Stark.

---

[30] James Leutze, op.cit., p. 239.
[31] Ibid., p. 239.

Admiral Hart waited and waited and waited for word from Washington and finally decided he could wait no longer. He had to tell his fleet of his decision that when war came, it would be fought from Manila Bay. He made the announcement to the Asiatic Fleet on 19 November, 1941. I remember the date well because those of us in *Stewart* wardroom began debating whether the decision was suicidal. It was also the day my promotion to lieutenant junior grade came through, with date of rank and back pay to 2 June, 1941. But the very next day 20 November Washington disapproved the plan to fight the war from Manila Bay. Back to square one. It almost seemed to be a diabolical plot to embarrass Admiral Hart and make him lose face in his own fleet.

In late November 1941 General MacArthur got his wing of B-17 bombers and bombastically announced he could defend the Philippines. You could almost hear the Japanese chuckling over that. Our feeling in the fleet was we are in for it now. Lookout! Again many of us took comfort in knowing we were not leaving our families and loved ones back in Manila to fend for themselves While we retreated and prepared to fight a delaying action in the islands to the south. The esteem of Admiral Hart in the fleet continued to shoot up sky high and was close to hero worship.

Of course there are always some individuals who think they can beat the system and outsmart the Admiral. Some few wives avoided being sent home by various subterfuges. Some got employment as teachers in Manila or other jobs which were excepted in the directive to return to the United States. Some kept their marriages secret. But some of them paid dearly by being rounded up by the enemy and spending years in hot, filthy prison camps. Some never made it back home.

Then on the 1st of December 1941 President Franklin D. Roosevelt sent out a strange directive[32] to Admiral Hart. The President wanted three small ships with minimum arms necessary for classification as men-of-war, to be sent out in the path of Japanese amphibious forces coming down in the West China Sea and the Gulf of Siam. While it could not be proven, there was hardly any doubt in anyone's mind including Admiral Hart that these small ships were intended as sacrificial goats to provoke the Japanese into starting the war.

---

[32] Ibid., p. 222.

One of the small ships designated for the mission was the USS *Isabel* (PY-10), a yacht used by the Commander-in-Chief, Asiatic Fleet for official ceremonies and entertaining in the Far East. Admiral Hart himself gave the skipper, Lieutenant J.W. Payne, class of 1935, his instructions which were top secret but unwritten. Lieutenant Payne had been an old shipmate for a few months on the light cruiser *Honolulu* and his executive officer was my classmate Lieutenant junior grade Marion H. Buaas. Later they filled me in on the hair-raising story of the mission. The *Isabel* sailed on the 3rd and on the 5th of December was off Camranh Bay, Indochina. She was of course immediately spotted by the Japanese and shadowed all day but not attacked. It doesn't take long to figure out why. The Japanese Fleet was then approaching Hawaii and they did not want to give away the game plan by early hostilities off Camranh Bay and spoil the surprise at Pearl Harbor. The sailboat *Lanikai* commanded by Kemp Tolley (later rear admiral) and one other small craft intended for the mission were getting ready but war came before they could sail.

On the evening of the 5th Admiral Hart recalled the *Isabel* during the time he was in the middle of a two-day conference with British Admiral Sir Tom Phillups in Manila. We shall hear more about the *Isabel* later. On the afternoon of the 6th as Admiral Phillips was preparing to leave, Admiral Hart told him he was ordering Destroyer Division 57 from Balikpapan to Singapore to operate with the British. This decision did not seem earth-shaking on its face but was fraught with all sorts of dangers and implications. The United States was not yet at war and such action might be just the move to bring on the war.

The matter of just how and when the cooperation with the British in the Far East would take place had not been worked out. Similarly there had been no "modus operandi" worked out with the Dutch. Conferences with the British and Dutch had been held but Admiral Hart had no authority to commit. Little or no guidance came out of Washington. The initiative and boldness of Admiral Hart in ordering the destroyers to Singapore were commendable. No doubt he was impressed and influenced by the willingness of the British to commit capital ships to the fight in the Far East. But with all this probably came the realization by Admiral Hart that he might possibly was being used to further President Roosevelt's and Secretary of War Stimson's desire to maneuver the Japanese into firing the first shot. This was an old tactic most notably used by President Lincoln in maneuvering the Confederates into firing the first shot at Fort Sumter to start the Civil War.

Of course Prime Minister Winston Churchill of Britain had been working hard for some time to get the United States into the war. It seemed to be an obsession with him as was President Roosevelt's seeming obsession with defeating Germany in Europe and in the Atlantic. With the attack on Pearl Harbor one might expect these obsessions to change. Mr. Churchill was delighted to get the United States into the war and his purposes only shifted a little to convince America to continue the highest priority to the European war. He even offered to commit Royal Navy ships to the Far East and did so in order to get Washington to commit the bulk of U.S. naval forces to the war in the Atlantic. But there was no observable change in the President's purposes, despite the terrible devastation in the Pacific Fleet and his highest priority continued to be the war in the Atlantic and Europe.

This was terribly disappointing in the Asiatic Fleet and gave rise to the suspicion that no reinforcements to the fleet were ever intended before the war nor would be forthcoming after war started. It became apparent to some of us and I believe to Admiral Hart and the rest of fleet personnel that the Asiatic Fleet was expendable as was the *Isabel* a few days before the war. There is nothing that concentrates the mind like the prospect of being the "goat" in a futile exercise likely to end in death or as prisoners of war. It was no wonder that esteem in the Asiatic Fleet for Washington including the President went from irritation to "cuss words." Back in Washington the name of the game was the "blame game." Fingers were being pointed in every direction on who was responsible for Pearl Harbor. Everybody was covering their rear ends. The Far East was so far away and nothing way out there could possibly be as newsworthy as the sensational Pearl Harbor disaster. National newspapers scarcely paid any attention. Thus it was that for two weeks into the war the Asiatic Fleet was in a sort of "limbo." For weeks before the war Admiral Hart was not permitted by Washington to make realistic operational plans with our potential allies because political agreements had not yet been reached. After start of hostilities it was a "catch-up" ball game, makeshift plans, jury-rigged communications, ship-to-ship relations by liaison officers and no fighter plane cover for the Allied ships—a recipe for disaster.

Chapter 4

Playing for Time

WHEN the Asiatic Fleet—at least most of it—got underway from Makassar, Celebes, early on 22 December 1941 we soon learned upon clearing the harbor that we were bound for Surabaya, Java. The news spread through the ship like wildfire. Not only was there a satisfaction that we were joining up with our new friends and Allies, the Royal Netherlands Navy, but also there were friendly port cities to visit and a chance for much needed rest and relaxation. There was a ripple of delight in the ship at the prospect of liberty and Christmas in Surabaya. Visions of sugarplums and beautiful girls danced in our heads.

But these thoughts were soon erased by lookouts reporting a strange looking ship over the horizon south of the formation. *Stewart* left the formation to investigate and for awhile it looked like a tall pagoda superstructure of a Japanese battleship. There was some delay before the navigator reached the bridge and reported that if it was a battleship it was sitting on top of the DeBril Bank Lighthouse. As the formation continued in a southwest direction for Surabaya there were the usual unidentified ships to be investigated by the destroyers. Floating mines were reported and several false submarine alarms.

Then we heard on commercial radio from Manila that enemy forces had landed at Lingayen Gulf north of Manila Bay. Later we learned that our submarines had contested the landings only to be frustrated by defective torpedoes. Also on the 22nd General MacArthur got his fourth star and renewed his vindictiveness towards Admiral Hart, the Asiatic Fleet and the Navy. It was extremely unfortunate that the faulty torpedoes and the inability of our submarines to do significant damage to the enemy gave the General more "ammunition" for his vendetta.[33]

On the 23rd shortly after noon the *Houston* and three destroyers were sighted in an easterly direction. *Otus*, *Pecos* and *Gold Star* broke off from our formation and joined the *Houston* group en route to Port Darwin, Australia. There were wistful looks after the *Gold Star* as she

---

[33] James Leutze, op.cit., 1981, p. 245.

disappeared over the horizon with all that beer cargo. Early on the 24th I had the midwatch and about 0300 we found ourselves in the middle of a fleet of fishing vessels some with and some without lights. By changing courses slightly with small amounts of rudder we weaved through the fleet. But one was very close and went bumping and scraping along the starboard side as we passed. There was no damage to the ship and apparently none to the fishing boat as I could see.

By mid-morning the formation was off the entrance to the harbor of Surabaya and ships began to take on pilots for passing through the minefields. At about 1400 we moored alongside the Rotterdam quay with *Bulmer* nested to starboard and took on fuel. There was real gaggle of ships present in the harbor: *Marblehead, Black Hawk, Holland, Langley, John D. Edwards, Parrott, Bulmer, Childs, William B. Preston, Isabel, Asheville, Tulsa, Lark, Heron* and *Whippoorwill*. In addition there were two Netherlands Navy cruisers *De Ruyter* and *Java*, several destroyers and small craft. In the outer harbor there were numerous merchant ships. Later, that evening *Boise, John D. Ford* and *Pope* arrived escorting the merchant ships *Sea Witch* and *Marechal Joffre*, the latter taken over from the French. We shall hear more about *Sea Witch* later.

But it was Christmas eve and a time for relaxation, subdued celebrations and thoughts of home. A limited number of the crew were granted liberty ashore. Others stayed on board for rest and catching up on sleep. I was content to retreat to my stateroom, write letters home and stay up until midnight for the opening of the few presents I had received prior to hostilities. On the 25th Christmas Day there were few ship movements but we did get underway early and anchored out in the harbor. Then in the afternoon I went ashore and sent a cablegram to my wife that I was alive and well. It was the first she had heard since start of the war and welcome news. Officers and men had a nice Christmas dinner thanks to the food we brought on board back in Makassar.

There was more bad news from Manila. General MacArthur gave Admiral Hart less than 24 Hours notice that he would declare Manila an open city.[34] Later we learned the Admiral boarded a submarine at midnight bound for Surabaya.

The next day there were few ship movements but *Stewart* and *Parrott* got underway late in the afternoon and left the harbor to search for a submarine reported 20 miles west of the entrance. We searched all

---

[34] Ibid., p. 240.

that night and most of the day on the 27th but found nothing. Late that afternoon we sighted a convoy coming out of the harbor and we were ordered to join. The convoy and escorts consisted of *Marblehead*, *Langley*, *Holland*, *Marechal Joffre*, *Bulmer*, *Parrott*, *Stewart* and *William B. Preston*. Minesweepers *Lark* and *Whippoorwill* broke off from the formation after clearing the minefields. After *Stewart* investigated a report of an unidentified boat and found nothing the formation settled gown on an easterly course en route to Port Darwin, Australia.

On the 28th and 29th of December the formation steamed steadily eastward at 12 or 13 knots. There were more unidentified ships to be investigated by the destroyers and several false submarine alarms. The *Bulmer* dropped four depth charges on what was later thought to be a false contact. We had yet to see or contact a real live Japanese enemy. But we knew they would soon be down-just give them a little more time.

It is a long haul from Surabaya to Darwin, over 1200 nautical miles and we passed just out of sight of a lot of strange and exotic islands. There was the island of Bali, famous for bare-breasted maidens. Then there was Lombok with its Komodo dragons, actually lizards as big as crocodiles. There was Sumbawa, Flores, Sumba and Timor, some with head-hunters and several with active volcanoes. For a geography buff like myself it was fascinating.

We navigated a lot of seas, there are many more than seven. There are hundreds. On this voyage we sailed the Java Sea, the Bali Sea, the Flores Sea, the Savu Sea, the Banda Sea, the Timor Sea, and the Arafura Sea. On some of the long night watches some of us would hum or sing an adaptation ditty to the tune of "The Farmer's in the Dell." It went something like this:

"Oh, we sailed the Java Sea, we sailed the Bali Sea, Hi Ho, the Merry-O, we sailed the Flores Sea."

Then there would be other verses until all seas were included. Or we might have a verse with just one sea mentioned and repeat the whole. But we usually omitted the Arafura Sea—too many syllables and didn't rhyme. We preferred the two syllable seas.

On the 30th of December at 1130 *Stewart* and *Bulmer* suddenly were detached from the convoy and ordered to rendezvous with *Houston* in Torres Strait at the extreme northern tip of Australia. We took off at 22 knots necessary to make the rendezvous on the 1st of January, 1942. Once again I had the thrill of feeling our sleek ship slicing through the waves at high speed. Soon we learned that at Torres Strait we with *Houston* would meet a convoy coming out from the states escorted by USS *Pensacola*, a heavy cruiser from the Pacific Fleet.

On we charged the last day of December 1941. At midnight as the new year 1942 began, the ship's log for the first watch entry was written in verse in accordance with a great old U.S. Navy tradition. The officer of the deck Lieutenant junior grade Francis E. Clark composed the verses and here are the first four: "Steaming swiftly on our way,

> Having come from the Sea of Flores,
> We'll arrive ere end of day,
> At the Strait by name of Flores.
>
> We steam through this foreign clime,
> A small part of our country's fleet,
> At sea we spend all our time,
> Always hoping the Japs to meet.
>
> We'll find the *Houston* at Torres,
> And get our orders from there,
> We hope our duties are forays,
> Against the enemy's lair.
>
> Now the speed is twenty-two knots,
> True course is one double naught,
> All the crew do sleep on their cots,
> Save those whom the watch has caught.

And on it continues for six more verses. In late afternoon we reached Booby Island in Torres Strait. But *Houston* and her destroyer screen were nowhere in sight. We looked around awhile and anchored near Booby Island for the night. I made a notation in my journal, "New Year's Day and a war to be won. On to Tokyo."

Early on 2 January 1942 *Houston* and destroyers *Alden*, *Edsall* and *Whipple* were sighted. They were anchored by noon and we went alongside the cruiser to fuel. At 22 knots we had consumed a lot of fuel and needed a whole bunch. Besides it was comforting to be close to one of the only two ships of the Asiatic Fleet with any decent firepower. I had an amiable classmate on *Houston*, Hal Hamlin and we had a nice chat while alongside. I like to think that had lot to do with the cruiser sending several tureens[35] of ice cream for our crew. There was no way we could make ice cream on board. There was another reason for our elation—the prospect of mail getting back home by way of the *Pensacola*. And we dared hope that she might bring us some mail. We remained at the anchorage overnight. Later we learned that Admiral Hart had arrived in Surabaya by submarine this same date.

The next day, 3 January, two Australian Navy sloops joined us early in the morning and about mid-morning the convoy from the states escorted by the USS *Pensacola* (CA-24) arrived. She brought no mail. In less than an hour *Houston* had relieved that ship as convoy commodore and our formation set course for Port Darwin. This convoy had been extremely controversial from the start. As early as 14 December the President, in response to squeals for help from General MacArthur had indicated his desire that no effort be spared to get this convoy through to Manila.[36]

The Chief of Naval Operations Admiral Stark and Admiral Hart both knew the scheme was not only not practical, but was impossible because General Mac had lost his air power the first day of the war. Poor Stark was caught in the middle and could only tell Admiral Hart to keep on trying, to do what he could to get the convoy through. Staff planners in Washington and in the Pacific bitterly opposed the mission as a waste of effort and supplies. But the President wanted it and what this old friend of the Navy wanted his beloved Navy would try to do.

It was a political and symbolic effort and there is considerable evidence to indicate that even General MacArthur knew it could not get through. But if he made the request and the Navy could not do it then he could blame the Navy to cover up his faulty strategy in the months before the war and his negligence in handling of his air forces on the first day of hostilities. There seemed to be a low opinion in the Asiatic Fleet for the General and FDR. We could hear radio Manila, Singapore, the BBC and sometimes San Francisco. The political posturing and bravado of these two were nauseating. Oh what the hell! We would do our duty anyhow but sometimes had to remind ourselves of that old Navy admonishment to junior officers, "Take heed what you say of your seniors, lest a little birdie ..."

---

[35] Tureens are metal pots used not for cooking but for transporting food prepared in the galley down to the mess compartment for the crew meals.
[36] James Leutze, op.cit., p. 240.

The alacrity with which the *Pensacola* turned on its heels and headed back down to Brisbane was disheartening. We were naive to hope this 8-inch gun cruiser might join with us in the Far East. This too fueled our suspicion that we might not get any more help and that we might have been written off as expendable. Navy Headquarters seemed not about to reassign another of the Pacific Fleet ships to the unwashed and doomed ships of the Asiatic Fleet. They had already given up the light cruiser *Boise* to our fleet and would do no more. It was like we were in a different Navy from different countries. It was a strange and weird feeling.

While the addition of *Pensacola* to our fleet might not have made any difference in the long run, her presence might have delayed the enemy timetable long enough for more of our ships to escape and live to fight another day. Besides we still did not know the full extent of the destruction at Pearl Harbor and continued to hope that at some point the mighty Pacific Fleet would come to our rescue. *Pensacola* would have helped us a great deal in playing for time until help arrived.

Back to the convoy—after clearing the anchorage at Torres Strait on the 3rd of January 1942 the formation settled down on westerly courses at a speed of 13 knots with the venerable Navy transport *Chaumont* as guide, en route to Port Darwin, Australia. This old ship had been in the Far East-stateside run for many years hauling personnel mostly and as far as we could tell was loaded with sailors and marines. Our signalmen with long glasses thought they saw some women on board. Then there was the Army transport *Willard A. Holbrook* loaded with troops. Next was the Dutch merchantman SS *Bloemfontain* loaded with trucks and other mechanized equipment. *Houston* took her station out in advance of the transports for sea room sufficient for plane operations. Destroyers *Alden, Bulmer, Edsall, Stewart* and *Whipple* screened ahead while the Aussie sloops screened the rear. The remainder of the 3rd and the 4th of January were uneventful except for launch and recovery of scout planes by the cruiser and transfer of charts from the Aussie sloops to two of the transports.

On the 5th the formation arrived in Port Darwin late in the day and it was 2100 before *Stewart* anchored. In addition to those in our formation, other ships in the anchorage were *Marblehead, Holland, Langley, Otus, Pecos, Trinity, Parrott, Peary, William Preston* and *Gold Star*. Ah-ha! We had caught up with all that good San Miguel beer. Big question-how to get some? It was all stowed way down below in cargo of *Gold Star* securely locked and only the captain had the key. It was rumored that the port captain would not allow the San Miguel beer to be off-loaded because the bar owners in Darwin did not want competition with the local beer.

On a more serious and happy note, all hands on the *Stewart* were delighted to find our sistership *Peary* in port. She had arrived from Manila Bay on the 3rd, just two days before our arrival in Darwin and word spread around the ship quickly that her new captain was our former executive officer Lieutenant John M. Bermingham. No one ever expected to see *Peary* again. When last we had heard of her she had been heavily damaged in the 10 December bombing of the Cavite Naval Shipyard with many casualties, dead and wounded. Some of us hoped we might have the opportunity to speak to her new captain.

During the day on the 5th we had also received an inspiring message about a seven hour attack of enemy seaplanes on our seaplane tender USS *Heron*. She had fought them off gallantly shooting down one of the enemy planes and damaging others while she suffered only one hit with two men killed and several wounded. Her commanding officer Lieutenant W.L. Kabler was immediately recommended for the Navy Cross medal and all hands were recommended for promotion. Our Captain Smith read the inspiring message to officers and men on the bridge and had it posted on bulletin boards around the ship for all hands to see.

We remained at anchor most of the day on the 6th and we were glad for the opportunity of making much needed repairs, cleaning and maintenance, resting and just plain catching our breath.

During the day *Boise*, *Black Hawk*, *Barker* and *Pope* entered the harbor. Before dark we went alongside a British tanker for fuel and remained overnight. On the 7th we anchored with *Barker* moored alongside. Mr. Clark was promoted to lieutenant. I got ashore briefly but made a U-turn back to *Stewart*. Darwin town was dismal with muddy streets looking like a movie set of a frontier western town. I half expected John Wayne to burst out of a saloon any minute for a shoot out with some pesky outlaws. I was satisfied San Miguel beer was not being dispensed over there.

The highlight of the day was entry in the harbor of USS *Heron* (AVP-2) looking all beat up after her ordeal of an all day enemy air attack. The gallant ship was given a rousing cheer when she passed close to our ships in the harbor.

Meanwhile we were hearing aircraft reports of enemy ship movements in and around the Philippines, Borneo and the Malay Peninsula. We would hear snatches of commercial radio broadcasts from Manila and Singapore. There were propaganda blasts from Tokyo and rumors galore. These would fly around the ship rapidly. They all seemed to add up to the massing of enemy ships getting ready to move further south. We knew they would be after us soon. On the 8th another convoy was cooked up. *Boise, Marblehead, Barker, Bulmer, Parrott, Stewart* and *Pope* departed Port Darwin escorting the Dutch merchant *Bloemfontein* en route to Surabaya. A pattern of convoying developed while we were playing for time, hoping, hoping more U.S. warships would come to help us. Meanwhile we in destroyers wanted to strike at the enemy ourselves.

Chapter 5

Saga of the USS *Peary* (DD-226)

BEFORE *Stewart* departed with the convoy on 8th January we were fortunate to have a visit on board of the captain, USS *Peary*. This was our former executive officer, Lieutenant Commander John M. Bermingham who had been relieved by Mr. Smiley several weeks before the war. He had completed his two and a half year tour of duty in the Far East and reported to the 16th Naval District Headquarters at Cavite for transportation stateside. It was great seeing him on board again and we now addressed him as captain and congratulated him on being promoted to lieutenant commander. It was heartwarming to watch the greetings of the men of *Stewart* as he walked around the ship talking to old shipmates.

Then we engaged him in earnest conversation as to how he had come to command of *Peary*. He told us that when *Stewart* left Manila Bay on 25 November 1941 he was still at Cavite awaiting transportation home. This was just at the time tension out there had reached fever pitch and thrown all means of transportation out of kilter. When war came on 8 December he was still there with nothing to do—in limbo—and no one to care about getting him back to the states. He volunteered to the district commandant and was put to work burning classified papers which he did in a waterfront park in the shipyard. He did this for several days out in the open with a great view of the bay, movements of ships, and the start of Japanese bombing. Burning page after page he took a keen interest in the formation, altitude and tactics of the enemy planes as well as their numbers and types. When the great raid of 10 December 1941 had practically destroyed the Cavite Naval Shipyard, he had wandered down to the docks where the *Peary* and *Pillsbury* were moored while undergoing yard overhaul prior to the attack. These two ships as well as others had been severely damaged in the bombing with many killed and wounded including the commanding officer of *Peary* who was hospitalized.

Captain Bermingham told us his visit to the shipyard docks was more out of curiosity and another officer nearby was also observing the damage. This was the Fleet Personnel officer Lieutenant Commander Alexander S. McDill. After an exchange of pleasantries the conversation went like this, "What ship are you attached to?" "Well, none, I was recently relieved as executive officer of the *Stewart* after completion of my tour." "Well, what are you doing now?" "Well, nothing except awaiting transport to the states." Then Mr. McDill's eyes narrowed to slits and he exclaimed "No you are not, you are the new captain of the *Peary*. Get aboard and take command. Your orders will be cut this afternoon and you will have them before sundown."

Then Lieutenant Bermingham walked across the brow, saluted the colors astern, stepped aboard and told the petty officer of the watch "I'm the new commanding officer. Log me in the notebook as reporting aboard under verbal orders of the Commander-in-Chief Asiatic Fleet, this date and time." It was perhaps the shortest orders and change of command on record. He was quickly spotted by the crew as a salty, experienced destroyerman by the way he took the ladders and how he ordered his coffee—black with no sugar.

Later we learned of his heroic effort to get the damaged *Peary* ready for sea, at least partially. She was under actual attack or threats of enemy bombing attacks every day in the shipyard. When Lieutenant Bermingham took command of the *Peary* late in the day on December 14th, the ship was in terrible shape and in no way seaworthy. Although her engineering plant had been cold iron on the day of the bombing, she now had one boiler on the line and could move into the bay if necessary. But much of her equipment such as sonar, radios, torpedo exploders, warheads and navigational instruments had been in the shipyard for repair and were destroyed. Scrounging parties were dispatched to search in the rubble of the shipyard for items that were desperately needed, including navigational charts, anchors and chain. By superhuman effort the *Peary* was barely ready for sea about the 17th except for the torpedo battery and still had no foremast. She was ready to go navigationally but not yet ready to fight.

Actually the *Pillsbury* had been ready for sea since the 14th but was not released to join our sisterships down in the Netherlands East Indies. Instead she was formed into a unit with *Peary* and a squadron of PT boats for use in and around Manila Bay as directed by Rear Admiral Francis W. Rockwell, Commandant of the 16th Naval District. There seemed to be a reluctance to let ships go to escape the untenable situation in Manila Bay. After the *John D. Ford* and *Pope* left the bay on the 10th, the *Bulmer* had been held back. And it was not until *Pillsbury* was ready for sea on the 14th that *Bulmer* was released to rejoin most of the fleet in the port of Makassar, Celebes on the 19th.

But now what to do about the terrible dilemma of *Peary* with no torpedoes? *Pillsbury* had her twelve and it was a gut-wrenching decision to split them between the two ships—six to each and to remove the two forward torpedo mounts on each ship. This was accomplished on the 20th and for the next few days both ships made separate patrols along Mindoro Island along with PT boats. Then it became almost a ritual that both skippers would go over each day and request Rear Admiral Rockwell to release them to rejoin the fleet down south. And almost ritually they were refused. No doubt there was a strong element of desire to keep some fast ships available for evacuation of staff and code personnel if necessary from harms way. But General MacArthur brought things to a head quickly by declaring Manila an open city on Christmas Day, 25th and moving his headquarters to Corregidor. Admiral Hart and his staff did the same but that night (early on the 26th) the admiral departed on the submarine *Shark* for Surabaya, Netherlands East Indies. The next day, the 26th, both captains of the destroyers went over to Corregidor to again make their ritual pleas for release. While they were gone enemy planes commenced their daily bombing raids and this time they seemed to target the two destroyers.

Both ships got underway with their executive officers at the conn and twisting, turning, slowing and accelerating managed to dodge stick after stick of bombs. There were near misses and shrapnel holes but no direct hits from the attacks which seemed to concentrate on the *Peary* as both skippers watched the action from the rock with a mixture of anxiety and admiration. After the enemy planes departed, Rear Adm. Rockwell called the captains back in the tunnel and late on the 26th released them to head south. At the same time he approved their plan for the ships to proceed separately, *Peary* inboard of Mindoro Island and *Pillsbury* outboard. When the captains got back to their ships and announced departure there were cheers and shouts of joy as preparations were made to get underway.

But before they could get underway there were messages from the rock to send boat for passengers and cargo. Then another said wait for passengers. There was that dreaded word "wait" which the crews feared would further delay departure. All hands instinctively knew their presence in Manila Bay was untenable and that they had better get the hell out of there right now. Soon a boat approached *Pillsbury* and disembarked several officers and men. Among the officers was Mr. Asiatic Fleet personnel himself, Lieutenant Commander A.S. McDill. There were two junior communication watch officers and several men including radiomen and an electrician.

Next the boat delivered two more communication watch officers, a chief yeoman and several more radiomen to the *Peary* along with a radio, electric coding machine, cryptographic aids and bags of official mail. These men and equipment were part of the Purple Code gang, an intelligence facility which Admiral Hart had at his disposal but which the Commander of the Pacific Fleet Admiral Kimmel did not have. Both ships were already underway as the boat cleared the side of *Peary* and soon were impatiently gaining speed and heading for the open sea.

The voyage of *Pillsbury* to Balikpapan, Borneo was without incident and she arrived at her destination on the afternoon of Sunday 28th December with no sightings enemy or friendly. But the voyage south of the *Peary* was entirely different and fraught with many perils. It is not quite clear why she chose to proceed south keeping Mindoro Island to port instead of starboard as was planned. Intelligence reports were coming in and there was no hesitation in changing the courses of action to suit the situation. Enemy forces were reported at the northern end of Palawan Island and enemy landings were in progress at Davao on the southern coast of the large island of Mindanao. There was no doubt it was a hell of a gauntlet to be run.

Skirting the west shore of Mindoro *Peary* set course southeast towards Negros Island and at 30 knots sighted the island of Panay at dawn on the 27th. Rounding the southern tip of that island she proceeded across the Panay Gulf and anchored about mid-morning close to the shore of Negros. About the same time a flight of five twin engine planes was sighted headed northwest and it was fervently hoped *Peary* was not seen. Spending the rest of the day applying green paint to the topsides, she was off again at sunset. Heading southwest across the Sulu Sea towards the southwestern tip of Mindanao, she had to navigate the narrow Basilan Strait, sure to be guarded and considered one of the danger spots of the journey. It was indeed fortunate that *Peary* passed Zamboanga and through Basilan Strait at midnight without enemy contact. But not for long.

Now *Peary* headed southeast across the Celebes Sea and rapidly passed out of Philippine waters towards the northeastern tip of Celebes Island, Dutch East Indies. But alas, her luck in being undiscovered ran out about 0800 on the 28th when a four engine enemy patrol plane picked her up and commenced shadowing at a distance. About 1400 two PBY planes were sighted at a distance to the east but contact could not be made. Shortly thereafter another enemy patrol plane joined the first one and commenced bombing runs on *Peary*. She evaded the bombs but a little while later two torpedo planes joined the attackers and made a coordinated attack on both bows. By violent twisting and turning and use of an old tactic—firing the surface guns at the attackers with the splashes interfering with the aim and altitude of the torpedo drops, managed to dodge all the torpedoes. It was a magnificent performance of Captain Bermingham and his crew.

At about 1630 all attacks ceased and a little peace was had but again, not for long. *Peary* still had not been able to establish radio contact with Rear Admiral Glassford, Commander Task Force 5. It was hoped that some word from him might indicate the wisdom of quicker rejoining the remainder of the Asiatic Fleet by passage south through the Makassar Strait. But now as *Peary* approached the northern coast of Celebes and observed the port of Manado burning, a decision had to be made whether to head west towards Makassar Strait or head east. The decision was made to head east through the Bangka Strait and then down to the port of Ambon on the Dutch island of Ceram. But while in the strait at about 1830 three twin engine planes commenced a menacing approach and were taken under fire by *Peary* until British markings were seen on the wings. Here was the cruelest of the quirks of warfare—attack by friendly forces, obviously Lockheed Hudson bombers.

Despite frantic efforts to show she was friendly, *Peary* had to open fire again when the planes split up and started bombing runs. Two bombs fell well astern with no damage. But then two bombs fell near the port bow and two more near the stern which did considerable shrapnel damage. One man on the director platform was killed instantly while two others were wounded. Then the planes commenced strafing runs and in the wild avoiding maneuvers one man fell overboard. He was wearing a life jacket, was thrown a life ring and when last seen was swimming towards the beach. Most of the material damage was numerous shrapnel holes in the steering engine room above the waterline, two depth charges split open and a machine gun destroyed. But more ominous was that the wheel ropes from the bridge to after steering were severed.

Soon the planes departed and *Peary* was left to lick her wounds while lying off the eastern shore of Celebes Island near Kema and trying to send off a damage report to ComTaskFor 5. This time she finally got through and was ordered to proceed to Port Darwin via Ambon, N.E.I. But even more ominous was that while the *Peary* was lying off Kema, the captain was informed that the starboard Kingsbury shaft bearing had been wiped. Nevertheless he proceeded on one shaft at 22 knots almost due east across the Molucca Sea and about 0500 on December 29th moored to palm trees between the small islands of Tidore and Mare just off the west shore of the large island of Halmahera, N.E.I.

While the engineers set to work on the wiped shaft bearing and the shipfitters began welding up the shrapnel holes, the rest of the crew set about camouflaging the ship with palm fronds. At the same time the captain had the two wounded men loaded into the motor whale boat and took off with them for the nearby Dutch village of Ternate for treatment by medical doctors. Meanwhile most of the crew set up camp on the beach a short distance away and needed no encouragement to partake of mangoes and other tropical fruit. Soon the captain returned with the wounded men and lots of beer, bread, more fresh fruit and some fine Dutch rum. The enthusiasm and appreciation of the crew was apparent.

The small Dutch village had no defenses to speak of and *Peary* gave them several small arms with ammunition. The Dutch officials assumed the ship would stay with them to help defend and seemed genuinely disappointed when told the ship must move on the next day. Indeed her very presence was the greatest danger even though well-hidden. In the afternoon two planes of PatWing 10 circled and landed after being waved down by the MWB because they could not pick out the hidden ship from the air. The captain and a Dutch official met the pilots and soon learned why *Peary* had been attacked by the Aussie planes. No one knew of the presence of *Peary* in those waters and she did not fit the profile of any allied ship. Of more importance was the misleading message sent out from the 16th Naval District that two destroyers were being released en route to Balikpapan but there was no mention that they were proceeding independently by separate routes.

After the PBYs took off the captain returned to the ship and at about 1630 he gathered the crew and explained why they had been attacked by Aussie planes the day before. Then he stated his intentions of getting underway at dusk the next day and the necessity of conserving fuel and fresh water in order to reach Ambon as well as maintaining a strict blackout to avoid detection by the enemy. Then the ship's company was called to attention for the purpose of burying the dead in accordance with Navy regulations. The captain gave a brief eulogy of Seaman K.E. Quinaux whose body was prepared for burial at sea. Then with the body placed in the bow of the MWB, the captain and a six man firing squad proceeded out to deep water and after three volleys consigned the body to the deep. It was a moving ceremony.

At dawn on Tuesday 30 December, 1941 reveille was quietly held but soon there was bustling activity on the ship and in the camp. The Dutch had kindly provided three pigs for barbecue and enthusiasm was the order of the day. Work continued on the shaft bearing and all hands were anxious to get moving. About noon two PBYs landed with messages and information. They promised to return the next day to act as escorts. In the afternoon the bearing was reported repaired and the captain made one more trip to Ternate for any last minute information on the enemy. Soon preparations for getting underway were made and at 1830 the moor was broken and *Peary* headed off almost due south for Ambon. At 2219 the ship crossed the equator and old salts on the bridge including the captain began to remember the first time they had crossed zero latitude. Most agreed the real life ordeal of the *Peary* crew was much worse than a fun and games initiation. At 2242 she passed the small island of Latalata but alas, the starboard shaft bearing again began running hot and was shut down. During the night *Peary* passed the small island of Obilatu and at 0730 on the 31st of December passed through Kelang Strait separating the Dutch islands of Buru and Ceram.

In the forenoon PBYs furnished the promised air escort and a Dutch pilot came on board for navigating the minefields off Ambon. Soon after noon *Peary* anchored in the port of Ambon and the captain commenced his official calls after first obtaining a doctor to look after his wounded. Fresh water was taken on board and at 1600 she went alongside a fuel pier for fuel. Then, wonder of wonders, liberty was granted for three hours. There wasn't much to see or do but there was some good but warm Dutch beer. And they got some answers to those age old questions of sailors in foreign ports-are the natives friendly? Yes! Is it safe to drink the water? No! An uneasy peace was declared with some Australian troops present and some comfort was taken from the news that quite a few hits had been scored on the Aussie planes.

At 0900 on Thursday, 1 January 1942, *Peary* was underway from Ambon and after clearing the minefields took a southerly course across the Banda Sea towards the small island of Teun at the eastern end of the Malay Archipelago or Barrier Islands as they were sometimes called. This time two of the Lockheed Hudsons which had earlier attacked them provided escort. During the night of January 1st *Peary* passed Teun Island and at midnight took departure on Sermata, also one of the barrier islands, and headed out on course 155 across the Timor Sea towards Australia.

Peary was still steaming on one shaft at 22 knots but heavy rains caused her to slow so that it was 1600 on the 2nd of January before she reached Australian waters. She then anchored in Clarence Strait separating Bathurst and Melville Islands from Port Darwin on mainland Australia. *Peary* had previously advised the task force commander that she had no charts of Australian waters and early on the 3rd of January our destroyer *Parrott* came out to greet and lead her through the minefields into Port Darwin. Shortly after 1800 she anchored and *Peary* was home, so to speak. She was back with her sistership and other ships of the Asiatic Fleet.

Peary remained at anchor the 4th, 5th and 6th of January for some much needed rest, relaxation and liberty. The arrival of the destroyer tender *Black Hawk* in Port Darwin on the 6th was extremely fortuitous for *Peary* for several reasons. Medical problems had just about caught up with the crew—injuries, sickness, fever, many ills needed attention of *Black Hawk* medical department. The terrible material condition of *Peary* got full time of the repair gang. *Black Hawk* was also wearing the pennant[37] of the boss destroyer officer of the fleet, Captain H.V. Wiley, Commander Destroyer Squadron 29. The commodore came aboard *Peary* and congratulated her on her epic voyage of 2100 nautical miles. He spoke of her escape from Manila Bay and running of the gauntlet down through the Philippines and the Netherlands East Indies to Port Darwin, Australia. The story is one of the great and inspiring sagas of U.S. naval history. Then he electrified the crew by stating that he was going to recommend *Peary* be sent home. Oh, how sweet it was! Stateside fever reigned. More about *Peary* later.

---

[37] Wearing is a British Royal Navy term meaning essentially the same as flying a flag or pennant. The term is permissible in the U.S. Navy but less frequently used. In this instance an officer below flag rank who commands a group of ships may be said to wear or fly his pennant from the mainmast of his flagship. But only flag officers have personal flags.

Chapter 6

Japanese Juggernaut Rolls South

AS our convoy departed Port Darwin, Australia on 8 January, 1942 en route to Surabaya, Java, we continued to get bits and pieces of intelligence indicating ominous enemy activity to the north. This time the convoy passed south of Timor Island and several other islands of the chain, but headed north through Lombok Strait between the islands of Bali and Lombok. Shortly after midnight on the 10th *Marblehead*, *Bulmer* and *Pope* were detached destination unknown. The remainder of the convoy arrived off Surabaya about noon on the 11th but *Boise* remained outside the minefields and was soon joined by *John D. Ford* and *Pillsbury* exiting the harbor, destination unknown.

Stewart remained in Surabaya for the next four days and it was a welcome respite from convoy duty. The crew were granted liberty and from all reports Surabaya was pronounced a good liberty port. One day we ran the degaussing range and one day in a tight spot we busted a propeller guardrail which had to be fixed in the Netherlands Navy Shipyard. I found a place in town to send a cablegram to my wife telling her I was alive and well. As commissary officer at that time I was being heated hot to get some fresh food on board. After five weeks of war and little re-supply, we were about out of fresh food items. I mentioned this to our Dutch Navy liaison officer. He said no problem and left. Pretty soon we heard some cows bellowing in the distance. Not too long afterward he returned with a truck dripping blood and full of newly butchered beef. We had our fresh meat all right but my was it tough and had that peculiar, unpleasant smell of fresh killed cows. This triggered another lecture by Commodore Binford on the proper hanging and ageing of beef. But we did not have the adequate cold storage for the purpose. Our cold box on the quarterdeck had very limited capacity. But in tropical waters we were fortunate the cold box furnished cold drinking water.

While we normally carried a 90 day supply of dry rations and had replenished at every chance, we were now running low and were out of some items. This included canned food and staples such as rice, potatoes, sugar, salt, dried beans, spices and many other items. So we went to see the man again—the Dutch Navy liaison officer. Again he said no problem. He departed and soon returned with a truck. We loaded up storekeeper Michael Hebert, two cooks, a good supply of sturdy bags and with requisitions in hand we headed for the city. We drove down main street and when we spotted a grocery store we pulled over and stopped.

The liaison officer then announced to the proprietor of the store that the U.S. Navy wished to purchase food for which the Dutch Navy would pay and in turn be reimbursed by the United States. We looked at the stocks of food on the shelves and in bins in the store and looked at our requisitions. Some items were there, some were not. It would take time to sort out, pick and choose among the items. But we didn't have much time. We looked at the liaison officer and he looked at us, and after a brief conference we decided—oh, what the hell we can use all this stuff. The liaison officer then announced to the startled owner that we are commandeering his entire stock. We proceeded to rake everything on the shelves into our bags—I mean we cleaned him out, bins and all. The liaison officer signed and handed the proprietor a chit and we returned to the ship in triumph. It was a creative style of provisioning ship. That evening in the wardroom we enjoyed a famous Asiatic Fleet meal—rice and curry.[38]

---

[38] Rice and curry was a favorite and famous meal practically throughout the Far East and India. There were arguments as to where it originated but in the Dutch East Indies it was known as "Rijstaffel." It's popularity in the Asiatic Fleet spread to the Atlantic and Pacific Fleets as well and wherever "old China hands" and Navy men met to dine. Essentially it was small chunks of meat cooked with curry powder—the meat could be beef, pork, chicken, lamb or what was available in the locality. But the manner of serving and eating was crucial to the enjoyment. A mound of boiled rice was placed in the center of a large dinner plate and the curried meat stew poured over it. Then as many spices and condiments as were available, the more the better, were added on top one after the other but never mixed. Some spices were "de rigueur" such as chutney and "Bombay duck" (bits of dried fish) and others of the area. In the Far East there were spices galore and it was not uncommon for a meal to include as many as thirty or more spices and condiments. A dinner invitation might read that one was invited to "Thirty-Boy Curry" meaning there would be thirty spices and condiments. If the host could afford it there would be thirty serving boys each with just one spice. Indeed it was a measure of the host's power and wealth as to how many serving boys he could bring in to impress his guests. The ultimate was considered to be "100-Boy Curry" which could only be afforded by kings,

continued...

On Thursday 15th January the fun was over and another convoy was formed. Shortly after noon we sailed along with *Barker* and *Isabel* escorting four small Dutch merchant ships from Surabaya to Batavia. It had been reported that some merchant ships had been sunk by Japanese submarines along that route the previous week. This voyage was uneventful and at mid-afternoon on the 17th the convoy arrived at Tandjung Priok, the harbor of Batavia. There we found several ships of the British Royal Navy—the light cruiser HMS *Dragon*, destroyers *Anking*, *Electra*, *Express*, *Janus*, *Jumna*, *Stronghold*, *Thanet* and *Yarra* in addition to Dutch light cruisers *Java* and *Tromp*. It was gratifying to see British ships committed to help us and especially nice to see *Dragon*. As a midshipman I had made a call on board her at Gibraltar back in 1935.

Shore leave was granted for officers and crew and it was reported to be a nice liberty port. Batavia was the capital of the Dutch Indies government and the Governor-General resided there. The city was neat and clean with impressive government buildings and a gracious old Indies Hotel with a long bar. This was a nice watering place for thirsty seamen and we found some excellent steaks there. But there was a nasty war to be won.

Early on the 19th we were off again with another convoy of six small merchant ships en route from Batavia to Oosthaven on the extreme southern tip of the large island of Sumatra. Again *Barker* and *Isabel* assisted us in escorting the convoy. We had the usual false submarine alarms but this time *Barker* actually took a shot at one of the phantoms. About 1800 we were near our destination and the merchant ships were released. We anchored shortly thereafter in the harbor of Teloek Betung as did *Barker* and *Isabel*. The next day 20th we shifted our anchorage a few miles away to Ratai Bay also on the southern tip of Sumatra.

There in addition to our ships we found the Australian heavy cruiser *Canberra*, HMS *Dragon* and destroyer *Jumna*. This heavy cruis-

---

...continued

maharajahs or other potentates. But no matter how high or low there was one particular "no-no" for all. The mound of rice, meat and spices was never to be stirred or mixed in any way. It was eaten by a vertical movement of the fork preserving the layers of ingredients intact. The result was a "color rainbow" of tastes never to be forgotten. To violate the no mixing rule was to court being ridden out of town on a rail, walking the plank, shot at dawn or other social ostracism. Enjoy.

er was a very welcome sight to we on *Stewart* and we hoped she would be with us when the showdown came as we were sure it would. There were also numerous British and Dutch merchant ships. The Commodore went over to *Canberra* for a conference and after he returned *Stewart* got underway in the afternoon and commenced anti-submarine patrols off the harbor entrance. This continued all night until noon on the 21st when HMAS *Canberra* and convoy stood out of Ratai Bay. We then joined *Barker* and HMS *Express* in screening a real big boy, the British ocean liner SS *Aquitania*, one of the largest in the world. She had brought about five thousand troops to assist in the defense of Singapore and had transferred them to the smaller ships for the last leg of the trip. We hoped the troops were not too late because we had heard enemy forces were closing in on the city.

When *Aquitania* exited from Sunda Strait and reached deep water she headed off to the southwest and started to build up speed. With the boilers we had on line we began to fall behind. At about 2000 the big ship released *Barker* and *Stewart*. As we left the formation we wished *Aquitania* "Bon Voyage" by signal light. She replied, "Good Luck and Good Hunting."

We were then well south of Java and our courses were generally northeast to head back through the Sunda Strait en route to Batavia. Early morning on the 22nd of January we sighted another British convoy headed north through the strait shepherded by the heavy cruiser HMS *Exeter* and several destroyers. It was the largest convoy we had seen with about twenty merchant ships. We guessed it carried additional troops, ammunition and supplies for Singapore. It was sort of a thrill to get a good look at *Exeter* of River Plate/*Graf Spee* fame back in the fall of 1939.

Later in the morning we passed through another convoy of two merchant ships escorted by the Dutch light cruiser *Tromp* and two Dutch destroyers. *Tromp* was a beautiful ship, fairly modern with nicely designed lines and some called her a destroyer leader. We would see her later under trying circumstances and we can attest to the fact that she was a fighting ship. By mid-afternoon we had passed through the minefields and moored to a wharf at Tandjung Priok. There in addition to *Barker* we found British light cruisers *Dragon*, *Durban*, British destroyers *Anking*, *Electra*, *Express*, *Stronghold*, *Tenedos* and Dutch destroyer *Evertsen*.

But we were not there long before we learned of another convoy being formed. On the morning of the 23rd we went alongside a Dutch tanker for fuel and upon completion we anchored in the outer harbor to await formation of the convoy. By 1700 we had the convoy shaped up and cleared the minefields. The convoy consisted of one British and five Dutch merchant ships escorted by *Barker* and *Stewart* en route from Batavia to Surabaya. But this time we were routed for passage south of the island of Java. Consequently we took westerly courses to reach and pass through Sunda Strait. It was slow going because the British ship either could not or would not make more than six and a half knots. It was billed as a nine and a half knot convoy so Commodore Binford and Captain Smith were mad as hell about the slow ship. It was 0300 on the 24th before we turned southwest to enter the strait.

Meanwhile amidst daily reports of more enemy activity up north including an enemy task force coming down Makassar Strait, we in *Stewart* had been receiving disturbing reports about turbine problems on board *Marblehead* which limited her speed and usefulness. We were very sensitive about our cruisers in the Asiatic Fleet because we felt with their bigger guns they could protect us as we made our torpedo attacks. And they would give us a fighting chance of living to fight another day. Then we learned with dismay that our newly acquired cruiser *Boise* on the 21st of January had grounded with considerable damage the extent of which we did not know. Then to add to our apprehension there were confirmed reports of enemy amphibious forces escorted by cruisers and destroyers coming down Makassar Strait. From our radio traffic there were hints that a task force of U.S. and Allied ships was being formed to counter the enemy advance down the strait. Lord, how we wished we could get in on the fight! But here we were stuck with a slow convoy and a long way from the action.

At our slow convoy speed it took just about all day the 24th to get through the Sunda Strait. During the day we passed a few miles away from the famous island volcano Krakatau. This volcano had erupted in 1883 which is recognized as the most violent in modern times and perhaps in recorded history. It was more like an explosion than anything else—sort of like the Mt. St. Helens eruption in our country a few years ago only many times bigger and powerful. One half of the island simply blew away. Tremendous tidal waves were formed and wreaked havoc thousands of miles away as well as nearby. Upwards of one hundred thousand people lost their lives. The sky was darkened and climates changed up to two years after the blast. From one bearing the volcano appeared as a perfect cone. From a bearing ninety degrees away it appeared one half of the cone was sliced away. It was very interesting but one hoped the next eruption would hold off for awhile.

It was late in the afternoon when we were finally through the Sunda Strait and turned east along the south coast of Java. During the evening one Dutch ship requested permission to leave the convoy and proceed by himself to Tjilatjap. Commodore Binford gave permission and he was gone. We guessed he was so disgusted by the slow convoy speed that the danger of submarine attack might even be lessened by proceeding alone at a higher speed.

On we plod at six or seven knots which is quite maddening to a destroyer sailor trying to provide effective anti-submarine protection for merchant ships. It is hard to imagine a more frustrating experience than a slow convoy. Thus passed the 25th. The only plus was that at that slow speed the sonar listening was more effective. But a modern submarine could catch us even if submerged. It was somewhat dispiriting to the officers and crew.

However, our spirits were lifted as reports and details began to trickle in about the very successful attack of four of our destroyers on the enemy transports at Balikpapan on the night of 23-24 January, 1942. The destroyers were *John D. Ford*, *Parrott*, *Paul Jones* and *Pope*, under command of Commodore P. H. Talbot, Commander Destroyer Division Fifty-Nine. More about these magnificent ships, their officers and their men later.

Meanwhile in the convoy, as we slogged along at slow speed there was the opportunity for cleaning and maintenance work. Early on the 26th of January I had the first watch at midnight and decided as officer of the deck to write the ship's log for the watch in rhyme. The first verse went:

At six knots along we poke,
Filling the ocean full of smoke.

Then it went on for several verses. But the next morning the navigator took a dim view and nixed my bright idea although he understood my effort to counter the boredom. On my watch we passed the port of Tjilatjap over twenty miles away and the big event of the day on the 26th was another merchant ship coming out from that port and joining the convoy. Incredibly we endured another full day of frustration on the 27th broken only by more good news about our destroyers in the battle at Balikpapan.

Then at midnight we got most welcome orders to leave the convoy at dawn on the 28th and proceed to Surabaya at 25 knots. We had already turned northwest towards Bali Strait and at 0600 we turned the convoy over to two PBY planes and rang up 25 knots. The navigator and quartermasters had distributed information about Bali Island and I studied with great interest the charts, pilotage books and sailing directions about this narrow passage between the islands of Bali and Java. At the narrowest part of the strait it is only a mile wide and following the channel meant we were only a thousand yards from the beach on either side. It was a beautiful day in the strait and all hands knew about the reputation of Bali having the lovely young bare-breasted maidens. Every long glass and every pair of binoculars, whether government issue or privately owned was pressed into service for the passage. There was some grumbling about the high speed preventing careful search of the beach. I saw nothing.

Soon after passage through Bali Strait on courses due north we turned west and by noon *Stewart* and *Barker* began entrance to Surabaya harbor. By 1500 we were moored at Holland pier with *Barker* alongside to port. In the harbor we found the gallant destroyers which had been in the battle at Balikpapan. Later in the day both ships fueled but the main business of the day was listening to the wild tales of the men who had been in the fight.

How this battle came about is an interesting story. While *Stewart* and *Barker* were forming up that slow convoy at Batavia on the 22nd for the voyage from Batavia to Surabaya by the southern route, information coming from the radio shack was to the effect that an Allied strike force was being formed to counter the enemy. Some of us had been thinking that it was about time. The cruisers and destroyers of the Asiatic Fleet had been so busy convoying it was difficult to see how a strike force could be formed to hit targets of opportunity. Besides convoying was such a passive/defensive strategy that it gave the enemy the advantage of the initiative leaving us only to reacting to his moves.

It had also seemed to some of us that there was a lull in Japanese activity since early January and we wondered why they did not come after us. There was no doubt in anyone's mind that they could overwhelm us at any time. True the enemy had made steady and rapid advances in the Philippines since the war started but these were operations planned long before the war along with the Pearl Harbor attack force. It is significant that the first invasion point selected in the Philippines was Davao on the southern coast of Mindanao. The Japanese seemed to have a special anxiety about Davao because of the 500 mile proximity to their big naval base at Palau in the Carolines.

Presumably they also thought Davao was a primary base of the Asiatic Fleet. Indeed their apprehension was so great it was the only port in the Philippines that was targeted for a surprise attack simultaneously with the attack on Pearl Harbor. Moreover it was of such importance to them that it was the only place other than Hawaii that an aircraft carrier with a squadron of dive bombers and fighters were allotted for the task. It was the second-class aircraft carrier *Ryujo* and the strike included only 20-22 planes. These may also have been second-class pilots because there was only one U.S. ship in the gulf and she was not hit although there were some near misses. This was the seaplane tender *William B. Preston*, a converted four-stack destroyer. But two PBYs were destroyed on the surface.

The first invasion of the Philippines came when Davao was captured on 20 December 1941. Then followed enemy landings on both coasts of the big island of Luzon on the 24th, Lingayen Gulf and Lamon Bay. On the same day Jolo Island in the Sulu Archipelago was taken. On the 25th of December Manila was declared an open city and Hong Kong surrendered. On the 2nd of January 1942 Manila and Cavite were captured. Then followed what to some of us appeared to be a lull in the action in early January although there were small enemy landings in the northern Celebes on 11 January and at Tarakan on the 12th. But I readily admit this may have only been the perception of a lull.

However, postwar historians have confirmed that there was indeed a period of readjustment of Japanese priorities and objectives at about that time. The spectacular success of the raid on Pearl Harbor and the virtual destruction of General MacArthur's air forces on the first day of the war was heady stuff to the enemy. The equally spectacular and breathtaking victory of the Japanese in sinking the *Prince of Wales* and the *Repulse* off Singapore on the 10th of December using shore-based air power and without risking a single one of their ships was a devastating and mind-boggling blow to our Allies.

These victories together with the destruction from the air of the Cavite Naval Shipyard on the same date, caused the enemy to rethink strategic objectives and priorities. It appeared that conquest of the East Indies and Allied strongholds in the Far East was going to be easier than they thought. It was like taking candy from a baby. Allied strong points around the Indies and the Malay Peninsula could be taken easily and the rest could be plucked like ripe plums. Singapore, Java and Corregidor would fall in due course. Japan's decades old dream of gaining access to the oil rich lands of the East Indies was about to come true.

It was three weeks after the capture of Davao on December 20th before modest enemy task forces sortied from Davao and Jolo for the capture of Tarakan, Borneo and Menado, Celebes. Their Pearl Harbor task forces had not yet returned to Japanese home waters or if they had returned were in port for voyage repairs and rest for the crews. None of them took part in the taking of Tarakan and Menado on 12 January where little resistance was encountered. But the arrival at Palau on 17 January of two aircraft carriers from Kure, the *Hiryu* and *Soryu*, which had taken part in the Pearl Harbor attack, signalled a new phase in the war in the Far East. It was a major step up in the pace of the Japanese juggernaut rolling inexorably southward. Could the Allies offer resistance?

Chapter 7

Destroyers Win One

THUS it was that an enemy invasion force of transports supported by cruisers, destroyers and minecraft departed Tarakan on the 21st of January and headed south. Rear Admiral William A. Glassford, Commander Task Force 5, had learned from reconnaissance by our planes and submarines on the 20th that enemy ships were assembling at Tarakan. Prior to that time on the 16th Task Force 5 had set out to attack enemy ships reported at Kema, near Menado, Celebes. But on the 17th these enemy ships disappeared and the task force commander ordered his ships to fall back to Koepang Harbor on the southwest tip of Timor Island.

Then followed a series of setbacks to U.S. ships which could be ascribed to the fortunes of war. First, *Marblehead* had a turbine casualty and had to shut down one shaft, limiting her speed to 28 knots. Later at about the time task force commander learned of the invasion fleet at Tarakan, he was advised that *Marblehead*'s speed was limited to 17 knots, above that would risk great damage. Then on the 20th the task force commander flying his flag in *Boise* was directed to proceed at 25 knots with four destroyers towards Makassar and prepare to attack the invasion fleet believed headed for Balikpapan. At about the same time *Marblehead* and *Bulmer* were to proceed north through Sape Strait and await further instructions.

But then came the second calamity. In the wee hours early morning on the 21st of January, while proceeding through the Sape Strait, *Boise* hit an uncharted shoal causing a 120 foot gash in her bottom. There was considerable damage to her engineering plant and could no longer participate in the operation. Shortly before *Boise* grounded, *Marblehead* received orders to proceed with *Bulmer* to Surabaya. But less than an hour later the task force commander decided to order both cruisers with their escorts *Bulmer* and *Pillsbury* to Waworado Bay on Sumbawa Island. There the task force commander transferred his flag and staff to *Marblehead* and she fueled from *Boise*. Meanwhile, Commander Destroyer Division (ComDesDiv) 59, Commander P.H. Talbot, flying his pennant in *John D. Ford* with *Parrott*, *Paul Jones* and

Pope was directed to continue on course to attain a position for attack if ordered.

Upon completion of fueling operations in Waworado Bay *Boise* with *Pillsbury* was ordered to proceed by a southern route to Tjilatjap. At first *Marblehead* and *Bulmer* had been directed to proceed to Surabaya but early morning on the 23rd were directed to take up a supporting position off the southeastern tip of Borneo in the event an attack by the destroyers was ordered. Shortly after noon on the 23rd, the final order for the destroyers to attack came from Asiatic Fleet headquarters. What had been planned as a two cruiser, six destroyer attack was now down to four of the old World War I four-stack destroyers. The enemy invasion force was reported to be escorted by a light cruiser and six modern destroyers, each of which had double the tonnage of our destroyers and over twice the firepower.

Undaunted our destroyers proceeded up the southwestern coast of Celebes Island and at 2000 took departure from Cape Madjene for crossing the Makassar Strait towards Balikpapan. It was a crossing with spray over the bow and up to the bridge.

On the 23rd Commodore Talbot had issued his battle orders and they featured standard doctrine of destroyers with torpedoes. It was simply, "torpedoes first, guns afterward." But he was quite emphatic that when it was time to use the guns, he wanted aggressive and determined action. His instructions did not go unheeded. After midnight and in the early hours of January 24th lookouts began to report searchlight beams or reflections in the clouds ahead or on the starboard bow over the horizon.

The course was northwest and at about 0235 a young officer in the crows nest reported what appeared to be several destroyers in column crossing ahead to port at about 3000 yards. The Commodore altered course slightly to starboard to clear and steamed on. The last ship in the enemy column challenged by signal light. Any answer would surely be wrong and would invite a salvo. If he did not reply that would also invite a salvo. The Commodore declined to risk an answer. All hands held their breath for awhile but there was no eruption of enemy gunfire. On the little ships sped at 27 knots. Soon the seas flattened out indicating the lee of Borneo ahead. Suddenly there were the enemy transport ships.

It was a destroyer sailor's dream—finding themselves right in the middle of the enemy invasion fleet, apparently no enemy combat ships to oppose and to the complete surprise of the foe. It was "Torpedoes Away!" for all ships. They had a field day in aiming and launching torpedoes on the port and starboard sides but there were always the nagging questions—were they getting any hits? Were the torpedoes running straight and true? Were they aimed properly, were they running at the proper depth and were they exploding when they hit? Our U.S. submarines had been reporting faulty torpedoes and there was concern that destroyer torpedoes might be no better. There was at least a partial answer at 0305 when a large enemy ship blew up. But considering the 48 torpedoes fired from the four ships at almost point-blank range, one would have to conclude the results were disappointing.

The other big worry in the minds of our destroyer sailors was those big, bad, modern Japanese destroyers. Since they had been avoided earlier in the morning, our men knew they were to seaward from the enemy transports. Now that the alarm was spreading among the enemy ships, searchlight beams and air bursts were observed to seaward. Postwar historians have confirmed that indeed the enemy destroyers did move further out to sea in search of submarines and were not able to counter our ships. The enemy could not imagine that four of our old, little World War I destroyers would dare try to attack their invasion fleet at Balikpapan.

At 0338 a lookout on *Ford* reported a destroyer and torpedoes on the port bow and her captain came left to offer less target by paralleling torpedo tracks. The Commodore immediately countermanded the orders but the engines were used to assist in the turns resulting in *Ford* slowing so that the ships astern sheered out to port and starboard and rushed by at close range. In the resulting confusion *Ford* became separated from the other three ships. But all four continued firing torpedoes at the enemy transports changing courses as necessary to bring both port and starboard torpedo mounts to bear. All four ships expended their torpedoes at about the same time but *Parrott* was the first to request permission to open gunfire which was immediately granted by the commodore. Others followed almost as quickly and in a split second the dark night was lit up with the gunfire of our little destroyers. While *Ford* was still separated from the other three ships, from the gun flashes there was no longer any doubt as to their relative locations to each other.

Now it was the destroyer gunners time to shine and that they did with a will. At almost point-blank range it was like shooting fish in a barrel. Four enemy transports and one patrol craft were sunk and several more were shot up badly. But one armed enemy transport with a well-trained gun crew after several misses finally got the range on *Ford* and scored a hit on her after deckhouse. No one was killed but four men were wounded. No. 4 gun on the after deckhouse continued firing and the fire started by the hit was soon put out. None of the other three ships were hit. At about 0400 with no enemy ships in sight the action was broken off and withdrawal to the southward was commenced according to plan.

The plan, the approach and the execution of the battle plan were a tremendous and spectacular success. The Dutch submarine K-XVIII had observed the battle off Balikpapan and sent a glowing report to Allied naval headquarters in Java that as many as thirteen enemy ships were sunk, burning or damaged. A U.S. Navy submarine reported six enemy ships sunk. Soon the BBC was on the air broadcasting to the world the great allied victory. The BBC even named the U.S. destroyers in the battle and indicated six enemy ships were sunk and others damaged. Officially Commodore Talbot and his gallant four pipers were credited with sinking the transports *Sumanoura Maru* of 3519 tons, the *Kuretake Maru* of 5175 tons, the *Tatsugami Maru* of 7064 tons, the *Tsuruga Maru* of 7000 tons and the patrol/assault boat P37 of 750 tons, all totaling 23,508 tons of shipping. They were also credited with damaging and setting afire the *Asahi Maru*. All were thought to be troopships except the *Sumanoura Maru* which blew up and was believed to be carrying aviation gas or ammunition. The sea around the sunken or sinking ships was full of enemy soldiers swimming or clinging to life rafts. Others were scrambling down the sides of damaged, burning and sinking ships. Some lifeboats may have been swamped by the bow wave and turbulent wake of the speeding destroyers. The lurid glare of burning ships was a terrible but satisfying sight to the grim but proud destroyermen. But now, ever watchful for the big enemy destroyers which were expected to pursue, our little ships raced southward at top speed until dawn when all four ships had each other in sight. Some of the ships worked up to a speed of thirty-two knots while all eyes were straining aft looking for pursuing enemy ships. At about 0645 *John D. Ford* rejoined the other three ships and took her station at the head of the column. Shortly after 0800 the *Marblehead* and *Bulmer* were sighted and only then could the destroyermen start to relax. And my were they glad to see that four stack light cruiser with her main battery 6-inch guns and 3-inch anti-aircraft guns and their sistership *Bulmer*. With the cruiser's help they now felt there was a good chance of holding off enemy pursuit. This was quite a switch from the disdain some of our destroyermen sometimes had for our cruisers.

Regrettably there was a tendency among our officers and crew of being too quick to pin the tag of "reluctant dragon" on any ship perceived to be not ready to go into action at any time. It was applied at various times to *Boise* and *Marblehead* and sometimes to our own destroyers. Perception is the operative word here and was too often based on lack of knowledge or lack of understanding of the facts why a ship might not be ready for action. Sometimes it might be just the opinion of crew members about their captain—whether they thought he knew his stuff, knew how to fight his ship and whether he was aggressive in action or inclined to be timid. When ships were nested together there would be interplay and talk-bridge to bridge, deck force to deck force, black gang to black gang or when meeting other sailors ashore.

Happily all this was put aside as the four little ships joined up with the *Marblehead* as she flew flag hoists signaling "WELL DONE." Back at headquarters British Army type staff officers even grudgingly admitted "it was a good show on the part of the U.S. destroyers and should put their tails up." Admiral Hart sent a "WELL DONE" to Commodore Talbot. Unhappily that gallant officer while resting in his bridge chair after joining up with *Marblehead*, had fallen ill by exhaustion and loss of blood from an almost unmentionable ailment—hemorrhoids. The long, sleepless night of tension, the battle action and the withdrawal to the south had proven more than his system could take. In trying to descend by himself the almost vertical ladder from the bridge to the well deck, he had fallen, bruised himself and had to be relieved from his duties. His replacement was Lieutenant Commander E. N.(Butch) Parker who as captain of the *Parrott* was renowned as a scrappy fighter from way back.

Shortly before noon on Sunday 25th of January the formation arrived in Surabaya Harbor and moored to Holland pier. In the afternoon Admiral Hart came to the harbor and visited the ships. My was he proud of them, especially so since he had been so discouraged by the poor performance of the submarine torpedoes. He went aboard each ship, chatting with the crewmen, visiting each wardroom and giving everyone a well done. He would later say it was the best day of the war for him. For the destroyermen who had taken part in the battle as well as those who had not participated, there was a swelling pride as the full realization of what the ships had done, began to dawn on them.

It was the first time U.S. naval surface ships had gone into battle against an enemy since the Battle of Santiago Bay in 1898. Admiral

Hart had taken part in that battle. At Balikpapan our little ships had covered themselves with glory. The attack was well-planned and magnificently executed with skill, courage and determination. It was a clear-cut victory, the first victory of any kind for the U.S. in the war and was a great morale builder.

Since Pearl Harbor the whole country back home had received nothing but bad news. Disaster after disaster had depressed the nation and the victory at Balikpapan was a shot in the arm for the folks at home as well as the entire Navy. This was especially true for the Asiatic Fleet. Even the Japanese recognized it as a U.S. victory but felt compelled to downplay and denigrate the attackers in any way possible. Postwar analysis of the writings of Japanese historians about the battle indicate an insufferable arrogance and inability to face facts. One claimed the Americans had it easy because the Japanese transports could be clearly seen silhouetted against the burning oil fires set by the Dutch. Another claimed the enemy ships were "relatively unguarded" when in fact they were covered by the light cruiser *Naka* and eight big modern destroyers.

The same source averred that the "Americans attacked quickly and boldly and a more stealthy and calculated approach would have probably yielded better results." That is classic double-talk and is essentially nonsense. Then this account goes into an elaborate explanation and justification of why Rear Admiral Nishimura flying his flag in *Naka* at the first alarm of an attack took his destroyers farther out to sea vainly looking for Allied submarines and aircraft. But it is more likely a lame alibi designed to cover his rear end.

Another source made much of the U.S. ships firing torpedoes but "in several approaches at short ranges, when 48 torpedoes are fired against initially little resistance, they are only able to sink three transports." Strangely this source never mentions U.S. destroyers gunfire which most observers agree wreaked probably more damage to the enemy transports than the torpedoes. This battle was a classic case of the difficulty of assessing the effectiveness of torpedo attacks. In gunnery, especially at short ranges you can see immediately whether you are shooting in the right direction, whether your shells are falling over, on or short of the target. And you can make quick corrections in time for the next salvo. Then you can see your hits immediately.

But in torpedo attacks there are so many variables you do not know what was wrong if your shot does not produce an explosion. Your torpedo might be aimed incorrectly, it might run too deep and under the target or it might hit and fail to explode. This points up the absolute necessity of constant testing of torpedoes for simplicity of design and effectiveness. Equally it points up the "penny wise and pound foolish" policies of the Navy Department resulting in furnishing the fleet unreliable submarine and destroyer torpedoes. The Japanese "Long Lance" torpedoes were masterpieces of simplicity and effectiveness. They were indeed lethal weapons. The men of our fleets deserved no less. See Table 1:

Table 1: Torpedoes

	Size	Speed	Range	Explosive
U.S.	21-inch	48 kts.	4360 yds.	135 lbs.
		32 kts.	8720 yds.	135 lbs.
Japan	24-inch	49 kts.	24,000 yds.	225 lbs.
		36 Kts.	43,600 yds.	225 lbs.

While the ships which had been in the battle arrived at Surabaya three days before *Stewart* and *Barker* arrived on 28 January, it was fun to watch the enthusiasm with which their crews retold the exciting stories of their part in the scrap. Their morale was sky high and they were justifiably proud of their part in the fracas. Their ships had been "bloodied" and now they were battle-scarred combat veterans. Men of the *Stewart* and other ships with no part in the battle hung on every word of the stories which got better as the days went by. All hands of *Stewart* were green with envy of those who had been in combat and wanted in on the action. The radio broadcasts of Tokyo Rose infuriated us and we were itching for a crack at the enemy. It was amusing to hear the banter between men of *Stewart* and the combat veterans. They lorded it over our men who had not yet been in battle and quite a bit of good-natured razzing went on.

Now after enduring that slow convoy for several days, I went ashore that night with my classmate Bruce Garrett. I cannot recall where we went and what we did but it is safe to say we found a watering place and hoisted a few mugs of good Dutch Heinekens beer. The next day, Thursday 29th, I wore my commissary officer hat trying to get supplies all day. It was tough going-other ships were doing the same thing and there were no supply ships present. Finally I succeeded in getting some fresh foods.

During the day a new young reserve officer, Ensign W.H. Harris, reported on board for duty. He seemed a very likable chap, pink-cheeked but so young and innocent leaving doubt whether he had ever shaved and lost his baby fat. Towards the end of the day our engineer officer Lieutenant junior grade Edwin L. Kyte was suddenly detached and subsequently ordered to USS *Tulsa* (PG-22) for duty. I never quite knew what precipitated his sudden departure but understood it was some error of omission that caused the captain to summarily order Ed off his ship and to call fleet headquarters to tell them Mr. Kyte was on the dock awaiting another assignment. Mr. Clark was reassigned as engineer officer. Soon rumors started to circulate that something big was coming up, a challenge to enemy invasion forces moving south. Practically all our ships were in Surabaya—*Houston, Marblehead, Pecos, Childs, Pope, John D. Ford, Pillsbury, John D. Edwards, Whipple, Paul Jones, Bulmer*, eight of our submarines as well as Dutch Navy cruisers *De Ruyter, Sumatra, Tromp* and several of their destroyers. There were also numerous merchant ships and small craft present. It would just not do to have such a concentration of ships for very long. And it did not last long. The Dutch were making incessant demands for more destroyer escorts for convoys around the Indies.

Then the rumors intensified and spread that *Stewart* with some other ships would soon be heading north for a fight with the enemy. Several of the crew sidled up to me and anxiously inquired which ships would be with us. This was a clear indication that our crewmen had formed perceptions as to which ships were real fighters or had bold, aggressive captains who could be depended upon for mutual support in battle. When one is going into battle you want the utmost confidence that the ship ahead of you or astern of you will give you maximum support as you expect to do the same for him. If he cannot or will not, it does not matter what the reason. You would rather have some other ship with you. If a captain of a ship is thought to be timid and unaggressive or the ship has a reputation for breakdowns in crucial situations, you don't want that ship with you in battle. It might not be the fault of the captain or the crew for an engineering casualty in a tight spot. It might have been faulty design or a bad installation of a good design on any particular ship. No matter, you want a ship you can depend on.

It was pretty clear that the officers and men of the *Stewart*, after hearing the stories of the men who had participated in the Battle of Balikpapan, had very definite opinions or perceptions of the combatant ships of the Asiatic Fleet, whether they had participated in the battle or not. One thing was certain, we all basked in the reflected glory of the ships which had been in the great victory and we were so proud of them. But, alas, Admiral Hart soon realized as did the rest of us, it was not enough. Our victory only slowed them down a little bit. It brings to mind those famous words of Robert Southey in his poem "The Battle of Blenheim."

"But what good came of it at last?"
Quoth little Peterkin
"Why, that I cannot tell," said he;
"But 'twas a famous victory."

Chapter 8

Impending Disaster

EARLY on Friday 30 January *Barker* and *Stewart* got underway from Holland pier and anchored out in Surabaya Harbor. At 0900 Captain Smith called the crew to quarters on the forecastle to give us information about threatening Japanese forces in the area. He reported an enemy carrier group coming south through the Molucca Sea, east of Celebes Island, with at least one carrier, possibly three cruisers, several destroyers and transports.

Then he went on to say that we will attack this force with *Marblehead, Barker, Bulmer, John D. Edwards* and *Stewart* with the odds against our five ships. There were some audible groans when he named the ships but it was impossible to tell which ships triggered the groans. Further he said, hopefully with the element of surprise we will engage in a night torpedo attack and if we get the carrier and the other large ships we will then try to mop up the small boys. He also said we could expect air attacks during daylight hours. The plan sounded somewhat overly ambitious with those odds and set some of us to wondering if the euphoria at Naval Headquarters over the success at the Battle of Balikpapan, had warped some judgments.

After noon all ships of the force got underway and headed out the western entrance to the harbor and through the minefields to sea. After forming up the anti-submarine screen on the *Marblehead* we settled on a northeasterly course at 20 knots. *Stewart* searched for a possible submarine contact but found nothing. At 1700 we slowed to 16 knots and at midnight turned due east.

All day and into the evening excitement seemed to be building in the crew and with it a firm determination to do our jobs, to do our part in defeating the enemy. Signalman second class William Kale wrote in his journal, "Everyone is quite pepped up—we will be pretty well rested up and rarin' to go. Crew is mighty happy. We'll do our damndest." Perhaps not the least of the motivations was the desire of our men to hold our heads high among the men of ships which had already been in battle. Mr. Kale also wrote in his journal that if successful "...we'll really laugh at those guys who razzed us yesterday."

On we steamed to the east on the 31st of January until noon then we changed to northerly courses and increased speed to 20 knots. Additional reconnaissance reports were coming in during the day and one of them reported two light cruisers and at least seven destroyers with transports off Balikpapan but no aircraft carriers. That group then became our objective as we changed course to almost due north. At 1600 we increased to flank speed, 25 knots. We had expected air attacks all day or at least enemy scout planes to find us but none came. We had knocked off all but essential work and made last minute preparations for battle during the day. Amongst the officers and men there was considerable soul-searching, thoughts of home, letter writing to loved ones and general philosophizing. But the grim determination to beat the hell out of the Japanese was paramount. It was getting to be an obsession and at the same time we knew that the enemy could overwhelm us. But we still wanted to hit him hard.

Later on the 31st another scouting dispatch reported three light cruisers and twelve destroyers against us. Still later a report had five light cruisers, twelve destroyers and seventeen transports in the enemy force. With that Captain Robinson of the *Marblehead*, the officer in tactical command, signaled "consider the odds to be too great, reverse course to 220 and change speed to 18 knots." Thus the attack was cancelled and the crew of *Stewart* were very disappointed they had missed another chance to strike back at the Japanese. But we all understood the odds and agreed it was a prudent decision not to attack. It was then 1900 and I noted in my journal, "There is a full moon tonight."

At midnight we slowed to 15 knots and continued our withdrawal to the southwest. Early on the 1st of February we sighted the *Houston*, *Paul Jones* and *Whipple* who merged with our group on a southerly course. At 0900 formation course was again changed to southwest and at noon *Barker*, *Bulmer*, *John D. Edwards* and *Stewart* were detached to rendezvous with oiler *Pecos* for fuel. We four ships took off at 25 knots headed due west for the tanker sitting in Bunder Roads northwest of Gili Radja Island. Shortly before 1800 we slowed to 20 knots on approach to a minefield and were soon moored, two ships on each side, of *Pecos* for fueling. All four ships were completed and underway by 2200 on an easterly course at 15 knots for a rendezvous with *Marblehead*. Now we felt that we were ready for another go at the wily enemy.

Early on the 2nd of February we rejoined the formation which steamed back and forth on east and west courses at 13 Knots the remainder of the day and until about 0600 on the 3rd when speed was increased to 18 knots. Then shortly after 0800 the formation started through the minefields and channel to Bunder Roads at the eastern end of Madura Island. We anchored at 0934 and found in addition to our formation, the Dutch cruiser *De Ruyter* flying the flag of Admiral Karel Doorman,[39] destroyers *Banckert* and *Piet Hein* and our tanker *Pecos*. There were conferences of ship captains and other top brass on board *De Ruyter* all day. Our commodore brought back hair-raising tales of the seeming lack of knowledge of the Netherlands Navy of the concepts of coordinated tactics, massing of forces for taking the attack to the enemy and for multiple destroyer torpedo attacks on enemy ships. Always the Dutch insisted on scattering what few warships we had all over the Indies convoying slow merchant ships hither and yon. Unfortunately the British Navy supported them in this so that whenever there was an opportunity to strike the enemy there were few ships available to do it—most were away on distant convoy duty. Meanwhile, except for our destroyer attack in the Battle of Balikpapan, the Japanese amphibious forces steadily moved south taking island after island and most importantly establishing airfields for air superiority. You could see the inevitable coming and it didn't take long either.

It was about this time that a new man for the crew was received on board *Stewart* who had an interesting story to tell. He had been a merchant seaman on a merchant ship which had been sunk by an enemy submarine. As a survivor of the sinking he had been offered the opportunity of enlisting in the Navy if he desired. He was an artificer shipfitter and was a welcome asset to our ship. The story he told was that his merchant ship had a cargo of tapioca and when the torpedo hit and exploded there was this tremendous cloud of brown dust which blotted out the sun. Then when the dust settled—he paused and said if you ever want to have a unique experience try swimming around in a sea of tapioca pudding. He was a pleasant and likable fellow but unfortunately he had some kind of a crippling disease not quite diagnosed and he was lost in a later sinking.

Late in the afternoon of the 3rd of February we fueled from the *Pecos* again and learned that enemy land-based bombers had attacked Surabaya. They may have sighted us also. There had been reports of unidentified aircraft during the day. At midnight we were underway approaching the Dutch cruiser *De Ruyter*, flagship, to pick up a Dutch Navy liaison officer. Shortly thereafter the combined Striking Force

---

[39] Rear Admiral Karel W.F.M. Doorman, Royal Netherlands Navy, Commander of the Combined Allied Striking Force.

was underway proceeding out the channel, through the minefield to sea from Bunder Roads. The Striking Force now included the Dutch destroyer leader *Tromp* and destroyer *Van Ghent* but *Pecos*, *Paul Jones*, *Pillsbury*, *Whipple* and *Isabel* were sent off on another mission. By 0600 on Wednesday the 4th we were formed up in the anti-submarine screen for the heavy ships and headed east at 15 knots.[40]

We never found out the objective of our strike force. Undoubtedly it was expected to be enemy amphibious forces coming down through the Makassar Strait or the Banda Sea. The objective was expected to develop during the day when aircraft reconnaissance reports came in. Events developed with a vengeance but not in the way that was intended. At 0950 a large group of unknown planes was sighted and a few minutes later were identified as twenty six two-engined Japanese bombers. They were far to the west and appeared to be headed for Surabaya when first sighted. But almost immediately they changed course and headed for our formation. At last we were looking at a real live enemy who were trying to do us in. It raised the hackles on my neck but it was hard to realize those beautiful, silvery planes up there flying perfect formation were trying to kill me.

The enemy planes were variously reported at eighteen thousand feet, sixteen, fifteen and on down to twelve thousand feet. Soon the enemy planes formed up into three groups, two of nine planes each and one of eight planes and commenced bombing runs seeming to concentrate on the U.S. cruisers. Standard doctrine at that time called for ships to scatter rather than stay in close formation under air attack. The tactics seemed to work for awhile as stick after stick of bombs missed as *Houston* and *Marblehead* twisted and turned independently. More enemy planes must have joined in the attack and one U.S. observer estimated their number as fifty-four Mitsubishi 96 bombers. After the war the Japanese reported there were thirty-seven planes in the attack. But so many sticks were dropped at the U.S. cruisers one could say the law of averages caught up with them and both ships were hit.

Later that day we learned *Marblehead* was hit by two bombs, one forward which started flooding and one aft which knocked out her steering gear. She also reported 13 killed and 70 injured.

The anti-aircraft fire of the *Houston* was good but would have been magnificent but for faulty 5-inch ammunition. It was estimated that 70

---

[40] F.C. Van Oosten, *The Battle of the Java Sea*, Naval Institute Press, Annapolis, 1976, p. 23.

percent of the rounds were duds. Even so one of the enemy planes was shot down, another was hit and disappeared trailing smoke. Several of the bombing runs were broken off or disrupted by the gunfire. At 1045 the enemy planes drew off and seemed to regroup returning to the attack about 1100. But this time they concentrated on the Dutch cruisers, dropping several sticks of bombs but got no hits. The smaller turning circles and rapid acceleration of the smaller Dutch cruisers made it easier for them to dodge the bombs. It appeared no bombing runs were made on any of the destroyers.

Meanwhile *Stewart* twisted and turned also, slowed and speeded up to foil any attempted run on us. Lt. Archie Stone requested the captain's permission to go aft, take charge of our one 3-inch anti-aircraft gun and fire several rounds for morale purposes. The captain knew the maximum trajectory of the 3-inch shells was about six thousand feet while the Japanese planes were several thousand feet above that but gave the permission anyhow. He knew our crew wanted to vent their anger at the enemy in any way possible. We opened fire at 1011 but ceased fire two minutes later, the first shots any of us had ever fired in anger. It was sort of amusing to hear comments near me as our air bursts appeared to be in line with the enemy planes but far below them. But some of our men did not seem to have good depth perception and were heard to exclaim, "You almost got one that time, keep it up," or "Attaboy, you are getting closer all the time."

When our 3-inch anti-aircraft gun opened up one of our .50 cal. machine gunners either thinking the open fire order applied to him or perhaps from anger also commenced firing. The other machine gunners thinking they had missed the open fire order also opened up. We quickly got them silenced but not before they had shot away some of our radio antennas. While we did not do any damage to the enemy, our men felt a lot better at having fired at the bastards. For me the experience of the air attack was liberation from an old apprehension—I lost all fear of horizontal bombing. Dive bombing was another matter and I hoped I would never see it.

At about 1145 the enemy planes departed and soon after the *Houston* headed for Tjilatjap for repairs and to off-load her dead and wounded. But it was the next day before we heard just how bad were her casualties, she lost 48 killed and fifty wounded. I noted in my journal how horrible it was. Most of her casualties were in number three turret in which powder bags were set afire by fragments from a 500 lb. bomb which hit the main deck nearby and penetrated the light armor of the turret killing all men inside instantly. The turret was completely put out of action. Some speculated that this deadly bomb was dropped in error too soon by a dumb pilot thereby negating evasive maneuvers. Before departing the area Captain Rooks of *Houston* gallantly offered to help *Marblehead* but Captain Robinson declined saying he believed his own personnel could handle the situation. But at about 1300 *Marblehead* signaled that she was using her engines to steer and could not hold a steady course. The formation consisting of *Marblehead, Barker, Bulmer, John D. Edwards* and *Stewart* generally retired to the southward towards Lombok Strait. The Dutch Navy ships remained in sight in a separate group also retiring to the south. At about 1500 *Stewart* was designated guide for the *Marblehead* and the formation for approaching and passing through the narrow strait between Lombok and Bali Islands.

We managed to get through during the night on various courses because the cruiser was all over the lot with her erratic steering by use of her main engines. It is very difficult to do and should never be attempted unless absolutely necessary. It was necessary to get *Marblehead* to a drydock quickly because she was down by the bow. We were able to make pretty good speed, sometimes 15 knots, sometimes 17, 18 and even 22 knots. At dawn on the 5th of February we changed course to due west en route to Tjilatjap. But alas, at dawn *Bulmer* was missing from the formation. Why was simple. With all ships darkened on a very dark night and with erratic courses and speeds of *Marblehead* she simply lost contact. No ships had radar. At 1100 an unidentified plane was sighted to the east and the formation steamed due south for several hours before again heading due west. At about 1500 lost sheep *Bulmer* rejoined the formation. At 1600 we headed northwest for remainder of the day and through that night.

At dawn on the 6th of February the formation reached the entrance and entered the harbor of Tjilatjap. It was sort of a miracle that *Marblehead* reached port. She was down by the bow and her forecastle was almost awash. Heroic efforts had been made by her damage control crew to stop and control the flooding but had not been able shut it off completely. *Marblehead* went immediately into a floating drydock for emergency repairs. The *Houston* had arrived the day before and buried her dead on the morning of the 6th. Admiral Hart came down to Tjilatjap to inspect the damage to his cruisers and determined that the combat usefulness of the *Marblehead* was so impaired she must return to the United States.

The Asiatic Fleet had already given up the light cruiser *Boise* when she hit a reef in Sape Strait and was so severely damaged she had to return home. Now the fleet was reduced to one cruiser, the *Houston* which was also heavily damaged. But the Admiral decided that *Houston* with her remaining six 8-inch guns was still a formidable fighting ship and would remain. It was a fateful decision. One bright spot was that *Boise* before her departure off-loaded some of her newer and fresher 5-inch anti-aircraft ammunition for *Houston* to replace her faulty/dud ammo.

During the day of the 6th we half-masted our colors as *Marblehead* landed her dead. *Pecos* escorted by *Pillsbury* entered the harbor and destroyers fueled alongside. Late in the day *Stewart* moored to Fortseiger pier with the other three destroyers alongside to starboard. In the evening destroyer captains came aboard for a conference with the commodore. On 7th of February *Barker*, *Bulmer*, *John D. Edwards* and *Stewart* were underway early from Tjilatjap for we knew not where. The best guess was that we were being stationed in the Indian Ocean south of Java to remain ready to join up with other U.S. destroyers and the Dutch ships for a strike at the enemy. At last the Dutch seemed to have come to the conclusion that they had better give up convoying for awhile and try to blunt the ever closer enemy thrusts towards Java.

On the 8th we were still at sea south of Java steaming back and forth, reversing course several times en route to an ever changing rendezvous with the other ships. It was during this time that there was some evidence of monotony and grousing among the crew about what some thought were unnecessary drills and the requirement for white uniforms. I remember the captain thought the drills were very necessary and he required a high standard of cleanliness and appearance of officers and crew. But soon all boredom and idle talk were gone when word came that an enemy carrier was at large. Once more excitement began to build, adrenalin began to flow and we were again looking for a fight.

Early on the 9th of February the *Alden*, *Edsall*, *Pillsbury* and *Whipple* joined up with us and soon thereafter the Dutch cruisers *De Ruyter*, *Tromp* and three RNN destroyers. We formed screen on the cruisers and steamed around all day in the Indian Ocean south of Java, back and forth waiting for air reconnaissance to tell us the enemy location. *Alden* and *Edsall* were detached during the evening en route to Tjilatjap. But the formation continued cruising back and forth the remainder of the night and on until about noon on the 10th. At that time *Barker*, *Bulmer*, *John D. Edwards*, *Stewart* and N.E.I. destroyer *Kortenaer* were detached. We took off at 25 knots for Prigi Bay, on the south coast of Java some miles east of Tjilatjap. We arrived before dark and all ships proceeded to fuel from Dutch tanker *Tan 8*. Upon completion all ships anchored for the night.

Early the next morning the 11th we were underway heading southeast to rendezvous again with our formation. But during the night one of our seamen had come down with what was thought to be acute appendicitis. We transferred him to *Kortenaer* which headed for Tjilatjap as soon as she cleared Prigi Bay to take the patient to a hospital. My journal entry for the 11th notes, "heading for rendezvous. Arrived but no one else here. Steaming around. Admiral Hart to be relieved. Singapore about to fall. Apathy in the U.S. What next?" I cannot remember how any of this bad news came aboard. Sometimes we heard radio Tokyo, Singapore, Manila and San Francisco. And sometimes we got news by official messages which is how we heard about our admiral having to go. I was not surprised by any of the bad news and rather expected it. I continued very pessimistic about the chances of any of us getting out of our situation alive or as POWs. And I continued on my guard to keep from passing on my pessimism to the crew. But most of all I was depressed by Admiral Hart leaving us.

What happened to Admiral Hart during about a year before the war up to mid-February 1942 should not happen to a dog. Aside from having to put up with the prima donna MacArthur with his ego, insults and bad judgment, he had extreme difficulty in getting high level guidance from the Navy Department especially in regard to relations with the British and Dutch in the Far East. And at times when he went ahead and made decisions, he was second-guessed by Admiral Stark, the Chief of Naval Operations. The CNO was himself being ground up by the millstones Secretary of War Henry L. Stimson and General George C. Marshall at the instigation of Douglas MacArthur.[41] After General MacArthur's air force was destroyed on the ground eight hours after the attack on Pearl Harbor, Manila Bay rapidly became untenable for Navy ships and Admiral Hart soon decided to shift his headquarters to the Netherlands East Indies. He departed Manila on the submarine *Shark* in the wee hours of the morning 26 December 1941. It was a hard 1000 mile journey on a crowded, hot submarine to Surabaya.

Admiral Hart arrived in Surabaya on 2 January 1942 and he could hardly have chosen a worse time to be on a submarine, submerged a

---

[41] James Leutze, op.cit., 1981, p. 239.

lot and out of touch. General Mac was steadily criticizing him and the Navy to Washington and other events were moving rapidly. Upon landing, there was an old message handed to him about establishing a unified naval command in the Southwest Pacific. Hardly any of us had taken any notice that at the end of January 1942 the Asiatic Fleet was no more. We were now Naval Forces, Southwest Pacific. There were other dispatches of recent days but which were already OBE—overtaken by events. But the big surprise that was about to hit him came two days later. The day after landing he took the night train from Surabaya to Batavia and on the morning of 4 January in the company of Vice Admiral C.E.L. Helfrich, senior Dutch naval officer, went to pay a call on the Governor General of the Netherlands East Indies, Alidius van S. Stachouwer and the Lieutenant Governor Hubertus J. van Mook. After the briefest exchange of pleasantries the governor general read a press release announcing the establishment of a unified Allied command to be known as ABDA—Australian, British, Dutch, American, whose naval commander would be Admiral Hart.

This was indeed surprising news to Admiral Hart and to learn of it in this way was particularly embarrassing. Obviously Vice Admiral Helfrich knew of the press release but did not deign to tell Admiral Hart before arriving to see the governor general. Then observing the discomfiture of Admiral Hart the Dutch asked him for his detailed plan of operations. It was difficult not to see this as a calculated set up growing out of their resentment that a Dutch admiral was not to be the naval commander. They knew damn well Admiral Hart could not possibly have a detailed plan of operations for a command he just found out about five minutes ago. The resentment of the Dutch was understandable because it would have been far more sensible to have a naval commander who was thoroughly familiar with the waters around the N.E.I. But their resentment was misdirected and should have gone to their home government. But they were fast learners and this is precisely what they did thereafter. In addition the Lieutenant Governor Mr. van Mook made a trip to Washington armed with "ammunition" which Admiral Hart had unwittingly supplied them. The admiral had made the mistake of joking about his age with the Dutch civil and naval authorities. No one had ever questioned his physical condition. He had recently had a thorough physical examination and was pronounced in excellent health at age 64. The surgeon who examined him joked that he would have to be killed with an axe. In fact he lived to be 94.

When the ABDA command was set up on 15 January 1942, the commander was Marshal Sir Archibald Wavell.[42] But his chief of staff was Gen. Sir Henry Pownall, a snotty bastard who felt that the Americans had to be put in their place. He thought U.S. naval officers on Hart's staff knew nothing of staff work and they in turn thought he was the best example of a "Col. Blimp" British officer that the British Royal Navy would never allow their ships to serve under. It was soon apparent that the British were primarily interested in saving Singapore while the Dutch placed their priority on protecting Java. And there were incessant demands for convoys. In staff meetings Admiral Hart explained this was a defensive strategy which gave the enemy free rein to advance, establish air bases and repeat the process on their way south. And that the best way to defeat or slow the enemy was to blunt their probes and hit their advances with quick striking forces which had to be ready for that purpose. Admiral Hart got along well with Wavell who under pressure from Pownall and other army types on his staff felt he had to give equal priority to convoy duty and the striking forces. It was a disastrous policy.

On the 28th of January Admiral Hart noted in his diary, "...for three days now, there has been an opportunity for a cruiser-destroyer foray to the northeast and we are unready because of the ships having been at sea so long. They are run to death and simply must have some time in port to get tuned up. At the conference this morning (I tell too many blunt truths for my own popularity), I said that we had made the mistake in all three navies of convoying and escorting interminably. That there would have been no losses if we had done none of that whatever, and that by exhausting our ships in that purely defensive work we had robbed ourselves of the power of offensive work, by cruisers and destroyers just at the time when a good chance for it arrived." Obviously that did not go over very well with Wavell and his staff who were trying to convoy more troops to Singapore.

But the idiotic policy of convoying went on and when there was an opportunity of striking at the enemy invasion forces, there was a frantic effort to collect whatever ships were available while others were off on distant convoy duty. Striking forces were sometimes inadequate and nearly always too late to catch the wily enemy. Our naval forces were also nearly always without air cover. The Allied air forces seemed to be having their own little private war without much coordination

---

[42] Ibid., p. 257-282.

with naval forces. Of all people the British should have known better having lost the *Prince of Wales* and the *Repulse* because of almost criminal negligence in failure to provide air cover. But it must be remembered we were seeing here the classic British colonial mindset of assumed superiority over the natives of their colonies. And this extended over into their contempt and disdain for the quaint little Japanese people with bad eyesight. Admiral Hart knew of course the formidable war machine the Japanese had put together and how best to fight it. But in staff meetings he was accused of overestimating Japanese efficiency. When various hare-brained schemes were put forth he explained why they were impossible, impractical or just unwise. For this British army types accused him of timidity, overcautiousness and not having a stomach for the fight. Apparently the British had not learned a damn thing from the disaster at Pearl Harbor and MacArthur's air forces on the first day of the war and the sinking of the *Prince of Wales* and *Repulse* on the 3rd day of the war.

Again Admiral Hart had continued the mistake of joking about his age and the British staff types used it against him. It was a "crime" that a very wise, experienced, four star U.S. admiral was not listened to in the early months of the war. Of course he should have been the supreme commander of ABDA because it was essentially a naval war. Why a figure like Marshal Wavell was chosen was political as every one knew. Some considered him as just another pompous general right out of Gilbert & Sullivan light opera who was created by the press. He was not quite that but he was available and famous so he got the job. Whether it would have made any great difference if Admiral Hart had been made supreme commander is a moot point. The result might very well have been the same-complete subjugation of Southeast Asia by the Japanese—although it might have been considerably delayed. Or perhaps blunted as later happened in the Battle of the Coral Sea and this would have depended entirely on whether more ships from the Pacific Fleet would be committed. This was too much to be expected so soon after the disaster at Pearl Harbor.

Meanwhile "weevils" were at work in London and Washington. The Dutch seemed to be motivated primarily by their resentment that their Vice Admiral Helfrich was not assigned to Admiral Hart's job. The British seemed to be afflicted by that age-old attitude towards Americans—you furnish the iron and we will furnish the brass—meaning you furnish the ships, guns, tanks, men and we British will command them. Inevitably the question of Admiral Hart's age was kicked upstairs to Churchill, the exiled Dutch government in London and to Roosevelt in Washington.

Some writers have speculated that President Roosevelt may have been reading about the problems Lincoln was having with his generals in the Civil War. He may have imagined himself as having similar problems, namely Admiral Kimmel and General Short. Of course he never realized he was part of the problem himself and was busy covering his rear end for the disaster at Pearl Harbor. Soon our shaken President had Admiral Ernest King, the new ComInch, send a message to Adm. Hart saying it would be best if he asked to be relieved for health reasons. This was the 5th of February and of course there was nothing more to be said. Admiral Hart sent the message although it was a lie, and his relief by Vice Admiral Helfrich was scheduled for 15 February 1942. It was a tragedy of epic proportions for us in the formerly Asiatic Fleet, now Naval Forces, Southwest Pacific. There was a feeling of we are in for it now, God help us!

On the 11th of February we arrived at the rendezvous point south of Java about 1600 but there was no sign of the Dutch cruisers and destroyers. We cruised back and forth in vicinity of the rendezvous the remainder of the night. At 0800 the next morning we four destroyers were ordered back to Surabaya via the Bali Strait and commenced northeasterly courses at 15 knots. Shortly after noon we entered the strait and increased speed first to 20 knots and then to 25 in order to reach Surabaya before dark. We just made it as darkness fell and moored to Rotterdam pier with *Barker* alongside to starboard, *Bulmer* and *John D. Edwards* astern of us. All ships fueled and took on such provisions as were available. It was a very dark night and Mr. Kale noted in his journal, "Lots of the guys are wandering off in the dark looking for beer, bad news, some might miss ship."

Early on Friday the 13th we were underway at 0430 and steaming on various courses and speeds out the western entrance to the harbor and through the minefields. Mr. Kale was right—several men were late returning to the ship and two missed sailing. Soon after 0800 we settled on westerly courses at 15 knots en route to Oosthaven, Sumatra. We continued to stand westward overnight and at 0535 on the 14th we increased speed. First we went to 20 knots then to 25 knots until about 1300 when we commenced various courses and speeds approaching the Oosthaven anchorage. Shortly afterwards we anchored in Teloek Betung Roads, at the southern tip of the large island of Sumatra, Netherlands East Indies, and found a whole gaggle of warships present.

There was talk of a strike north to catch an enemy force of transports protected by cruisers and destroyers.

Soon after 1600 all ships were underway and proceeding out of the harbor. We steered generally northeast courses at 20 knots headed for Gaspar Strait between Bangka Island to the west and Billiton Island to the east. Before dark we formed night cruising disposition with the cruisers in column—*De Ruyter* (guide) wearing the flag of Rear Admiral Karel Doorman, RNN, HMAS *Hobart*, HMS *Exeter*, HNMS *Tromp*, HNMS *Java*. The Dutch destroyers PIET HEIN, VAN GHENT, BANCKERT and *Kortenaer* screened ahead at the limit of visibility. *Stewart*, *Barker* and *Bulmer* formed column broad on the starboard quarter of the flagship while *John D. Edwards*, *Parrott* and *Pillsbury* were in column on the port quarter. I had the 20 to 24 watch that night and after being relieved made an entry in my journal, "Went through Gaspar Strait, bad business. Expect action tomorrow and welcome it." One report we got was that we were up against two *Kako* class heavy cruisers, two *Mogami* class light cruisers, one or two other light cruisers and several destroyers. We felt like we would give them quite a scrap. But one big question loomed in our minds-would we have air cover? We all were very aware of the sinking of the *Prince of Wales* and the *Repulse*.

Chapter 9

The Beginning of the End

IT was a dark and stormy night and early morning on Sunday, the 15th, *Stewart* formed astern of two Dutch destroyers to lead us through the small islands and reefs in the Gaspar Strait. But alas, the *Van Ghent* just ahead of us hit a reef near Bamijo Island at 0525 and we had to back down and swing hard to port to avoid her and the reef. We rejoined the formation in the antisubmarine screen at 0700. The *Banckert* remained with *Van Ghent*. We expected to make contact with the enemy before noon and all morning we were ready to do battle. But the morning stretched on with no contact. We later learned the enemy force heard we were coming and withdrew. As the morning wore on there was much discussion among the crew about the double bad news—the replacement of Admiral Hart by Vice Admiral Helfrich and the surrender of Singapore. All of us on the *Stewart* had unbounded admiration and confidence in Admiral Hart but none for Helfrich. There was sadness, discouragement and defiance but this soon turned into a deep anger and more grim determination to defeat the enemy. And the fall of Singapore—how can this be? Hadn't we all been told all our lives that it was impregnable?

Well, we got our enemy contact before noon but it was bombers not ships. At 1150 seven Japanese bombers attacked from southward and the formation broke up with individual ships maneuvering to evade bombs. At first the bombers went after *Exeter* but she put up spirited anti-aircraft fire and the bombs missed. The attacks went on all afternoon in small groups, three, six, seven or nine each at heights variously estimated from eight to 12,000 feet. At 1220 *Stewart* opened fire with our 3-inch anti-aircraft gun but the planes were far out of our range. We ceased fire at 1222 after only a few rounds. At 1246 fleet course was changed to southeast at 24 knots to commence retirement. At one point a group of planes went after the *Tromp* but she was a very fast ship with tremendous acceleration and the bombs missed badly. Then they tried for the *Hobart* and again missed badly. Next a group of seven seemed to be coming after *Stewart*. Signalman Kale was on his back spotting and when the planes were over us and bombs away, Captain Smith ordered hard left rudder. We were making 25 knots at the time and when the bombs hit the sea we were 500 yards away. Then a stick of bombs intended for *Barker* also missed when she turned sharply. Next a group of planes went after the cruiser *Java* but she too put up such hot anti-aircraft fire they turned away. At 1417 we opened fire again with our anti-aircraft gun but ceased fire after five rounds expended. Our air bursts were far below the bombers. At 1515 all the bombers seemed to have disappeared and shortly thereafter the formation settled on a due south course at 24 knots, heading for Gaspar Strait.

But about two hours later when we were in the narrow part of the strait, dodging small islets and reefs, here come the bombers again. This was a group of seventeen planes attacking from the east. Again the formation scattered but there was little room to twist and turn to evade the bombs. This time they seemed to go after the *Exeter* again and *Stewart* was fairly close to her at bombs away. This was a large stick of bombs but Captain Smith reached into his bag of tricks and backed down full speed. They all missed *Exeter* but we were straddled with some bombs fairly close. But there were no hits and no apparent damage, just a bit of jarring. Another stick aimed at *Hobart* also missed because her skipper backed down and sheered to port. *Bulmer* had a near miss but no great damage except perhaps to her dignity. Shortly before 1800 all the bombers disappeared and the force reformed heading due south at 27 knots. It was quite a battle and the number of planes in the attack was variously estimated from eighteen to 75. They got no hits on us but one plane was seen to be hit and smoking although no splash was observed. Later it was learned most of the attackers were from the light, second class aircraft carrier *Ryujo* although some land-based two engine bombers may have participated. Signalman Kale had at one point reported some of the planes were three-engine bombers, but which were most likely two engine jobs. In any case we were all glad they were not dive bombers and because they got no hits on us we were glad they were perhaps second class pilots. Postwar historians have confirmed that two-engine land-based bombers participated.

Shortly after 1800 formation course was changed to southeast and speed reduced to 16 knots—later further reduced to 14 knots. Soon we passed a terrible sight, the burning and blackened Dutch destroyer *Van Ghent* which had run aground just ahead of us early this morning. Some of us wondered why she could not have been pulled off the reef and salvaged. The *Banckert* had removed her crew and set off demolition charges to render her unusable. It is never pleasant to see a proud warship destroyed. It was a cogent reminder to all of us that war is death and destruction. War is hell and we should all hate it. Now we were on night cruising formation which we continued through the night on southerly courses en route to Batavia. About 0600 Monday morning the 16th our orders were changed. Part of the force continued on to Batavia while Dutch cruiser *Java*, RNN destroyers *Kortenaer* and *Piet Hein* together with *John D. Edwards*, *Parrott*, *Pillsbury* and *Stewart* were ordered to Oosthaven, Sumatra.

Shortly after 0630 *Stewart* and other ships in our newly formed group anchored for awhile waiting for the Batavia group to clear the formation. But at about 0715 we were underway again on northwesterly courses at 10 knots en route to Oosthaven. In the forenoon we passed a large troop transport escorted by HMS *Encounter* on an opposite course heading out from Oosthaven. In the afternoon two more convoys were headed out and we soon learned they were evacuating British and Dutch troops from Sumatra. As we approached Oosthaven we could see the town of Teloek Betung burning and great columns of black smoke from burning oil tanks. The town and harbor were the terminus of the railroad from all points of Sumatra and obviously was being destroyed to minimize any usefulness to the enemy.

Stewart and other ships of our group anchored in the harbor shortly after 1500. Before us was a terrible sight. Trains on tracks running right down on the piers were discharging evacuees of all types—soldiers, civilians, men, women and children all eager to get aboard ships at the docks or anything that floats in order to get out of Sumatra. All were falling back on Java, the last hope of the Dutch in the Netherlands East Indies. These were people who had spent their lifetimes in Sumatra, and now were leaving, abandoning their homes, plantations and businesses. They were also losing their way of life. The sights and sounds of the people ashore milling around in the rain with anxious looks on their faces searching for any means of reaching Java, were enough to convince anyone this was an awful and terrible war.

After anchoring in Teloek Betung Roads we did not stay long. In less than half hour we were underway again and formed column on the Dutch cruiser *Java* en route at 15 knots to Ratai Bay for fuel. It was 13 miles over to the bay. We anchored soon after 1700 and stood by to fuel from a Dutch tanker. In the late afternoon I put on my commissary officer hat. We were again desperate for fresh foods of any kind. With storekeeper Michael Hebert and ship's cook Norman Sims we got in the motor whaleboat and went ashore looking for anything. Over at the docks there was utter confusion and people were milling about frantically looking for transportation away from Sumatra. Everyone we asked turned out to be a refugee.

There were no stores open, no wares or food of any kind of display and for sale except several bunches of bananas. We bought and loaded in the whaleboat as many as we could and went back to the ship disappointed and apprehensive of a dressing down from the captain. But he was delighted. We hung bunches of bananas on the quarterdeck and invited all hands to help themselves—which they did with gusto. It seemed to raise spirits.

Early on the following morning Tuesday 17th February our force got underway shortly after 0700 and proceeded out of Ratai Bay on various courses and speeds. Soon we settled on a southwesterly course at 18 knots heading through the Sunda Strait towards the Indian Ocean. The Dutch cruiser *Java* was the guide screened by RNN destroyers *Kortenaer* and *Piet Hein* together with U.S. destroyers *John D. Edwards*, *Parrott*, *Pillsbury* and *Stewart*.

When we got underway it was estimated that advance columns of enemy troops were only about 32 kilometers away. In order to foil possible enemy reconnaissance of our movements the plan was to transit the strait in daylight and then double back through the strait at nightfall and proceed to Surabaya along the north coast of Java. But at nightfall orders were changed and the Dutch Navy ships were ordered to break off and proceed to Tjilatjap along the south coast of Java. The U.S. destroyers were to adhere to the original plan. At 1845 our ships broke off, formed column, slowed to 15 knots and headed back through Sunda Strait. We completed the passage to the Java Sea at midnight and turned due east en route to Surabaya along the north coast of Java.

We remained on the course due east for the remainder of the night and all day on Wednesday, the 18th. At 1700 we slowed to 11 knots and continued at that speed all night. Meanwhile we continued to get reports that the Japanese were getting closer all the time. Day after day there were persistent reports that enemy amphibious forces with strong warship escorts were coming down through the Gaspar Strait between Borneo and Sumatra and also down Makassar Strait. We did not know what our Naval Headquarters were thinking but we felt that we were being positioned for some kind of strike at the enemy.

By 0600 on Thursday, the 19th, we were due north of the western entrance of Surabaya Harbor, turned due south and increased speed to 15 knots. Soon we were maneuvering on various courses and speeds passing through the minefield and the channel. At 0847 we moored starboard side to Holland Pier and shortly thereafter *Parrott* came alongside to port. The other two ships moored to the east side of Holland Pier, and all ships fueled. We also got some provisions which was mostly dry stuff but very, very welcome.

It had been rumored that we might get mail and that liberty might be granted for the crew. I guess this was mostly wishful thinking—none of it materialized. Surabaya had been having frequent air alerts and another came at 1145. It appeared to be two fighter planes one of which was reported to be the famous Messerschmitt 109 which seemed highly unlikely. We were not yet familiar with the Japanese Zero fighter. Several shore based anti-aircraft batteries and *Parrott* opened fire but with no apparent results. No bombs were dropped and the enemy planes were undoubtedly on a reconnaissance mission. The all clear signal came at 1300 but now more ominous reports were circulating. It was reported that enemy transports were landing troops on the south coast of Bali Island.

It was also rumored that we were going after the enemy landing on the south coast of Bali. Shortly after 1500 all four of our U.S. destroyers present—*John D. Edwards*, *Parrott*, *Pillsbury* and *Stewart* were underway proceeding out the east entrance of the harbor and through the minefields. Upon clearing the minefields we commenced closing the Netherlands light cruiser *Tromp* at high speed. Then the captain electrified the crew by confirming that we were indeed going in to attack the enemy transports and escorts south of Bali. Excitement started to build.

At last it appeared that we might have a good chance of getting in some good licks of our own against the Japanese. We had been frustrated so many times by abortive thrusts at the enemy only to be disappointed. We had fired at the enemy nothing more than an unauthorized burst of .50 cal. machine gun fire and a few rounds from our single 3-inch anti-aircraft gun which had been designed in World War I. For the enemy it was nothing more than a toy pop-gun. As gunnery officer I was eager to get at them with our four 4-inch deck guns. But most of all the entire ship's company was hoping to hit them with our main battery—our twelve torpedoes in four mounts of three each, two mounts on each side.

The plan of attack had been devised by the Dutch successor to Admiral Hart, Vice Admiral Helfrich, Commander of all Naval Forces of the ABDA supreme command, and the Commander of the Striking Force Rear Admiral Karel Doorman, RNN. The plan was simple-there would be three waves or phases for the attack. The first would be the

Dutch cruisers *De Ruyter* with Rear Admiral Doorman embarked, the *Java*, Dutch destroyers *Kortenaer* and *Piet Hein* plus U.S. destroyers *John D. Ford* and *Pope*. This wave would come in from Tjilatjap along the south coast of Java and hit the enemy transports landing troops on the south coast of Bali or wherever they might be found. They would strike the enemy before midnight, 19th-20th of February, then proceed northward through Lombok Strait and retire along the north coast of Bali/Madura Islands.

The second wave—us, the Dutch light cruiser *Tromp* plus *John D. Edwards*, *Parrott*, *Pillsbury* and *Stewart* would come in from Surabaya, pass down through Bali Strait, turn east along the south Bali coast and hit the enemy about two hours later. This would be after midnight on the morning of Friday, 20 February 1942, a day I would never forget. The third wave was a force of nine Dutch motor torpedo boats—MTBs, who were to strike about two hours later than the 2nd wave.

At first glance and on paper the plan looked good. But the trouble was that the first wave would be the only attack with the element of surprise. It was inevitable that some wag would dub the plan as not only simple but also simple-minded. And it was duly noted that the commander of the task force was in the first wave with the element of surprise. We were equally apprehensive that we did not know what we were up against. Vague intelligence reports were that enemy transports with escorts were landing troops on the south shore of Bali. In *Stewart* our big question was what escorts? Were they large or light cruisers, large or small destroyers or small craft? Our kingdom for this knowledge!

The whole operation seemed to be dogged with bad luck from the start. During the sortie of the first wave ships from Tjilatjap, the Dutch destroyer *Kortenaer* ran hard aground and was lost to the operation. Next, the Dutch cruisers on entering Badoeng Strait were so far ahead of the destroyers *Piet Hein*, *John D. Ford* and *Pope* that they were unable to give mutual support. Consequently there was no surprise left to the Japanese after a brief exchange of gunfire with the *Java* at 2225 in which *Java* was hit on the stern with minor damage. *De Ruyter* never engaged and both cruisers proceeded up through Lombok Strait.

Then the three destroyers led by *Piet Hein* were soon in a wild melee firefight of guns and torpedoes with an enemy who was thoroughly aroused but of unknown types and numbers of ships. The drift of the fight was to the southeast with our ships firing to port. There appeared to be one or more transports, certainly destroyers and probably cruisers but it was so dark nothing could be made out for sure. A fragment from a near miss cut the falls on *Ford*'s whaleboat. At about 2235 *Piet Hein* was hit by a lethal salvo or a torpedo and seemed to explode and sink quickly. *Ford* and *Pope* continued on a generally southeast direction towards the island of Noesa Besar which is separated from Bali by Badoeng Strait, intermittently firing guns, torpedoes and making smoke.

Suddenly at about 2256 *Ford* was illuminated by a powerful searchlight close by and seemingly high up, thought to be a cruiser and followed very quickly by near miss shell splashes. Desperately *Ford* got off torpedoes and gun salvos at the large ship which could be seen by the reflective light of the searchlight on *Ford*. Miraculously neither *Ford* nor *Pope* were hit in this exchange and the searchlight was soon extinguished, either shot out or doused by its owner. The two destroyers continued in a southerly direction and soon lost contact with the enemy. It was a good thing because they had only two torpedoes left and were having engineering casualties. At 2315 searchlights and furious gunfire were observed to the north and it was concluded that the enemy ships were firing at each other, since it was too early for the second wave to start their attack. Commodore Parker, Commander Destroyer Division 59. flying his pennant in *John D. Ford* with *Pope* and wishing to stay well clear of the second wave attack continued on south until 0100 on the 20th. Then turning southwest and later to west, the two ships headed for Tjilatjap. Efforts were made to raise Commander Destroyer Division 58 on the TBS radio but were unsuccessful. *John D. Ford* and *Pope* were lucky to have gotten out of that melee with only minor damage—a fragment hit on a whaleboat of *Ford*. But the two little destroyers had done well. No doubt they survived because they fought so well.

Chapter 10

Baptism of Fire

USS *Stewart*

NOW let us turn our attention to the second wave of the attack. At about 1900 on 19 February all ships of the second wave were clear of the harbor of Surabaya and heading east towards the Bali Strait. At 2105 we turned south and then commenced various courses and speeds through the strait. Ships were in column led by the Dutch light cruiser *Tromp* followed by U.S. destroyers *Stewart, Parrott, John D. Edwards* and *Pillsbury*. The Commodore of the destroyers was Commander Thomas H. Binford, who as Commander Destroyer Division 58 was flying his pennant in *Stewart*. But the senior officer present and in tactical command of the second wave attack force was Captain de Meester of *Tromp*.

At midnight we were through the Bali Strait and commenced southeasterly courses while the *Tromp* took up her battle station astern of the destroyers. Earlier in the evening we saw searchlight beams and gunfire across the Tafel Hoek peninsula on the southern tip of Bali Island. We heard snatches of TBS radio talk between *Ford* and *Pope* but could not establish contact. We heard enough to know they were in hot combat. But about 2300 things quieted down and we on the *Stewart* had about an hour of peace for reflection and writing letters home to sweethearts, wives, and mothers. I wrote in my journal, "Funny feeling going into battle." At 15 minutes after midnight early on the 20th we went to General Quarters and soon passed the Dutch MTBs awaiting their turn as the third wave attack. About thirty minutes later we changed course to due east and at 25 knots soon passed the Tafel Hoek peninsula abeam to port distance three miles. At 0110 we changed course to 020 to head up to the area where the enemy ships were reported to be landing troops.

At 0134 we sighted what appeared to be two ships broad on the port bow and we changed course to 030. It was a very dark night and the ships were extremely hard to make out. They only appeared as a little different shade of black against the dark mountains of Bali to the north. But they were close in and estimated at 2000 to 2500 yards. With my large binoculars the ships appeared to be small and on an opposite course. By this time the hackles on my neck had risen and my adrenalin was flowing as I thought to myself this is it. This is the enemy and it is now or never.

I could see that the fire control director did not seem to be pointing quite in the same direction as my binoculars were looking. I asked our director trainer seaman Eugene Stanley, "Are you on target? Do you see the ships?" He replied, "No, I do not." I tried coaching him on, "Come right! Come right!" Just at that moment the enemy ships commenced challenging us with signal lights which looked to be close to the water. Instantly seaman Stanley sang out "On target" as the signal lights enabled him to pinpoint his aim. The pointers and trainers at the guns were continuously matching the director bugs and the gun crews were already standing by with shells cradled in arms ready to load.

Meanwhile the portside torpedo director was tracking the enemy ships and when the signal light challenge came a fast decision had to be made by Commodore Binford and Captain Smith.

There was no point in trying to reply to the challenge by signal light because it would surely draw a salvo from the enemy. The best reply was obviously a torpedo salvo from our ships and it had to be quick. The commodore wasted no time with his decision and in less than two minutes from the first sighting *Stewart* and *Parrott* at 0136 launched all six of their portside torpedoes. The *Pillsbury* launched three. Torpedo mount captains on *Stewart* reported all "fish" running hot, straight and normal.

Lieutenant Stone, torpedo officer at the port director, started his stop watch on launch for the running time countdown to the expected first hits and hoped for explosions. Now it was nail-biting time. The tension could have been cut with a knife. Hardly anyone dared to breathe and it seemed like an eternity. At the end of the running time there were loud oaths and groans of disappointment. Apparently all fifteen torpedoes missed or did they? What could have gone wrong? No one could know.

Then standard doctrine of destroyers came into play that gunfire would not be resorted to until after torpedoes were launched. The captain asked me through his talker on the sound-powered phones if the guns were ready? I had been having a running commentary on our phone headsets with my gun captains. Gunner's mate Charles Gilchrist on gun No. 1 on the forecastle, gunner's mate James Lindly at guns nos. 2 and 3 on the midship deckhouse and gunner's mate Pershing Sales at gun no. 4 on the after deckhouse, all assured me they were ready. I told the captain we were on target and ready. I had a good understanding with the captain that the first salvo would go out simultaneously with opening shutters on the searchlight. Then the commodore climbed up to the director platform and spoke to me to assure himself we were on target and ready. No doubt he and the captain knew that what we were about to do would open up Pandora's box or a can of worms(or any words to avoid the cliché that all hell was about to break loose). They also knew as did we all that we had to hit the enemy in any way we could.

The order came quickly to "Commence Firing" and at 0143 *Stewart* opened searchlight shutters and got off the first three gun salvo at the same time. That way we hoped to tear up his topsides, knockout his gunfire control systems and disable his means of ship control before he could react. The searchlight beam caught him immediately and—WOW! What a ship we exclaimed! He looked as big as a cruiser and we felt we were looking up above the horizontal to his bridge and superstructure. The tendency of our 1200 ton destroyers to squat low in the water at high speed may have added to this optical effect. None of us could ever explain why the signal lights challenging us looked so low near the water-perhaps also an optical illusion.

Our searchlight beam showed there were two ships and we were aiming at the right or rear ship of the two which were on a course opposite to ours. But we could not tell whether they were a cruiser and a destroyer or perhaps two large destroyers. After our initial broadside we were getting off salvo after salvo of our three 4-inch guns on the portside and after the fourth salvo I could see that we were hitting. Seaman Ralph Layl on the bridge annunciator was positive the first salvo hit the enemy amidships.[43]

But in less than a minute after we opened up the enemy opened his search light shutters on *Stewart* and we could see the flash of his guns. Both our searchlights furnished nice points of aim for the opposing gunners. In naval gunnery 2000 to 2500 yards is practically point-blank range and we could hardly miss. Then the destroyers astern of us were into the fray. *John D. Edwards* tried a spread of six torpedoes but two of them jammed in the tubes and again there was no indication of hits. All ships were now engaged in furious gunnery. The enemy had been

---

[43] Ralph Layl, Letter of 17 March, 1999.

aroused by our first wave ships, were at their battle stations and mad as stinging hornets.

Soon the air around *Stewart* was alive with screaming shells some whizzing by but others appeared to be air bursts which sprayed the portside of the ship with fragments. Then very tall splashes from near misses began to appear. There was a sensation of being in a forest of tall trees and I felt these splashes must be from big guns—6-inch or possible larger. Indeed it was recorded in the ship's log that at 0146, just three minutes after we opened fire, that fragments from 8-inch shorts sprayed the bridge structure. But I don't think so. I am pretty sure that I saw the air burst at 0146 just forward of the port beam about mast high and 10 to 20 yards away which knocked several holes in the topside and hit my director trainer seaman Eugene R. Stanley.

The 0146 burst also wounded our executive officer Lieutenant Clare B. Smiley who was on the navigation bridge and who was conning the ship. The fragment that got him had ricocheted around the bridge area and finally wounded him in the right leg. He was bleeding profusely and over his protests the captain sent him below to be patched up by our pharmacist's mate Donald McClune. We did not know how badly seaman Eugene Stanley had been wounded but fire controlman Fred Allison replaced him immediately as director trainer. I reported to the bridge that we had a casualty on the director platform and requested that our pharmacist's mate McClune be sent up for assistance. He quickly arrived, examined seaman Stanley and reported to me and the captain that he had been hit squarely in the chest by a fist-sized fragment and killed instantly. A stretcher was brought and his body was gently lowered to the quarterdeck.

Meanwhile we continued firing with the replacement director trainer. There was no time to be afraid. We were too busy aiming, loading, firing and just keeping things under control. Then at 0147, just four minutes after we opened fire at 0143, we were straddled and hit by what we guessed was an 8-inch salvo. There was hardly any jolt and at first no great apparent damage. But we could see aft the bow section of the motor whaleboat on the port side had been shot away and what remained was hanging from the after falls. It looked like a fish which had been bitten in two by a shark. It was reported that there was a hit aft but the damage was not immediately discernible.

By 0148 the enemy ships were drawing well aft and our guns would no longer bear. We ceased fire having gotten off 12 salvos.

At the same time we changed course to 065 and increased speed to 28 knots. Shortly a shower of sparks were seen close to the enemy searchlight then it flickered and died out. I am sure the searchlight must have been shot out by one of our destroyers astern of us. They too ceased firing and there seemed to be a lull in the battle. I wondered how the ships and my classmates had made out back there.

During the lull, Lieutenant Francis E. Clark, formerly torpedo officer and now was the chief engineer who had been assigned a temporary battle station on the starboard torpedo director, was sent aft by the captain to report on damage to the ship. In addition to the hit on the whaleboat, he reported the steering engine room had been hit and that it as well as the crew living quarters just forward were full of steam and so hot they could not be entered. The hit appeared to be a hole over a foot in diameter under the port propeller guard but above the waterline and no water was being shipped. Miraculously the steering seemed not be affected. The steering engines on these ships were run by steam from a long steam line from the boilers. It was later determined that the steam line had been nicked just enough to leak steam every where but enough pressure remained to operate the engine. On we charged but the lull did not last long. At 0157 we changed course to 075 and at 0201 the remains of the whaleboat were cut away. At 0205 the *Tromp* astern of us was engaged in a furious fire-fight with the enemy on his starboard. The ships we had engaged had apparently crossed astern of us but ahead of *Tromp*. This gallant ship's fire appeared to be very effective but we could not be sure. It was like having a ringside seat at a giant 4th of July fireworks celebration. At times they appeared to be firing giant roman candles—probably 40mm machine guns. At other times it looked like they were throwing bright oranges at each other. It was quite a show. Later we learned *Tromp* had been hit ten times mostly on her topside with several of her crew killed. But we felt she gave as good as she got.

During this time I inquired of Ensign John T. Brinkley in the crow's nest on the foremast how he was doing up there. He replied that he was doing just fine but I think I detected a slight quaver in his voice as he reported several fragment holes in the crow's nest. He did an excellent job as foretop spotter.

Then came action from starboard for *Stewart* and the other destroyers. At 0212 a salvo fired from broad on the starboard bow landed well ahead and way over. We quickly changed course right to 085 and it appeared to be three enemy ships at a range of about 5000 yards who illuminated us with searchlights. More salvos landed ahead and over. At 0219 we launched all six of our starboard torpedoes and a minute later opened up with our 4-inch guns. Enemy shells came a bit closer but missed by hundreds of yards and soon stopped. Then a small craft passed down our starboard side reportedly raking us with machine guns. There was no apparent damage. I did not see this boat and doubt that it happened. At 0221 we ceased firing after six salvos and at that range could not observe any effect. But we believed we got a torpedo hit on the left ship and possibly the next one to the right. We observed great columns of smoke rising from the left hand ship so we knew great damage was done to one enemy ship.

Meanwhile, in the first phase of the battle with the two enemy ships to port and amidst turns and evasive maneuvers, *Parrott* and *Pillsbury* had come close to colliding and the latter became separated off on the starboard quarter and lost to our sight. Now in this second phase of the battle with the continued sporadic illumination and gunfire off to starboard when none of our ships were supposed to be there, we were set to wondering where was *Pillsbury* and was she one of the three ships we thought were enemy? Quickly we concluded it had to be *Pillsbury*.

Later we learned that indeed it was *Pillsbury* and that she had done great execution work on an enemy destroyer with her guns. A timeline analysis of the second phase of the battle indicates that the enemy ships *Stewart* had engaged to starboard at about 5000 yards were themselves suddenly surprised when *Pillsbury* laid into them at a much shorter range. This accounts for these enemy ships abruptly ceasing their fire on *Stewart*. Nevertheless we were sure we had contributed with our guns and torpedoes. But I am glad we had ceased firing. In the wild confusion of a night battle it again pointed up the importance of knowing where your friends are.

Then with the enemy falling well aft on the starboard quarter we commenced a series of zig-zag turns generally to the northeast and at 0224 the captain sent an important message to the acting engineer officer Chief Machinist's Mate Paul R. Seifert, temporarily replacing Lieutenant Clark for the night. The message was "give me every thing you've got." It should be remembered that at that time the captain thought the enemy included one or more cruisers. Chief Seifert quickly started speed buildup. When the ship was new about 1920 and with a clean bottom this would have meant 35 knots. But with the age of the ship and a foul bottom we would be lucky to reach 32 knots.

Shortly before commencing our speed buildup, the rudder of *Parrott* jammed over full left at 0219. She found herself headed for the Bali beach at full tilt and only by backing down full was she able to avoid hard grounding. Even so she lost a man overboard who later turned up back in Surabaya. *Parrott* was able to back off the soft grounding and started to rejoin. By then she was far astern. We did exceed 30 knots before we again slowed to 28 at 0251 and headed due north through Lombok Strait.

Soon Commodore Binford started efforts by UHF radio to get the destroyers together. *John D. Edwards* had been sticking close to *Stewart* but *Parrott* and *Pillsbury* were somewhere astern. The Commodore also came up to the director platform and asked my opinion whether we should pass back through the area in search of the enemy. I told him I did not think it was a very good idea because we were out of our main weapons—torpedoes. I am sure the captain and commodore had already made up their minds and just wanted corroboration. Anyhow I am glad they took my advice. At about 0317 we changed course to 290 to head for Surabaya and secured from General Quarters. However we stayed in condition two with half the guns manned and making 28 knots. At last some of our officers and crew could get some rest. But there was high excitement on the ship and little conversation buzz groups everywhere. Soon *Pillsbury* rejoined and when dawn came at 0550 *Tromp* was sighted several miles astern and *Parrott* four miles on the starboard quarter. What a relief it was to see that our sisterships and the gallant *Tromp* had survived.

With daylight a more careful inspection of the ship revealed that the only damage of any consequence was the hit in the steering engine room at frame 167. The hole was three feet high and 28 inches wide with the bottom of the hole four inches above the waterline. At the same frame on the starboard side were one 3-inch hole and two 2-inch holes. Because of the steam and the heat the steering room could not be entered immediately but all hands were thankful steering had not been lost. The scary part about this hit was that if it had been about two feet higher it might have detonated depth charges on the fantail. This would have blown the stern off the ship and possibly sank her.

There were numerous fragment holes on the portside near the bow, on the bridge structure, the stacks and in the vicinity of the whaleboat which had a direct hit. There were four holes in the crow's nest and Ensign Brinkley wondered how he got out of it alive. We teased him by asking where he was standing when those holes were made. The main deck and bridge deck were littered with shell fragments and the hit on the boat created a lot of sawdust.

I was teased by wags suggesting the red spots on my face and hands were caused by powder burns or dust particles that made me eligible for the Purple Heart. I declined.

Then as we realized that our damage was not fatal and could soon be fixed to fight another day, pride in the ship swelled to the highest ever. Morale went sky high. We had gotten in there and slugged it out with what some thought was a Japanese cruiser and one or more large destroyers. We had been bloodied with one man killed and one officer wounded but we hung in there and took it to them with torpedoes and gunfire. No longer could the crews of other ships razz the combat veterans of *Stewart*. We believe we gave as much or more than we got.

I believe we survived a much superior force because of aggressiveness, high speed and presentation of a lower, smaller target to the enemy. We initiated the fight with torpedoes and gunfire along with illumination and achieved a measure of surprise. Gunner's mate Lindly told me I had to be the gutsiest, bravest man in the fleet for turning a searchlight on a Japanese cruiser. But then an officer shipmate put an irreverent spin on it by saying "either the bravest or the dumbest."

At dawn on the 20 February 1942 en route to Surabaya we learned that it would be noon before arrival. So we break our story and fast-forward to October 1945. Ever since hostilities had ceased U.S. Navy interrogation teams were busy questioning Japanese naval personnel about gaps in our knowledge, what enemy units were involved in the various campaigns and battles, what their losses were and all manner of mysteries that needed to be cleared up. As late as October 1945 there was still confusion on both sides about the Battle of Badoeng Strait. First, the Japanese stoutly maintained that no cruisers were present. What was present according to them was one transport the *Sasago Maru* and four destroyers, the *Asashio*, *Oshio*, *Arashio* and *Michishio*.[44]

These four were part of the Bali invasion force which had escorted two transports, the *Sagami Maru* of 7200 tons and the one mentioned above of 8200 tons, from Makassar to the Bali beachhead arriving late on 18 February. Rear Admiral K. Kubo was in overall charge and covered the landing with the light cruiser *Nagara* and three other destroyers north of Bali. On the 19th, one Japanese source says both transport ships were hit and slightly damaged by Dutch planes. Another source said the invasion force was harassed by sporadic B-17 raids and the *Sagami Maru* was seriously hit. But she was able to get underway in the afternoon of the 19th for Makassar escorted by the *Arashio* and *Michishio*.

---

[44] P.S. Dull, *A Battle History of the Imperial Japanese Navy, 1941-1945*, p. 55.

More confusion of sources—when the Allied first wave went in one source says the *Java* engaged in gunfire with and was hit on the stern by *Oshio*. Another source says *Java* engaged *Asashio* and *De Ruyter* engaged *Oshio*. But we know *De Ruyter* never fired a shot. One source says *Java* hit *Sasago Maru* several times, the other never mentions it. This type of confusion is common in night battles. But the important thing was that Admiral Kubo on hearing of the Allied attacks broke off *Arashio* and *Michishio* from escort of *Sagami Maru* and sent them flying back down through Badoeng Strait to the landing area on Bali to help protect the *Sasago Maru*. That accounts for the challenges to *Stewart* et al by signal light of the *Asashio* and *Oshio*: They were expecting friends, the *Arashio* and *Michishio*. We were thus fortunate that this allowed us to achieve surprise and get in the first salvos as well as launching all six portside torpedoes, before the enemy opened up. Let us look at these enemy ships. They comprised the 8th Destroyer Division and were among the newest, modern and largest destroyers of the Japanese Fleet. According to *Jane's Fighting Ships*, 1943-44 Edition, they were 356 feet long, had high freeboard and superstructures and displaced over 1500 tons. How much over was variously estimated at 500 to 1000 tons. At 2500 tons they would be twice as large as our old destroyers. That is why they looked so big in our searchlight beam. More importantly they had eight torpedo tubes with those lethal "Long Lance" torpedoes for which we learned to have utmost respect. Also they had six modern, rapid fire 5-inch guns in enclosed twin mounts. We were no match with a broadside of only three 4-inch guns.

In one interrogation of Japanese Vice Admiral K. Shirachi he stated that two Allied ships and one Japanese were sunk in the battle. But we know the Dutch *Piet Hein* was the only ship sunk. The admiral may have been thinking of *Stewart* damaged but by no means sunk and *Michishio* damaged. The latter had come down from the north along with the *Arashio* to join the fray in the second phase of the Allied second wave attack. While these two ships got off the first salvo at us at 0212, they were promptly hit with an avalanche of torpedoes and gunfire from *Pillsbury*, *Stewart* and *John D. Edwards*. *Michishio* was heavily hit, slowed and soon was dead in the water with 96 dead, dying or wounded. *Tromp* soon passed her and gave more parting shots. *Michishio* had to be towed north for repairs. In the first phase of the Allied second wave, *Asashio* and *Oshio* were also hit by gunfire, the latter with seven dead. *Stewart* along with *Tromp* claim those hits.

The damage to the *Tromp* has already been mentioned but the battle was by no means one sided as Japanese propaganda claimed. They also claimed that none of our torpedoes hit any of their ships. But we on *Stewart* believed that one or more of our starboard spread of six "fish" hit *Michishio* and along with *Pillsbury* gunfire caused the fire and smoke we observed. The enemy report of the battle while containing an element of truth was a model of propaganda, lies and arrogance.

We now cease fast-forward and return to *Stewart* en route to Surabaya on the morning of 20 February 1942. We also return to our state of mind at that time without the benefit of hindsight.

Soon after 0800 we slowed and about 0930 we went on various courses and speeds at channel entrance. Soon we learned the third wave attack went as scheduled but the nine Dutch MTBs which swept the battle area found no targets. *Stewart* anchored at 1204 in the harbor of Surabaya and not a minute too soon. The steam leak from the hit aft was taking its toll and the consumption of fresh boiler feed water had reached alarming proportions. The prospect loomed of having to shut down the boilers and the main engines.

*Seaman Second Class Lodwick H. Alford
Attached Battleship USS Mississippi, 1933*

Lt. (j.g.) Ed Kyte, Chief Engineer, USS Stewart, in the Stewart's wardroom, circa June 1941.

*Captain Albert H. Rooks
Commanding officer, USS Houston*

Admiral Thomas C. Hart
Commander-in-Chief, U.S. Asiatic Fleet
25 July 1939-4 February 1942

USS Mississippi (BB-41)

USS Stewart (DD-224)

USS Houston (CA-30)

USS Marblehead (CL-12)

USS Paul Jones (DD-230)

USS Asheville (PG-21)

USS Peary (DD-226) sinking in Darwin Harbor, 19 February 1942

USS Canopus (AS-9)

USS Heron (AVP-2)

USS John D. Ford (DD-228)

Casualties from Marblehead carried ashore to a hospital train in Tjilatjap, Java.

HMAS Perth

HMS Exeter

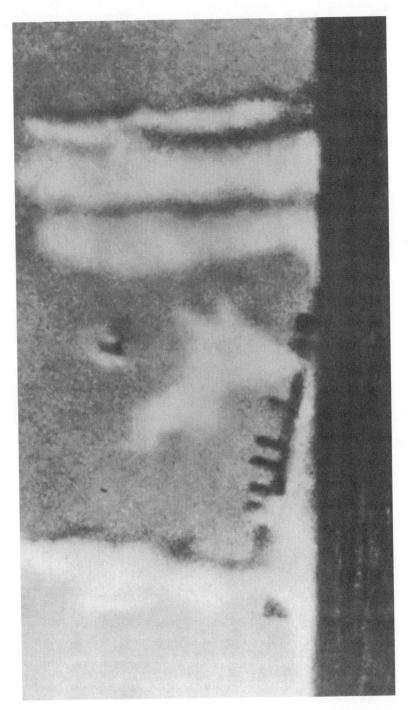

USS Pope (DD-225) sinking, Java Sea, 1 March 1942

USS Langley (AV-3)

USS Perch (SS-176)

USS Isabel (PY-10)

HMNS Tromp

USS Babbitt

USS Blackhawk

USS Boise

USS Marblehead

USS Isabel (PY-10), southwest Pacific, early 1942

USS Isabel (PY-10), southwest Pacific, early 1942

USS Houston

USS Houston at Tjilatjap, Java, 6 February 1942, seen from Marblehead which was passing close aboard. Houston's colors are half-masted pending return of her funeral party, ashore for burial of men lost when a bomb hit near her after eight-inch gun turret two days earlier during a Japanese air attack in Banka Strait. The disabled turret is visible in the center of the view, being trained to port.

USS Houston (right center) at Darwin, Australia, probably on 15 or 18 February 1942. The destroyer astern of Houston may be Peary. Among the ships in the background, to the left, are HMAS Terka and the SS Zealandia.

USS Stewart

S-38

S-39

USS Stewart in dry dock at Surabaya after slipping off the blocks

Japanese PB102 (ex-USS Stewart) after her recapture and re-designation as DD-224 (no name)

Chapter 11

Abandon Ship!

AFTER anchoring in Surabaya harbor and allowing a little time to cool off, the steering engine room was opened for a detailed study of the damage. The living compartment just forward was also opened and it was found that the bulkhead between had been holed in three places by shell fragments. The uniforms and personal effects of the crew living in that space were ruined by oil and steam condensate. It was something of a miracle that the steering engine and controls were intact and that the steam line though nicked by a fragment still had enough pressure to run the engine. It was soon decided in a conference of the commodore, the captain and the Dutch Naval authorities that the ship should be dry-docked for patching up and for quick repairs. In view of the rapidly deteriorating war situation in Java and the Netherlands East Indies, there was no time to lose. Japanese amphibious forces were expected to commence invasion of Java at any time. A commercial floating drydock was available and the repairs were variously estimated to take from three days to a week. At 1320 a harbor pilot came aboard and tugs began to tie up alongside.

A few minutes later the Dutch light cruiser *Tromp* passed close aboard to port and we had a good look at some of her topside damage from several hits. They did indeed look like 8-inch shell holes but I guess could have been caused by exploding 5-inch shells. Attention was called to port for an official salute and *Stewart* crew on deck gave the intrepid *Tromp* a rousing cheer which was reciprocated by the Dutch sailors. We knew she was a staunch fighting ship. We had seen her in action.

Meanwhile arrangements had been made for the burial of our crewman who was killed in the first phase of the second wave Allied attack in the Battle of Badoeng Strait. At 1545 colors were half-masted and we saluted as the body of our shipmate Seaman Eugene R. Stanley was transferred off the ship. How sad-he was one of the finest young men I have ever known—neat, clean-cut, friendly, likable, smart and an all-American boy type. At the same time our executive officer Lieutenant Clare B. Smiley who had been wounded in the battle left the ship for Central Burger Hospital, Surabaya for treatment.

At 1605 with the ship now resting on the keel blocks and timber supports in place from the ship to the sides of the drydock, the special sea detail was secured and the in port watch set. The Captain called a conference of all officers in the wardroom while the drydock was still being pumped out and the *Stewart* raised from the water. At 1615 the pumping out had not yet been completed and the wardroom conference was still going about the urgent repairs to be made, when, suddenly, Oh My God! The ship tipped over to port about half way on its side. We found ourselves over against the portside of the wardroom scrambling to get out of there against what seemed to be a 45 degree list. It was later measured and determined to be 37 degrees.

At first we jumped to the conclusion that the ship and drydock had been bombed. There were enemy air raids on Surabaya every day. When it was found that the ship had not been bombed, some jumped to the conclusion that it was sabotage. While the naval authorities were Dutchmen, nearly all the drydock workmen were native Javanese and it was thought perhaps the enemy had subverted some of them. But this was mere speculation amidst rising anger at the Dutch naval authorities. The air became blue around little knots of crewmen hanging on to lifelines along the slanted decks and railing against the Dutch.

It sounded like some of the words of a well-known doggerel which goes something like this—"Oh, there's the Veendam Dutch and the Amsterdam Dutch, there's the Rotterdam Dutch and the goddam Dutch" and so on. The rage and frustration were understandable. But then cooler heads prevailed as we remembered our comrade-ship-in-arms, the gallant *Tromp*. I am sure our captain was the hardest hit of all. Captain Smith looked like he was brokenhearted and I am sure he was. After all we had been through, the air raids, the convoys and the big battle off Bali, then to have his ship roll over in drydock. It was the last straw.

Actually the RN Navy authorities had been furnished with a set of "The Booklet of General Plans for USS *Stewart* (DD-224)" so that the keel blocks and bilge blocks could be properly placed in the drydock for receiving the ship. But this was a commercial drydock and the workers were used to docking merchant ships with flat-bottomed hulls. They were not used to the slim, curved underwater hulls of these destroyers. Even so there was no valid excuse for the drydock not being properly prepared. An official RN Navy report stated "the *Stewart* tipped over in drydock because the bilge blocks had not been fastened onto the ship, so that when the drydock was being raised *Stewart*'s hull was supported by only a few side supports. These side supports could not carry the entire load since the drydock itself was being raised with some list due to the manner in which the destroyer had been docked. As a result, the side supports broke and the ship slipped down along the stocks, causing these stocks to penetrate the ship's hull plating at several places, and for the port propeller to puncture the floor of the drydock." There was no explanation why the bilge blocks were not properly placed.

There may have been a breakdown in communications between the Dutch naval authorities in passing the booklet of plans to the commercial drydock authorities or a failure within that organization at the level of the dock workmen. But at this point there was nothing to be gained by recriminations or finger pointing. The captain and the commodore had to assess the damage, make estimates as to how long it would take to make the minimum repairs that were absolutely necessary and make recommendations up the naval chain of command. Actually the official Dutch report did not include all the damage to the ship. In addition to that mentioned, the port shaft and the struts were badly bent. Both engine rooms and one fireroom had leaks and two fuel tanks were leaking oil onto the drydock.

Estimates for the time to make *Stewart* seaworthy varied from thirty days to three months. In addition to the enemy air raids every day, Japanese invasion of Java was considered imminent.

Things looked bleak. Meanwhile, just after the mishap our crewmen put out wire hawsers on the starboard side and the dock crew erected shoring on the portside to prevent further listing. Late in the afternoon officers and crew moved off the ship to a barracks(with cots) and began subsisting on the *John D. Edwards*, *Parrott* and *Pillsbury*. There was no way I could see of getting out of this mess and I feared the ship would be lost. Again I took care to conceal my pessimism.

The next day Saturday, 21 February 1942, we were trying to get organized to save the ship. At 0700 the drydock workers started pumping out and raising the ship a bit more out of the water. The port list was actually reduced two degrees to 35. But at 0730 pumping was stopped and the dock officials decided that the ship had to be cradled and the bilge keel removed before raising her anymore. Some of us wondered what "cradling" meant. Little work was done however because of intermittent air raids all day. This work would require even longer time to make the ship ready for sea. Officers and men sensed that this spelled doom for the ship. We knew the enemy was expected to land troops on Java any day.

Into this milieu of dejection came word of the loss of our sistership, the destroyer *Peary* in Darwin harbor by a massive air raid of aircraft carrier planes on 19 February. There were few survivors and the captain went down with the ship. Thus was lost Lieutenant Commander John M. Bermingham, our former executive officer. He was much liked on *Stewart* and all hands felt a personal loss. We last left *Peary* after chronicling her epic voyage and perilous voyage of 2100 nautical miles from Manila Bay to Port Darwin, Australia. She had just arrived in Darwin on the 4th of January 1942 and on the 6th had gone alongside the destroyer tender/repair ship *Black Hawk* for desperately needed repairs and medical attention for her crew.

The big boss commodore of all the Asiatic Fleet destroyers, Captain Herbert V. Wiley, Commander Destroyer Squadron 29 had come on board, congratulated the crew and pinned a medal on the captain. It is not clear what this medal was but subsequently it became known that he was awarded the Navy Cross though again it is not clear whether or not the award was posthumously. But of great importance to the crew of *Peary* was that Commodore Wiley had told them he was recommending the ship be sent home. This of course electrified the crew and stateside fever was rampant on the ship. What happened to the recommendation has been lost in the mists of time, sunken ships and demise of the Asiatic Fleet.

Meanwhile persistent demands on *Peary* for convoy duty in and out of Port Darwin continued and it seemed a day to day affair of maybe just one more convoy won't hurt. Although she was of limited usefulness—she had no foremast, only half (six) of her torpedo tubes, short on depth charges, but her sonar gear had been updated. This situation continued on through January and to mid-February. In a way it was a "crime" that *Peary* had not long since been sent on her way stateside. At last she was ordered to accompany heavy cruiser *Houston* from Port Darwin to Java to participate in last ditch efforts to defend the island.

On exit from Darwin on the 18th of February *Peary* gained sonar contact on what was thought to be an enemy submarine. *Houston* continued her voyage while *Peary* worked over the contact and it was well after dark when further search was considered to be fruitless. She was then sent back to Darwin to top off on fuel but this could not be accomplished until the next morning. *Peary* got underway on the morning of the 19th and was preparing to go alongside a British tanker for fuel.

At about 1000 a massive air attack was made on the port and ships in the harbor. It was a combination of land-based bombers and carrier aircraft including dive bombers. With no effective air or ground resistance the enemy aircraft methodically proceeded to work over ships and port facilities. Casualties, destruction and damage were horrendous. Captain Bermingham of the *Peary* twisted and turned, zigzagged and altered speed as best he could in a crowded harbor with other ships also fighting for their lives. But with his machine guns blasting away at the enemy planes, *Peary* soon received two bomb hits aft doing tremendous damage. Near misses caused numerous shrapnel damage to the sides. Incendiary bombs made an inferno of the galley on the main deck amidships. Ship's firefighters soon had that fire under control.

But the odds were too great. Shortly another bomb penetrated to the forward ammunition magazine blowing out the whole side of the ship. An incendiary made a shambles of her engine room. The dead and wounded were everywhere. It was too much. Her anti-aircraft guns firing to the last, the ship soon broke up and sank in a welter of oil, fire, black smoke and struggling survivors. Eighty heroic officers and men went down to their deaths including Captain Bermingham. Forty men survived and were picked up by small craft.

If ever a man deserved the Medal of Honor, Lieutenant Commander John M. Bermingham, United States Navy, should have been awarded the highest honor the nation could bestow. Whatever awards he may have received, the Navy Cross or other, whether posthumously or not, they were not enough. That it has not been done even to this day will forever remain until corrected, a dark blot on the Navy and the honor of the nation.

The mindset of Washington at the time may be inferred from this passage in the book by W. G. Winslow, *The Fleet the Gods Forgot*:

> So ends the saga of the USS *Peary* (DD-226) and the magnificent Americans who manned her. Hopelessly outgunned, but always tenaciously fighting back, they exhibited a raw courage and steadfast devotion to duty that should constitute an inspirational chapter in our navy's history. Yet when the smoke of battle cleared, the little four stack destroyer USS *Peary*, without so much as a "well done" for her heroic crew from the Navy Department, was summarily scratched from the lists, to be forgotten by all but a handful of survivors and the loved ones of those who died fighting for their country.

Back to the terrible situation of *Stewart* lying partially on her side in a drydock in Surabaya on Saturday 21 February, 1942, we anxiously looked for anything we could do to save the ship. We remembered those immortal words of Captain James Lawrence on the banner high on the walls of Memorial Hall back at the Naval Academy—"Don't Give Up The Ship." Several ideas were put forth, the most plausible of which involved putting quick patches on the holes in the hull and steering engine room, floating the ship and getting the hell out of there on one shaft headed for West Australia. The condition of the ship and various alternative courses of action were being presented to naval headquarters by the captain and commodore but no decisions had been made.

In the afternoon of the 21st I took an honor guard of fifteen men to Surabaya for the burial of our shipmate Eugene R. Stanley in Kembang-Koenig Cemetery. He was buried in a common grave along with the dead from the Dutch light cruiser *Tromp* which included some Javanese of the Muslim faith. The different burial ceremonies of the various faiths were interesting, sad and very impressive. I was not ashamed of my tears along with those of my shipmates of the honor guard.

That night I went to a soiree at the home of a Dutch destroyer captain. The Netherlands Navy officers were very kind to include officers of the *Stewart* and other ships in their social events. This was a welcome respite to the bad news we had all day and the grim prospects for the next day. But I remember a profound sense of sadness that these gentle people seemed not to be aware of the terrible fate about to descend upon them—death, imprisonment, destruction and complete collapse of their world and way of life.

The next day air raids started at dawn but we were down on the ship trying to do what we could to save it. During the morning I had the opportunity to chat with my classmates on the other ships and they were unanimous in thanking me for turning on our searchlight during the battle thus drawing enemy fire away from them. I replied "you are welcome, any time."

But there was precious little the ship's company could do to get the ship ready for sea. It was Sunday 22 February and no shipyard drydock work was done on Sunday. Our situation was more desperate than ever and I began to wonder if my guardian angel would pull me out of this as she had before the war when I almost ran the ship on the rocks at Bataan and more recently when seaman Stanley was killed at my elbow during the battle.

Then came the big news at 1330—ABANDON SHIP! No further efforts would be made to raise and repair. It was a terrible and gut-wrenching decision but had to be made if the crew were not to be sacrificed as prisoners of war. It was certain the ship would soon fall into enemy hands. The ship's company was directed to be roughly divided three ways for *John D. Edwards*, *Parrott* and *Pillsbury*. These three ships were also directed to remove ammunition, stores and such other equipment as they needed from *Stewart* which could be readily obtained or dismantled in the time before some of the ships would depart.

Captain Smith recommended to Naval Headquarters that he remain behind with a small contingent of men to demolish the ship and render her useless to the enemy. He was refused and told that other arrangements were being made to accomplish her destruction.

Then those of us transferred to *Parrott* and *Pillsbury* were told to get our clothes and whatever effects we could from *Stewart* and get aboard the ships to sail at 1600. There was no time to pack up or any niceties. We got mattress covers to use as bags and just raked everything on desks and in drawers into the covers. Then with that 35 degree list it was tough getting off the ship with a big bag load just like Santa Claus with his sack. Alas, I had a record player and a pretty good collection of jazz records but could not bring them. Thereafter when I heard Tokyo Rose broadcasting music I used to have, I swore she was playing my records. There were other things I had to leave behind.

Then the sailing of *Parrott* and *Pillsbury* was delayed until 1730 and I had time to make another salvage trip to *Stewart*. This time I came away with the wardroom radio. We were glad to sail because everyone felt the the city and Java were doomed. While no one spoke of it we were kind of fleeing for our lives and a chance to fight again another day. *Parrott* and *Pillsbury* had no more torpedoes, were low on ammunition and there was no further point of keeping them in harms way. Commodore Binford shifted his pennant to *John D. Edwards* which still had torpedoes and she remained in Surabaya for later action.

At 1730 on 22 February we were underway for Tjilatjap via the Sunda Strait and we had on board *Parrott* Captain Smith, Lieutenant Stone, Ensign Brinkley and myself. Lieutenant Clark and Ensign Harris were on board *Pillsbury*. As *Parrott* pulled away from the dock I gave one last look at *Stewart*. She had been my home for over a year and I had learned to love the ship. I had ridden her into battle several times and she had brought me out of it each time. That night I made a notation in my journal, "It was with a twinge of sadness that we abandoned the *Stewart*, a proud and happy ship with great morale."

In the wardroom of *Parrott* after dinner came my first opportunity to talk to Captain Smith about the battle, the terrible drydock mishap and the desperate efforts to save the *Stewart*. He had been so busy along with Commodore Binford in dealing with the Netherlands Naval authorities, the drydock officials and U.S. Naval Headquarters, there was no time to talk to anyone else. We talked of how the battle went and cleared up questions he had of what went on in my gunnery department that he had not observed. He was very interested in the circumstances of how seaman Eugene Stanley was killed in the battle.

Captain Smith had high praise for the ship's company of *Stewart* and wrote in his report that the officers and crew behaved like veterans. He went on to write that their courage and skill in carrying out their various duties was all that could possibly be desired. This was praise indeed because during my fourteen months on board I had heard Captain Smith declaim many times against the practice of handing out medals and decorations to people for just doing their jobs.

Then in his battle report Captain Smith commended our executive officer Lieutenant C.B. Smiley who kept the conn, though painfully wounded and bleeding badly. For awhile Mr. Smiley denied injury and insisted on remaining on the bridge.

When Captain Smith discovered his condition, he was sent below over his objections. Later Mr. Smiley sent messages during the second phase of the battle requesting that he return to the bridge to help, since his leg had been bandaged. He was a candidate for the Purple Heart Medal.

Captain Smith also had his highest words of praise in a special commendation for Chief Machinist's Mate Paul R. Seifert who for years had kept *Stewart*'s engines in the finest condition. For the night of the battle he was in charge of the entire engineering plant while the engineer officer was temporarily assigned to the starboard torpedo director. Chief Seifert's night long patrol below, his skilful handling of all feed and fresh water, and of the evaporators, and his assurances that he could do it, allowed *Stewart* to steam on, though losing feed water at a dangerous rate through the damaged steam line to the steering engine, and keep her station as division leader.

I mentioned to him several of the stalwart petty officers in my gunnery department—gunner's mate Charles Gilchrist, gunner's mate Henry Grothe, gunner's mate James Lindly, gunner's mate Robert Stange, gunner's mate John Stewart and others. Captain Smith mentioned several—torpedoman Frank Berry, torpedoman John Kinsella, torpedoman Ellsworth Westfall, machinist's mate James Brodie, machinist's mate Grady Burns, watertender Malone Hendry, watertender John Parkin, radioman Victor Frondorf, pharmacist's mate Donald McClune, quartermaster James Hawkins, signalman Lawrence Cushman, signalman William Kale and others.

We agreed these were magnificent men, steady under fire who knew their stuff and were a tremendous example to the men under their supervision. There were many others too numerous to mention. Captain Smith stated with emphasis what a privilege and honor it was to have led such men into battle for our country. Then he related an anecdote about signalman Kale whose General Quarters battle station was as helmsman. In the noise of battle with guns firing and enemy shells exploding it was impossible for the helmsman to hear orders for course changes. Captain Smith said he simply tapped Kale's right or left shoulder to indicate whether he wanted right or left rudder. And all the while signalman Kale was mumbling or moaning something to the effect that they are aiming at my belly.

On Monday, 23 February, as *Parrott* and *Pillsbury* were approaching Sunda Strait, we passed *Houston*, British heavy cruiser *Exeter* of River Plate fame, Australian light cruiser *Hobart*, *Alden*, *John D. Ford*, *Paul Jones* and *Pope* entering the Java Sea from the strait. It was rumored they were headed for a rendezvous with Netherlands Navy ships for a showdown with enemy amphibious forces and escorts. Soon *Parrott* and *Pillsbury* entered Sunda Strait. While aboard *Parrott* Captain Smith also wrote up his report of the bungled drydocking of *Stewart* and her abandonment. In a later chapter we shall take up the story of the *Stewart* after the Japanese took over the shipyard at Surabaya. Upon exiting the strait our two ships headed east for Tjilatjap. The next few days would be the most terrifying of my whole life.

Chapter 12

Allied Defeat!

ON the morning of Tuesday, 24 February, *Parrott* and *Pillsbury* arrived at Tjilatjap on the south coast of Java and found our tanker *Pecos*, destroyers *Edsall* and *Whipple* in the harbor. It had been sometime since some of us had been in company with those sisterships. The destroyer tender *Black Hawk* was gone, on down to West Australia. It was fervently hoped that we too would soon be directed to head for Fremantle. But we had no information on what was intended for *Parrott*, *Pillsbury* and the *Stewart* personnel temporarily attached. Captain Smith departed for Naval Headquarters to get some information and things started to happen fast. Lieutenant Francis E. Clark was ordered by Naval Headquarters to proceed overland back to Surabaya to prepare for the demolition of *Stewart* when ordered. That night I made an entry in my journal, "Japs raising hell everywhere." The situation looked more ominous than ever.

At about noon on the 25th orders came for more or less permanent assignments of *Stewart* officers. Captain Smith was assigned to the Naval Headquarters staff and subsequently escaped to Australia on the submarine *Seadragon*. Lieutenant Stone was assigned to the *Pecos* and I was ordered to the *Isabel* (PY-10), the so-called relief or ceremonial flagship of the Asiatic Fleet. Ensign Brinkley already aboard *Parrott* was then permanently assigned. Ensign Harris went to the *Asheville* (PG-21). In the afternoon I reported on board *Isabel* and was delighted to find her skipper was Lieutenant J. W. Payne, USN, my old shipmate on the light cruiser *Honolulu* back in 1938. I was also pleased to find my classmate Marion H. Buaas as executive officer.

I was promptly made gunnery officer and first lieutenant. The trouble was the ship had no guns to speak of. There were two 3-inch 50-cal. guns, one on each side, which could elevate only to thirty degrees and were mainly used as a saluting battery. There were also a few machine guns. But the officer quarters were better and comfortable compared to the four stack destroyers. Before leaving *Parrott* my classmate Obie Parker and others talked me into swapping the wardroom radio I had salvaged from *Stewart* for theirs which they thought was not as good. I still have the old Hallicrafters receiver but it was

1999 before I had the courage to plug it in for fear it would go POOF! It works fine.

Meanwhile, on February 25th Vice Admiral Helfrich of the Dutch Navy who had relieved Admiral Hart on the 14th commenced forming a Strike Force at Surabaya under command of Rear Admiral Karel Doorman, RNN. The 25th was also the day that General Wavell, the supreme ABDA commander, had dissolved his command and left for India. Remember that the Asiatic Fleet had ceased to exist on 30 January and we were now U.S. Naval Forces, Southwest Pacific. But it made no difference to us on the ships. We were still the proud Asiatic Fleet and we along with the British and Australian ships were committed to the Dutch in defense of Java and the other islands of the Malay barrier. There were some who still felt we were playing for time in hopes the Pacific Fleet would come to our rescue. Our commander was Vice Admiral William A. Glassford who cooperated to the fullest with Vice Admiral Helfrich, RNN.

Late in the day on the 25th the Strike Force made a night sweep along the north coast of Java but found nothing and returned to the anchorage in Surabaya in the early hours of the 26th. At that time the force consisted of the Dutch cruisers *De Ruyter* (flagship), *Java*, USS *Houston*, Dutch destroyers *Kortenaer* and *Witte de With*, U.S. ships *Alden*, *John D. Edwards*, *John D. Ford*, *Paul Jones* and *Pope*. During the day on the 26th, Rear Admiral Doorman called a conference of captains and unit commanders to take place at 1500 at Dutch Navy Headquarters, Surabaya. Commander T. H. Binford, Commander of Destroyer Division 58 and Commander E.N. Parker, Commander of Destroyer Division 59 were the U.S. reps, leaving the captains to get some rest and ensure their ships got fuel. Commodore Binford later related to me what happened next.

While proceeding to the conference the two U.S. commanders noticed three British destroyers entering the harbor and following at some distance two cruisers. These turned out to be our old friend HMS *Exeter*, heavy cruiser with 8-inch guns and a new Australian light cruiser with 6-inch guns, HMAS *Perth*. Ahh—reinforcements, things began to look better. If only *Houston* had her third turret and if *Boise* were available it would have been quite a formidable Strike Force. Even so it was a powerful force but handicapped by poor communications and lack of air support.

The Strike Force Commander delayed the conference to 1700 to give the captains of the incoming ships time to arrive. The British destroyers were HMS *Jupiter*, a nice new ship and the somewhat older ships *Electra* and *Encounter*. After introductions all around the conference started. Admiral Doorman began by stressing the absolute necessity of defending Java and that intelligence indicated there might be two invasion forces approaching. One was coming down through Bangka Strait towards the western end of Java and the other from Jolo in the Philippines down through the Makassar Strait towards the eastern end of Java. Unfortunately there was little information about the enemy warships covering the invasion fleets. There was just this grim determination to get after the enemy transports with troops. The Dutchmen felt their backs were against the wall. Any idea of the acceptance of the invasion of Java was unthinkable.

Later in conversations with Commodore Binford he related how the Dutch naval officers would approach him with statements like "our honor requires that we go down fighting." Then they would look him straight in the eye and ask "Are you with us?" The commodore asked me how I would answer such a question. He said he patiently explained to the Dutch officers that although our U.S. Navy ships would be with them to the end, we had a somewhat different concept of what was "the end." We did not consider "the end" as death or POW camps. We considered the end was the point at which further sacrifice of men and ships would no longer serve any useful purpose. And that it was better to save the ships and live to fight another day. But it was easy to understand the feelings of the Dutch naval officers—their wives and children were on the island of Java.

After agreeing to the order of ships according to size and seniority of the cruiser captains and trying to arrive at a practical means of tactical communications from the hodge-podge available, the conference broke up at 1800. Sortie was set to begin at 1900 and promptly at that time the Dutch destroyers led out through the minefields followed by British destroyers and the cruisers. The U.S. destroyers brought up the rear but *Pope* signaled she could not get underway because of repairs to a main steam valve. After clearing the minefields the cruisers formed column in order, *De Ruyter* (Flag), *Exeter*, *Houston*, *Perth* and *Java*. Screening ahead were the British destroyers, one on each bow and one dead ahead. The two Dutch destroyers paired with the British destroyers on the bows while the U.S. destroyers were astern in column, *John D. Edwards* (Flag), *Alden*, *John D. Ford* and *Paul Jones*.

After well clear of the harbor into the Java Sea, the Strike Force swept eastward along the north coast of Madura Island. Then Admiral Doorman reversed course of the formation and swept westward as far as Tuban on the Java coast. Reversing course again, the Strike Force about noon on the 27th was approximately north of the entrance to the harbor of Surabaya when, the enemy not having been found, the decision was made to return to port for refueling. But after daybreak and during the forenoon of the 27th there were several sightings of enemy aircraft including float scouting planes indicating the ominous presence of Japanese cruisers or battleships presumably not too far away.

While in the minefield channel heading towards Surabaya Admiral Doorman in *De Ruyter* received an aircraft reconnaissance report about 1430 that the enemy fleet had been sighted near the Bawean Islands which were about 100 miles north of Surabaya. At once Admiral Doorman had *De Ruyter* reverse course in the minefield channel and led the formation back out to sea but not without some anxious moments of the meticulous navigators of the force who felt the flagship had gotten into the minefield. After clearing the mines course was set approximately northwest at 25 knots and excitement began to build in the exhausted crews of the ships. Most of them had been at battle stations or with half the guns manned for days now as sweeps were made north of Java looking for the enemy. Now with the immediate prospect of getting at the Japanese enemy, the adrenalin began to flow freely.

At about 1615 one of the British destroyers in the van reported two battleships off to starboard. This was quickly corrected to two heavy cruisers after a few apprehensive moments. The enemy and Allied formations were on approximately opposite courses with the range closing rapidly. Soon the heavy ships were in sight of each other and the enemy were identified as *Nachi* class heavy cruisers with ten 8-inch guns in five turrets and eight torpedo tubes each. They were indeed the *Nachi* flying the flag of Rear Admiral Takeo Takagi, Commander of the 5th Cruiser Division, and her sistership *Haguro*. At about 1617 *Nachi* opened fire at an extreme range variously reported from 28,000 to 30,000 yards. Our heavy cruisers opened up return fire a couple of minutes later. Meanwhile at about the same time as the first sighting the British destroyer *Electra* in the van sighted and reported one light cruiser and several large destroyers bearing 330 degrees, hull down and apparently on a southwesterly course. This was the four stack light cruiser *Jintsu* flying the flag of Rear Admiral Tanaka, Commander of Destroyer Squadron 2 plus four of his destroyers. Dutch sources reported this was the first sighting but it did not matter which sighting was first, either way it was bad news for Admiral Doorman and the Allied ships.

It meant there was more to contend with than just two enemy cruisers and that the enemy transports had not yet been found. Two days earlier Admiral Doorman had told Commodore Binford that his ships 4-inch guns would be useless against enemy cruisers and he wanted our destroyers to remain astern of his cruisers in readiness to engage enemy transports when found with torpedoes and gunfire. This limited perception of the role of destroyers in a naval battle raised a lot of eyebrows in the U.S. destroyers.

But there was no time for ruminations. The range was closing rapidly and it was quickly realized by Admiral Doorman that both groups of enemy ships were about to cross the "T"[45] of his formation. At first he changed course 20 degrees to port and then to 260 to eliminate this tactical advantage to the enemy while continuing to close and bring the enemy within the range of the 6-inch guns of his light cruisers. At the first salvos of the heavy ships, the British destroyers in the van wheeled around to port to the disengaged side of the Allied ships. The two Dutch destroyers were still on the port quarter of the heavy ships and the U.S. destroyers remained in column astern but quickly moved over to the port quarter of our cruisers. And almost immediately it became apparent that the enemy cruisers were screened to port by four destroyers belonging to the *Jintsu* group.

Simultaneously a forest of masts appeared to the north and to the starboard of the enemy cruisers. Aha! U.S. destroyermen thought to themselves, could this be the enemy transports and how can we get at them? The answer was not long in coming. It was more enemy destroyers headed due south and coming on fast. It was six destroyers with the four stack light cruiser *Naka* flying the flag of Rear Admiral Nishimura, Commander Destroyer Squadron 4 proceeding at high speed for a favorable position for torpedo attack. At about 1617 or soon after the enemy opened fire his cruisers turned towards the southwest as did *Jintsu* with her flotilla of destroyers more or less paralleling the Allied ships.

But the *Naka* group with six enemy destroyers kept on barreling south until about 1630 when they too turned southwest and at 1633 commenced launching torpedoes. The British destroyers were out there to meet them and sharp fire-fights ensued. To the men of the U.S. destroyers it was a grand spectacle as they observed the gallant British destroyers charging in with guns blazing and flying as high as

---

[45] F.C. Van Oosten, op.cit., p. 46.

possible their largest white ensigns in one of the finest traditions of the Royal Navy. The enemy flotilla managed to get off additional long lance torpedoes at about 1640 and 1645, then made smoke as they continued westward. The enemy heavy cruiser *Haguro* also got off a salvo of eight torpedoes about 1652 at the range of about 25,000 yards. But at the extreme ranges at which the torpedoes were launched and gunfire exchanged there had been no hits scored.

Meanwhile the gunnery duel between the cruiser battle lines continued apace. The first salvo of the enemy fell 2000 yards short but succeeding salvos rapidly adjusted to the range and straddles began to fall. The enemy salvo patterns were small and there was no doubt that Japanese gunnery was excellent with the assistance of spotter planes which had almost unlimited space over the battle. An occasional spot plane was driven off by Allied anti-aircraft fire. But the Allied ships were denied the advantage of spotter planes because Admiral Doorman had expected only night battles and made the decision to leave spotter planes ashore in order to reduce the fire hazard of aviation gas. Even so the opening salvo of the *Houston* called forth from the foretop spotter "no change" in the range. The sixth salvo was a straddle and on the tenth *Houston* drew first blood on the second cruiser in the enemy column. Additional hits were observed and fires were noted forward and amidships on the enemy cruiser. She turned away into a thick smokescreen.

For a quarter of an hour or so after the enemy cruisers opened fire, they seemed to concentrate their fire on the first two ships in the Allied column, *De Ruyter* and *Exeter*, especially the latter. *Houston* and ships astern of her seemed to be ignored. But after *Houston* had scored hits on the enemy cruiser, she began to be straddled herself. And soon after the enemy cruiser which had been damaged returned to the battle line and resumed fire albeit at a slower rate of fire. Evidently the enemy damage control was very effective or the hits scored had not been very destructive. Then *Houston* and *Perth* came under a concentration of fire. They were straddled salvo after salvo but seemed to bear a charmed life. But inevitably hits were scored on the Allied cruisers. Both Dutch cruisers were hit, *De Ruyter* twice and *Java* once. Early on *Exeter* had one hit and after almost 45 minutes of the gunnery duel *Houston* received two hits both of which were duds and did little damage. Up to that point it was the same with the other Allied cruisers, either duds or superficial damage.

All this time the men of the U.S. destroyers from their position on the port quarter of the Allied cruisers were goggle-eyed at the spectacle and puzzled by the tactics of Admiral Doorman. They were guessing about his intentions. In conversations with Commodore Binford later, he related to me how they wondered whether Admiral Doorman had forgotten about the U.S. destroyers, was too preoccupied to consider using them to his advantage in the battle or whether he had no concept of the proper use of destroyers in a major naval engagement. But our men were itching to get in the fight although they knew that ship for ship our little four stackers could not match up with the large Japanese destroyers. Perhaps the admiral was waiting for the propitious time to "send in the destroyers."

Then calamity struck. At 1708 *Exeter* took a hit which knocked out six of her eight boilers and wreaked havoc on board. She sheered out to port and lost speed rapidly down to about ten knots. The ships astern of her also turned thinking they may have missed a signal but the flagship *De Ruyter* momentarily continued on course and confusion reigned for a few minutes. *Perth* began to lay a smoke screen around the stricken *Exeter* and the British destroyers joined in this effort. Order was soon restored and the flagship regained her position at the head of the Allied column on a generally southward course. Meanwhile at about the time *Exeter* received her destructive hit the U.S. destroyers had reached a position on the port beam of the cruisers and were also confused by the Allied ships turning to port.

Then calamity struck again. At about 1713 the Dutch destroyer *Kortenaer* was struck by a torpedo, most likely one of the lethal long lance types launched in the first torpedo attack by the enemy. There was a tremendous explosion, she turned bottom up, jack-knifed and sank within two minutes, taking down with her 56 of her crew of 150. Adding to the confusion were torpedo tracks observed and the maneuvers to evade as well as the automatic explosions of the torpedoes at the end of their runs. The *John D. Ford* narrowly escaped a torpedo which overtook and passed her a few feet on her portside. The U.S. destroyers generally followed the movements of the cruisers, first turning southwest and then southeast at about 1725. Meanwhile the enemy destroyer flotillas appeared to be forming up for another torpedo attack. Admiral Doorman ordered the British destroyers to counterattack. At about the same time the *Exeter* was directed to return to Surabaya for repairs escorted by the Dutch destroyer *Witte de With*. Further adding to the confusion enemy bombers attacked but no hits were scored. Heavy smokescreens in the area alternately obscured and sometimes clarified the situation.

As the enemy destroyers bored in for the torpedo attack, British destroyers *Electra* and *Encounter* rushed through a smoke screen to meet them. At that moment HMS *Jupiter* was a bit too far away for support. Suddenly at about 1730 *Electra* and *Encounter* emerged from the smoke screen into brilliant sunshine with six enemy destroyers and the light cruiser *Jintsu* at almost point blank range. In the savage firefight which followed *Electra* scored hits on the enemy ships but she was hit by an avalanche of shells and was soon blasted into a flaming hulk, sinking about 1800. Meanwhile *Jupiter* had come up and joined in the savage melee but soon realizing the odds against them, *Jupiter* and *Encounter* ducked back into the smoke screen.

Then enemy destroyers were in range of our cruiser guns and under heavy fire withdrew to a safer distance but not before three of their destroyers were heavily hit. Indeed the destroyer *Asagumo* was dead in the water for about forty minutes and had to withdraw to join the enemy transports not yet in sight. By this time our remaining cruisers were reformed with *De Ruyter* leading followed by *Perth*, *Houston* and *Java* on a generally south to southeastward course. And remarkably the U.S. destroyers were now between the Allied and enemy cruisers. At about 1806, miracle of miracles it seemed to our destroyermen, Admiral Doorman ordered Commodore Binford with his destroyers to attack. But the order had to pass through the jury-rigged communication system, TBS radio, liaison officers, flag hoists and finally blinker lights. As the U.S. destroyers were forming for the charge the order to attack was cancelled and there was a new signal to make smoke.

Then came a third message variously interpreted as "I am going to attack—follow me," "cover my retirement" or simply "follow me." By this time our destroyermen were thoroughly confused and not only wondering what the signal meant but what were the overall intentions of Admiral Doorman. Commodore Binford related to me afterwards how he decided in conversation with Captain Eccles on the bridge of *John D. Edwards*, to go ahead and make a torpedo attack on the enemy cruisers. He reasoned that the best contribution the U.S. destroyers could make for the Allied force would be to attack the enemy battle line with torpedoes, the destroyer main battery. Here the U.S. destroyers were already in between the cruiser battle lines, it was getting close to sunset, fuel was getting low and it was now or never he reasoned. Besides he knew our destroyermen were anxious to get into the fight.

Giving the order to form for torpedo attack he headed off to the northwest to close the range on the enemy cruisers then about 22,000 yards off to starboard and appearing to be heading southwest on a course about 250 degrees. It did indeed appear that the enemy cruisers were trying to head in for the kill on our outgunned cruisers then on a northeast course of about 070 degrees. Boring in for the attack at 28 knots our men lay to their tasks with enthusiasm. This too was a destroyerman's dream—to make a determined torpedo attack on the enemy battle line to sink his ships if possible, disrupt his gunfire, distract his attention, make him turn away, or anything to give our battle line an advantage. It was standard destroyer doctrine and in peacetime the training maneuver was practiced many times.

But this was war for real and here they were with adrenaline flowing and acting out that old U.S. Navy fleet tradition when the word comes to "Send in the destroyers." Commodore Binford signaled for a starboard torpedo salvo at a range of about 10,000 yards. On they charged as the secondary batteries of the enemy cruisers opened up and splashes began to fall around our destroyers. But no hits were scored due in part to the long range and the low silhouette presented by our four pipers which tend to squat low in the water at high speed. To add to the wild scene, enemy bombers made runs on our destroyers but got no hits.

At 1817 it was "torpedoes away" as the torpedo mount captains reported the "fish" running "hot, straight and normal." The starboard salvo consisted of a 20 torpedo spread launched at ranges variously estimated from 10,000 to 13,000 yards. *John D. Edwards* had only three "fish" for the starboard launch and there was a misfire on *Paul Jones*. Promptly the Commodore changed the course of his column of four ships to about 080 degrees so the portside torpedo mounts would bear and prepared for another salvo. It was sunset at 1820 and shortly after at 1827 it was again "torpedoes away" for a portside spread of 21 "fish."

Unfortunately no hits were observed but the enemy cruisers turned away to northward and broke off contact just as a shell hit on the stern of *Haguro*, second ship in the enemy column. The cruiser gunnery duel had continued during the destroyer torpedo attack and the hit may have come from *Houston* or *Perth*. The hit caused a brilliant fire on the stern of the enemy cruiser and was attributed by the Dutch to ignition of aviation gasoline. Evidently the enemy cruiser damage control party was able to put out the fire without great effect on her fighting ability.

Curiously the Japanese battle reports made no mention of the hit and resulting fire. Also curiously there was no mention of the U.S. destroyer torpedo attack. But perhaps one should say characteristically the enemy could not and would not bring himself to admit a non-crippling hit on a cruiser nor that he had turned away because of the destroyer torpedo attack. We saw before this enemy reluctance to admit any damage in their reports on the Battle of Badoeng Strait. But the Japanese commander, Admiral Takagi was at pains to explain why he had turned away and headed north-he was afraid of running into the Dutch minefield north of Java and was afraid of Allied submarines he said.

However the Japanese did magnanimously give the credit to the gallant British destroyer *Electra* for very damaging hits on their destroyer *Asagumo* causing her to go dead in the water for a long while. Of course *Electra* herself sank as a result of that fire-fight and the Dutch battle reports suggested that *Exeter* and *Witte de With* may have contributed to the hits on *Asagumo*. Samuel Morison in his book about destroyer operations credits our four stackers with gunnery hits on the *Asagumo* during the torpedo attack. Whatever the credits, the torpedo attack of the old four stack U.S. destroyers on the enemy battle line was a classic destroyer combat maneuver which was smartly executed with courage, dash and elan. And it was a tactical success. Lieutenant Commander L.E. Coley, captain of the *Alden*, the men of which with very few exceptions had not been in combat before, reported that his crew behaved like veterans. It is no wonder that the performance of the old World War I destroyers of the Asiatic Fleet in the early months of World War II has been sometimes compared to the "Charge of the Light Brigade" in the Crimean War made famous by Alfred Lord Tennyson's poem by the same name.[46] It was easy to make the poetic transition from the approximately six hundred men in those four destroyers that day in 1942 to those who in 1854 "Into the valley of death, Rode the six hundred." For his part in leading the daring and courageous destroyer attack, Commodore Binford was awarded the Navy Cross.

By the time the torpedo attack was completed about 1830, it was getting dark and Commodore Binford sought to rejoin the Allied cruisers then due east and headed north. Soon the trademark signal "Follow Me" was picked up by blinker light from Admiral Doorman and rendezvous was made about 1840 at which time the force headed northwest at 28-29 knots. The U.S. destroyers took up station in col-

---

[46] J. D. Mullin, *Another Six Hundred*. Privately published, inside back cover.

umn on the starboard quarter of the cruisers while the two remaining British destroyers were on the port bow.

Meanwhile all hands in the Allied force except perhaps those on the flagship were wondering what were Admiral Doorman's intentions. He had earlier indicated he thought the enemy cruisers were headed west and most guessed that Admiral Doorman was trying to take a round about way to get at the enemy transports. If so all hands including the Admiral were disabused of the idea of end-running the enemy warships when at about 1930 the enemy ships were sighted on the port beam at some distance. They were keeping pace with the Allied Strike Force with their aircraft reporting every move of our ships.

Perth fired star shells but they did not reveal the enemy. Then the British destroyers engaged in a brief fire-fight with *Jintsu* which launched four torpedoes, made smoke and withdrew northwest. This was followed by a short gunnery duel of the cruisers which was inconclusive. Then at 1937 Admiral Doorman changed course at first to the east and then southeast. But soon after several enemy parachute flares one after the other lighted up the Allied ships revealing their new course and speed. It was an ominous portent. At 2008 course was changed to due south and continued until 2100 when the dark mountains of Java loomed ahead indicating shallow water would soon be encountered. Then course was changed westerly at about 280 degrees and at the same time Commodore Binford with the four U.S. destroyers were detached to return to Surabaya for refueling and rearming with torpedoes.

The remaining ships continued west into increasingly shallow water when at 2125 *Jupiter* suffered a tremendous explosion, probably a mine planted a day or two before by a Dutch minelayer. Jupiter sank quickly as the course of the Allied strike force was immediately changed to north to get out of the shallow water and to avoid any further danger of mines. Now the force was down to one last destroyer. At about 2200 the Allied ships again passed through the waters where *Kortenaer* was sunk and *Encounter* was directed to pick up her survivors and return them to Surabaya. Still Admiral Doorman was determined to get at the enemy transports and continued on a northerly course.

Shortly after 2300 two enemy heavy cruisers were sighted to port on a southerly course and there followed a brief exchange of gunfire starting with star shells. Apparently there were no shell hits but *Houston* was dangerously straddled. More importantly at 2322 the *Nachi* launched a spread of eight of those lethal long lance torpedoes and the

Haguro a spread of four. At 2332 *Java* was hit by a torpedo and was almost instantly enveloped in flames and dead in the water. Two minutes later at 2334 *De Ruyter* was also hit by a torpedo and flames rapidly spread from forward aft the entire length of the ship. At about 2352 *Java* sank with heavy loss of life. Only about 19 of her crew of 528 survived. At about 0100 *De Ruyter* also sank with heavy loss of life. Only 92 of her crew of 437 survived.

But alas, Admiral Doorman did not survive. His last message sent to *Houston* and *Perth* after *De Ruyter* was hit, was make no effort to pick up survivors but head for Tandjong Priok, the port of Batavia. The Allied Striking Force had been soundly defeated.

Chapter 13

The Enemy Mops Up

WITH the sinking of the Netherlands Navy cruisers *De Ruyter* and *Java* late in the evening of 27 February 1942, time had run out. There was no longer any reason or pretense for U.S. Navy ships in the former Asiatic Fleet to claim they were playing for time until the Pacific Fleet came to the rescue. It was time for surviving ships, U.S. and Allies to get out of the Java Sea. We last left U.S. destroyer *Pope* in Surabaya harbor with main steam line repairs. She was joined late in the evening of the 27th of February by Commodore Binford in *John D. Edwards*, with *Alden, John D. Ford* and *Paul Jones* returning from the Battle of the Java Sea having expended all their torpedoes and in dire need of fuel.

Earlier that evening heavy cruiser HMS *Exeter*, severely damaged by enemy gunfire, had also returned to Surabaya escorted by Dutch destroyer *Witte de With*. Even later British destroyer *Encounter* returned to port after picking up survivors of Dutch destroyer *Kortenaer*. All night of the 27th and all day on the 28th *Exeter* made emergency repairs to her shell-damaged engineering plant while all ships fueled and the U.S. destroyers frantically looked for torpedoes. But none were to be had.

Early on the 28th word began to come in that the Dutch cruisers had been sunk and that *Houston* and *Perth* were en route to Batavia for refueling prior to exiting the Java Sea via the Sunda Strait. Avoiding the Java Sea trap was the watchword then and the U.S. destroyers were directed to escape through the Bali Strait to West Australia. Late on the 28th Vice Admiral Helfrich, RNN, ordered HMS *Exeter* to sail with escorts HMS *Encounter*, RNN *Witte de With* and USS *Pope*. The latter was the only U.S. destroyer in Surabaya having torpedoes. Captain Gordon of *Exeter* quickly called a conference of captains and briefed them on the plan to escape from the Java Sea and proceed to Ceylon. It was to depart by the harbor western exit, run along the north coast of Madura Island then head north passing east of Bawean Island and on reaching the Borneo coast, to steer west along the coast until it was time to head south for a night passage through Sunda Strait.

It was hoped to end run and avoid the powerful covering force for the enemy landings expected that night in eastern Java. At the time of the conference nothing was known of the impending landings on the western tip of Java. Departure was set for 1900 but the captain of *Witte de With* said that he had granted shore leave to his crew and could not round them up in time. Captain Gordon directed him to do the best he could and catch up at best speed. *Exeter*'s engineering troubles continued and at first she expected only sixteen knots. It was hoped that about midnight she could make 22 knots and later push that up to 26 knots.

Thus it was that at dark on the 28th of February three groups of Allied ships were set to try to escape from untenable places in the Java Sea. The *Houston* and *Perth* were departing Batavia for Sunda Strait. The U.S. destroyers except *Pope* were departing Surabaya for Bali Strait and we leave them now to follow the fortunes of the third group— *Exeter* and escorts. The sortie went according to plan except *Witte de With* never sailed. According to Dutch sources she had mechanical troubles. At 2230 with *Encounter* on the port bow and *Pope* on the starboard of *Exeter*, the three ships were 20 miles east of Bawean and headed north. They did not know enemy aircraft had spotted them leaving Surabaya.

About 2230 radio traffic intercepted by POPE indicated a surface engagement close to Sunda Strait. It was obvious the battle was *Houston* and *Perth* fighting for their lives. About 0200 past midnight on March 1st all radio contact of *Pope* with the embattled ships died out. This was confirmed by *Exeter* indicating the two gallant ships had lost the fight. There followed an agonized rethinking of the escape plan using Sunda Strait and speculation as to whether an exit through Lombok or Sape Strait might be a better plan. About the same time unknown ships were sighted off to port and course was changed to east.

A few minutes later however course north was resumed. At 0400 *Exeter* turned due west indicating Captain Gordon still intended the original escape route. At 0730 masts were sighted over the horizon to the west and soon another group of masts to the northwest. More ominous, ship-based float planes were sighted indicating enemy cruisers nearby. At 0935 *Encounter* and *Pope* engaged two enemy destroyers to the northwest and at 0945 *Exeter* opened a gunnery duel with two enemy cruisers of the northwest group. These were the heavy cruisers *Ashigara* flying the flag of Vice Admiral Takahashi and the *Myoko*. *Exeter* then began irregular zigzagging generally headed eastward with *Encounter* and *Pope* making smoke around her. The other two enemy cruisers turned out to be our old "friends" *Nachi* and *Haguro* which had wreaked such havoc on the Allied force late afternoon and evening of the 27th. Then ensued a long running gun battle to the east at 25 knots with *Ashigara* and *Myoko* to port and *Nachi* plus *Haguro* to starboard. *Encounter* and *Pope* continued to engage the enemy destroyers now augmented by three more as the enemy groups closed in. *Exeter* alternately fired at both groups and she was bracketed and straddled by cruiser gunfire. A hit was observed on an enemy destroyer which turned away smoking. When the range got down to 7000 yards, *Pope* launched two torpedoes at the port group which turned away and increased range to 11,000 yards. Now the starboard group starting closing in and were taken under fire by *Encounter* and *Pope*. At 1105 *Exeter* fired torpedoes at the port group and at 1110 *Pope* launched a spread of four torpedoes at the enemy cruisers to port at a range of 6000 yards. She then swung around and fired her last torpedoes—a spread of five at the enemy to starboard. A large explosion was seen on an enemy destroyer which appeared to drop out of the fight.

But the odds were just too great-four to one with the heavy cruisers and better than two to one with the destroyers. At about 1140 or before *Exeter* was heavily hit by gunfire and shortly thereafter *Encounter* was hit. Both ships slowed radically and were smoking heavily. *Exeter* continued firing but her salvos appeared inaccurate. Then the enemy destroyers came charging in with gunfire and torpedoes. *Encounter* was hit again and *Exeter* was smothered with shell hits. Captain Gordon ordered abandon ship. Dutch sources credit the Japanese destroyer *Inazuma* with the coup de grace—a torpedo into the bowels of the cruiser which rolled over and sank at about 12 noon. Thus ended the illustrious career of HMS *Exeter*, of River Plate/*Graf Spee* fame. *Encounter* sank a few minutes later at 1206. Survivors including the gallant Captain Gordon were picked up and made prisoners of war.

Miraculously *Pope* had not been hit and seemed to bear a charmed life. She plowed on and plunged into a merciful rainstorm which hid her from the enemy. This provided a much-needed respite for making some urgent repairs and shifting of ammunition to guns which had emptied their magazines. But nothing could be done about boiler brickwork which had been jarred loose by concussion from near misses. *Pope* changed course to 060, ran out of one rainstorm and into another. At about 1215 she emerged from the second squall into bright sunlight and there was not a ship in sight. Was this too good to be true? Alas it was. *Pope*'s luck had run out—a float plane spotted her and was soon joined by others who commenced bombing runs. All missed but then came more trouble in bunches—dive bombers! Carrier planes, by God!

Bombing run after run was made on the ship while the single 3-inch anti-aircraft gun on the fantail and the .50 cal. machine guns did their best to fight them off. At least twelve bombing runs were made with no direct hits but there were several near misses which did considerable damage. Fragments from a near miss off the bow wounded some of the forward gun crew. A near miss aft knocked the port shaft out of alignment and a hole below the waterline.

Soon a gun casualty silenced the 3-inch anti-aircraft gun, speed was down almost to zero and the ship began to feel "loggy" from progressive flooding aft. Upon receiving a report from the damage control officer that the flooding could not be controlled, Captain Blinn ordered preparations to abandon ship.

While preparations were going on, two or three more bombing runs were made on *Pope*, all misses. We now know these planes were from the second class aircraft carrier *Ryujo* whose planes had attacked Allied ships near Banka Island 13-14 February without any hits and American sailors once more had reason to be glad these were perhaps second class pilots. At about 1250 abandon ship was ordered and went off in orderly fashion. Sadly the explosion of a demolition charge was larger than expected and one man was killed. All others of the crew got off safely in the two boats and life rafts. Not a single man was lost to enemy action. Then an enemy seaplane appeared to be making a run on the boats when some misguided soul with a BAR stood up and took shots at the plane. This was all the enemy pilot needed to make strafing runs on the boats and rafts for about half an hour. Again miraculously no one was hit. But good fortune had run out.

Soon shell splashes appeared around *Pope* and the men knew the enemy cruisers had caught up with them. The stern was under water and lifting the bow of *Pope* clear when an 8-inch salvo from a range of about 4000 yards hit home. *Pope* slid under stern first leaving just a ripple on the surface. The time was about 1330. Then a strange thing happened. The enemy ships formed up and disappeared over the horizon seemingly without paying the slightest bit of attention to the crew of *Pope* in boats and rafts. What was to be made of this? Did the enemy mean they would come back and pick them up later or did they mean to leave them at the mercy of the sea? Perhaps the enemy had gone back to the scene of the sinking of *Exeter* and *Encounter* to pick up those survivors first. No record has been found to indicate what were the intentions of the Japanese. Whatever they were Captain Blinn and his crew now found themselves in the middle of a big ocean and wondering what next. Some messages had been gotten off on radio before sinking, raising hopes that Naval Headquarters had intercepted and would send a U.S. or Dutch submarine to the rescue. Captain Blinn had the engines started and commenced a very slow tow southwards towards Java. But it was more of a boost for morale rather than for any progress made. A muster was taken and all 151 were accounted for. The wounded were kept in the boats and men hanging onto the life rafts took turns resting in the boats. Thus the night of March 1st was endured and men wondered if their survival chances would hold and they might yet be rescued. The next day the engines were again started and ran until all fuel was gone. Kapok life jackets were beginning to get waterlogged and weaker men were moved into the boats. Hard biscuits and abandon ship rations were carefully and sparingly used. Water from the five gallon wooden kegs was carefully rationed as was the case of medicinal brandy removed from the *Pope* wardroom before sinking. Some fervent prayers were said.

All day and night of March 2nd came and went. On the 3rd of March it was still an empty ocean and Captain Blinn gave up any hope of a submarine rescue. The men pondered and wondered. Perhaps they were left to slowly perish at sea. Fortunately the sea was calm and warm but it was hot and the sun bore down on any exposed bodies of the men. Nightfall and darkness fell and soon the beat of high speed propellers was heard. When bow wave luminescence was sighted, Lieutenant Wilson, gunnery officer, fired off a flare. A searchlight beam flashed on and soon found the huddle of rafts and boats. It was enemy destroyers and one of them approached cautiously. Lieutenant Wilson who had been a naval attaché in Tokyo, hailed the destroyer in Japanese and swam over to the sea ladder. He was allowed to come aboard and kept up a continuous conversation in Japanese with the sailors of the destroyer until all his shipmates were rescued.

The destroyer was His Imperial Japanese Majesty's Ship *Inazuma* which had delivered the coup de grace to *Exeter* and it was to her credit she stopped and picked up men of *Pope* because she was extremely wary of Allied submarines. The officers and men of *Pope* were "guests" on board *Inazuma* as prisoners of war. Among them was my fine classmate Lieutenant junior grade William O. Spears, Jr. After the war we spent many hours talking about *Pope* and our experiences on the four stack destroyers. He related how surprised he and his shipmates were about their treatment on board *Inazuma*. Although closely guarded they were kept together on the main deck and kindly treated.

Corned beef, biscuits and tea were brought out at first and according to him chocolate bars. Thereafter the prisoners received the same rations as the Japanese crew. The ship's medical men with *Pope*'s pharmacist's mate moved among the prisoners treating the wounded and weak. Some clothing and blankets were distributed and the Japanese destroyermen seemed to be friendly towards the American sailors. Some tried speaking English with the prisoners and generally showed respect for the effort of the little four stacker.

But when the prisoners were landed at Makassar two days later, and delivered into the hands of brutal army type prison guards, it was a different story. It was the start of "hell week" which never stopped. The POWs were moved about from one wretched camp to another and always forced into slave labor. Living conditions varied from one camp to another but generally were terrible-lack of food, unsanitary facilities, exposure to the weather, lack of clothing and medicines. Malnutrition and diseases were rampant and 27 men of the *Pope* died during the two and a half years of captivity. POW survivors of the *Houston* including my classmate Hal Hamlin had the same story to tell. He told me of the epic battle of *Houston* and *Perth* near Sunda Strait in which they were overwhelmed and sunk. Some senior officer survivors of *Exeter*, *Houston*, *Encounter* and *Pope* were sent to Japan. But most of the POWs remained on tropical islands—Celebes, Java, Taiwan—for the remainder of the war and many had horrible stories to tell of brutal treatment and sometimes of unspeakable cruelty.

With the sinking of *Exeter* and *Encounter* it was the last of the Royal Navy ships in the Java Sea. It was also the last of the Allied cruiser force assembled to resist the invasion of Java and it failed completely. Amphibious landings on the island came off pretty much on schedule. For the Allies it was complete and utter defeat. Some remnants of the Netherlands Navy remained but were soon wiped out. The destroyer *Evertsen* in a running gun battle with two enemy destroyers was beached and destroyed on March 1st. On the 2nd of March destroyers *Banckert* and *Witte de With* in Surabaya harbor were bombed and then scuttled. With the sinking of the *Pope* it was the last U.S. Navy ship in the Java Sea. The U.S. destroyers which had taken part in the battle on 27th February escaped Surabaya late on the 28th. *Stewart*, stricken from the Navy Register and abandoned, forlornly lay partially on her side, in a damaged floating drydock in Surabaya.

The victory for the Japanese Navy and Empire was so complete, so devastating and so efficient in the proper use of ships, submarines, aircraft and landing forces in modern war, that their proud ships might have borrowed an ancient seafaring tradition from Holland. Their ships might have hoisted brooms to their mastheads signifying a clean sweep of their enemies. The tradition was established in the glory days of the Dutch Navy in the 17th century when doughty Dutch Admirals such as Tromp, de Ruyter and de Witt regularly dominated the seas and sometimes beat hell out of ships of the British Royal Navy. The Dutch Navy of the Indies in early 1942 and their Allies had courage but outclassed ships and weapons. Sometimes courage is not enough.

Chapter 14

Escape From the Java Sea

WHEN last we left the four U.S. destroyers in Surabaya harbor late in the afternoon of 28th February to follow the ill-fated fortunes of HMS *Exeter*, HMS *Encounter* and USS *Pope*, the four were preparing to depart late in the afternoon to escape from the Java Sea. The plan was to exit the east entrance of the mined harbor, proceed east through Madura Strait then head south and sneak through the Bali Strait to the Indian Ocean thence to West Australia. They knew they would be opposed. For several days intelligence reports had been coming in that heavy Japanese forces were operating south of Java. But it was a desperate gamble that had to be made. There was no other feasible way.

At 1700 *John D. Edwards* flying the pennant of Commander Thomas H. Binford, Commander Destroyer Division 58, with *Alden* got underway and headed towards the eastern entrance to the harbor. A minute or two later *John D. Ford* flying the pennant of Commander E.N. Parker, Commander Destroyer Division 59 got underway and headed for the west entrance. About twenty minutes later *Paul Jones* got underway and *Ford* reversed her course to proceed with *Paul Jones* to the east entrance. In this way it was hoped to confuse enemy planes or coast watchers. After dark the ships formed column in order *John D. Edwards*, *Alden*, *John D. Ford* and *Paul Jones* and at 22 knots proceeded on various courses through Madura Strait and the southern(eastern) minefields.

At about 2030 all ships manned their battle stations but all hands knew their 4-inch guns would be no match against Japanese cruisers or those big modern destroyers. All hands also were acutely aware that the destroyers main battery—the torpedoes, were gone—expended in the Battle of the Java Sea. No more replacement torpedoes could be found. The best that could be done would be to fire booster charges making the enemy think torpedoes were being launched. While the crews of the ships had been close to exhaustion for days, the adrenalin was flowing now and their best allies seemed to be speed and darkness. At about midnight the ships cleared the minefield channel, increased speed to 25 knots and turned almost due south to enter the narrowest part of the Bali strait—only about a mile wide.

Clearing the narrows the ships continued to hug the Java coast which juts off to the southeast at the easternmost tip of the island. With the full moon close to the starboard beam it was felt that staying close to shore would reduce the silhouette effect to the east. Now the course was 130 then 135 then something else but generally southeast as anxious navigators kept eyes on the depth finders hovering around 30 feet. Speed crept up to 26 knots as the engineers showed their anxiety about getting the hell out of there. About five minutes after two in the morning an enemy destroyer was sighted on the port bow at an estimated distance of about 5000 yards and approximately on an opposite course although at a slow speed.

At about 0210 the enemy destroyer was observed to reverse course indicating his sighting of our ships was about the same time. But by the time he had reversed his course and picked up some speed he was already abaft the port beam of our ships. But then two more enemy destroyers were sighted to the southeast at 0215. They appeared to be forming up in column with the first destroyer and also on a southeast course. At 0222 the enemy opened fire and the first salvos were uncomfortably close. Apparently they were able to use their rangefinders effectively with our ships silhouetted in the bright moonlight. Our ships returned the fire but were unable to get good ranges. They had to resort to rocking ladders aiming at the enemy gun flashes. At the same time our ships torpedo mounts began to fire the booster charges. But it was obvious the darkness was no longer an ally of the U.S. destroyers and speed was their one remaining asset.

Perhaps the enemy had been fooled by the booster charges and had lost speed maneuvering to avoid imagined torpedoes or the enemy ships had just wasted too much time forming up and reversing course. Maybe the enemy ships just could not get up steam quick enough to overhaul our ships. Whatever the reason, our engineers had pushed speed up to 27 knots and the enemy were falling well aft. Now the advantage to the enemy of the moonlight was diminishing. At 0236 when the turning point was reached at the eastern tip of Java where the U.S. destroyers could round the corner without danger of running aground, course was changed southwest to about 205 degrees. Now the enemy were dead astern, falling further behind and all firing ceased. On the ships raced and there was momentary elation among the crews that so far they had run the gauntlet and still survived.

Their elation soon turned to anxiety as the awful reality hit that the enemy destroyers they had just left behind would at that very moment be alerting their compatriots on nearby islands and units of the Japanese fleet operating in the Indian Ocean south of Java. Surely enemy aircraft from Bali and Timor would be after them in the morning. Our destroyers would have been even more apprehensive if they had known the truth about the massive forces of the Japanese Fleet in the Indian Ocean blocking their way.

On the 25th of February the 1st Carrier Air Fleet consisting of four aircraft carriers under Vice Admiral Nagumo, plus two battleships *Hiyei* and *Kirishima*, two heavy cruisers *Chikuma* and *Tone*, the light cruiser *Abukuma* and eight destroyers had sortied from Kendari, Celebes and passed through Sape Strait (where *Boise* came to grief) into the Indian Ocean south of Java. But these were not second class carriers. This was the first team—the aircraft carriers *Akagi*, *Kaga*, *Hiryu* and *Soryu* with their air squadrons which wreaked such execution on battleship row at Pearl Harbor. Perhaps it was merciful our destroyers did not know.

These were soon followed into the Indian Ocean by another force under Vice Admiral Kondo consisting of battleships *Haruna* and *Kongo*, heavy cruisers *Atago*, *Maya*, *Takao* and three destroyers. On Commodore Binford and his four destroyers raced through the night more fearful of land-based aircraft on Bali than of surface forces whose whereabouts were unknown. About an hour after cease fire at 0236 gun flashes and the rumble of gunfire over the horizon astern were observed. There was no explanation for it other than perhaps the enemy destroyers had encountered a Dutch patrol boat or commercial vessel. Dawn was approached with fear and trepidation. Everyone dreaded the enemy bombers who would then call in surface forces for the kill. At daylight the horizon was anxiously searched and there was nothing in sight. Oh, for a rainstorm or any kind of bad weather which would keep enemy planes from taking off from carriers or airfields. But the weather was clear and high anxiety continued.

High speed was maintained and no one dared suggest reducing it but the captains and the engineers were beginning to worry about fuel consumption. Also the sustained high speed was beginning to result in engineering breakdowns. These were handled as expeditiously as possible with temporary slowdowns and then resumption of speed. All day on the 1st of March this went on and at nightfall there was a guarded sigh of relief. It was pretty much agreed our destroyers were now out of range of the land-based bombers. There is no doubt the enemy made air searches but just could not believe the U.S. ships had escaped so far south. As darkness came the captains were increasingly concerned about running out of fuel and during the night speed was reduced to 15 knots. A reduced condition of readiness for the guns was set.

This continued all day on the 2nd of March as the ships continued south with no sightings of any kind. But the weather began to change with squalls, moderate seas, salt spray and most welcome—cooler temperature, a relief from the stifling heat up in Java. Meanwhile bits and pieces of radio traffic and calls for help from merchant ships under attack was convincing proof that the enemy was raising hell in the Indian Ocean. On the morning of the 3rd the ships were spread out on a broad front to give a better chance of spotting any possible survivors of sunken ships. Then shortly after noon on the 3rd a lighthouse was sighted to the southeast, probably near the entrance to Shark Bay, and this electrified the crews. At last they had sighted Australia and this meant maybe they would get through this thing after all.

Excitement was building and course was gradually changed to southeast and speed increased to 22 knots although seas were getting rougher with salt spray coming on board. No matter, they could handle that. On the afternoon of Wednesday 4th of March a friendly aircraft was sighted—a very welcome sight. Late in the afternoon of the 4th the four ships anchored off the port of Fremantle, West Australia. They had escaped the jaws of death.

Upon arrival in Fremantle Commodore Binford with his four destroyers found the destroyer tender *Black Hawk* had already arrived. Then Commodores Binford and Parker with their four ship captains paid an official call on Commodore H.V. Wiley, Commander Destroyer Squadron 29. But the officers and men of the ships after heaving a big sigh of relief and grabbing something to eat, took to their bunks for the deep sleep of the exhausted. Never was a good rest more richly deserved.

Chapter 15

Ordeal of *Edsall* and *Whipple*

MEANWHILE back in Tjilatjap on board USS *Isabel* we remained at anchor all day on the 26th of February while many merchant ships were leaving the harbor. Late that afternoon came a rumor that the old carrier *Langley* might be under air attack 40-50 miles south of Tjilatjap. If so it would be a setback for the Allies because she had a deck load of thirty two ready-to-fly P-40 fighter planes sorely needed for the defense of Java. The rumor may have been sparked by sighting of a reconnaissance aircraft.

On Tuesday 27th *Edsall* and *Whipple* were underway early and proceeding to rendezvous with *Langley* to escort her back to Tjilatjap harbor with the fighter planes. Captain Abernethy of the tanker *Pecos* for some time had been trying hard to get Naval Headquarters to allow him to leave Tjilatjap. He knew enemy air would hit the harbor any day. Now that *Pecos* was at the pier where *Langley* had to berth in order to offload her fighter planes for towing to an airfield, Captain Abernethy got permission to leave and departed early on the 27th. As soon as *Pecos* cleared the harbor hatches were battened down and course set for Ceylon.

Then because of message foul-ups and backtracking caused by changes of escorts and rendezvous points, *Langley* changed her ETA at Tjilatjap from early on 27th to 1700. She would be in the dangerous part of her voyage during daylight. Sure enough she was spotted by an enemy patrol plane. Shortly before noon *Langley* was attacked by seven or more land-based bombers from Bali. Coming in at 15,000 ft, far out of range of her anti-aircraft guns and those of her escorts *Edsall* and *Whipple*, the enemy pilots made leisurely bombing runs. With her slow speed and slow turning *Langley* was a sitting duck. She was hit by at least five heavy bombs and then strafed by fighters. In less than two hours she was a flaming, sinking hulk and abandon ship was ordered by Captain McConnell. *Edsall* and *Whipple* did a good job in taking aboard the survivors. But once this was done *Langley* seemed reluctant to sink. Destroyer gunfire and torpedoes were used to put her out of her misery but while listing heavily and sinking slowly, still she would not go down. By this time the destroyers with survivors on board became alarmed that enemy planes might stage a return engagement and cleared the area to leave the "old lady" to die alone. A Dutch patrol plane later reported that he saw her sink about sundown. Alas, Vice Admiral Glassford took a dim view of what he felt was premature abandonment of the *Langley* by Captain McConnell and wrote a nasty letter. Admiral King, COMINCH had to rescue the captain and save him from opprobrium.

Back to the *Pecos*, after sortie from Tjilatjap she wasted no time heading west at maximum speed to get clear of the area. But during the bombing of *Langley* she was only about thirty miles away and soon was directed by Naval Headquarters to rendezvous with *Edsall* and *Whipple* near Christmas Island to take on board the *Langley* survivors. On the morning of the 28th the ships met just north of the island and were making preparations for the transfers when they were surprised by three twin engine enemy bombers. The ships ducked into some nearby rain squalls while the equally surprised enemy pilots seemingly paid them no mind but proceeded to work over the phosphate plant on Christmas Island.

By this time Commodore E.M. Crouch, Commander, Destroyer Division 57, flying his pennant in *Whipple*, senior officer present, decided to clear the area as quickly as possible and headed due south. He knew the enemy would be after the three ships in a hurry. He hoped to get out of range of the land-based bombers and make the transfers early on the morning of March 1st. By some accounts Naval Headquarters directed the three ships to clear the area by proceeding west. But this was the morning after the utter defeat of the Allied ships in the Battle of the Java Sea and there was confusion at Naval Headquarters. The message may never have been sent or may simply have been overruled by Commodore Crouch.

It proved to be a wise move and no further sightings or attacks occurred during the afternoon and night. But the sea got rough with winds around 25 knots. However at dawn conditions had moderated and the transfer of *Langley* survivors to *Pecos* was accomplished by superb seamanship of a *Pecos* boat captain. The transfers took less than two hours and were completed by 0825 after which all three ships went their separate ways. *Whipple* headed almost due west to the Cocos Islands to fuel from a waiting oiler. Why she did not fuel from *Pecos* and remain with her has never been explained. *Pecos* was told on completion of the transfer to proceed to Exmouth Gulf on the northwestern coast of Australia. But Captain Abernethy wanted to continue southward for awhile and settled on course 160 to further escape the range of the enemy land-based bombers.

But *Edsall* in one of the most bizarre, stupid or courageous moves of the entire war, depending on your point of view, was directed to deliver some Army Air Force personnel to Tjilatjap. These were pilots and men who had been aboard *Langley* for operation of the P-40 fighter planes once delivered to Tjilatjap. But now that the ship with the planes had gone down there seemed no further point in placing *Edsall* and the men on board in harm's way. The cause was lost. Japanese amphibious forces had landed on both ends of Java and the island was doomed. *Houston* and *Perth* had been sunk near Sunda Strait the night before in the first hour of the 1st of March. *Exeter*, *Encounter* and *Pope* had been sunk later on the 1st. Sending *Edsall* to Tjilatjap was futile.

But the Dutch were frantic and desperate for anything that could be done to defend Java. The Air Force men on board *Edsall* were intended for manning the 27 P-40 fighter planes packed in crates on board the U.S. merchant ship *Sea Witch* which had arrived in Tjilatjap on the 28th of February. That ship had been in the same convoy en route from Fremantle to Ceylon from which *Langley* had broken off to make her ill-fated dash to Tjilatjap. *Sea Witch* had broken off at a different time and she made it to port but *Langley* did not. So there was some logic in getting those Air Force men to where the P-40 fighters were located—Tjilatjap.

More than likely however our boss Vice Admiral Glassford, who most of us considered a solid, level headed commander, would never have allowed *Edsall* to try returning to Tjilatjap if he had seen the directive and had time to consider the implications. Remember this was March 1st, the day the last Allied ships which had survived the Battle of Java Sea were finally wiped out. Utter confusion reigned at Naval Headquarters. Vice Admiral Glassford and his staff were preparing to evacuate for Australia. They were leaving by ships, submarines, planes and merchant vessels. But whatever the circumstances surrounding the issuance of the order, who approved it or signed off on it, brave Captain Nix of the *Edsall* dutifully sailed with his crew and airmen passengers to carry out his orders. She departed company with *Pecos* and *Whipple* about 0830 on estimated course 010 for Tjilatjap, disappeared over the horizon and was never seen or heard from again.

It was as if she had sailed off into oblivion, a void, a nothingness and it hurt. It was as if she had disappeared into the mists of time and like the legendary "Flying Dutchman" she was doomed to sail the seven seas forever, on perpetual patrol, never touching port again. It was many years later, after the war, that a Naval Technical mission determined that *Edsall* had been caught by Vice Admiral Kondo's battleships and cruisers at about 1733 on the 1st and sunk at 1901 with no indication whether there were any survivors. It was 1952 before an amateur movie film was found taken from the heavy cruiser *Ashigara* showing the little ship being sunk by gunfire. Another account says that after the war a common grave was found on the south shore of Java with the bodies of five men sufficiently identified as POWs from *Edsall*. But they were beheaded. On learning this I wept.

Back to the *Pecos* after receiving *Langley* survivors on board she continued on course 160 for an hour and a half after the transfer until about 1000 when an enemy scout plane was sighted. I had more than a passing interest in the fate of *Pecos* because our former communications officer on the *Stewart*, Lieutenant Archibald Stone, was now one of her ship's officers. With Commander McConnell alongside him on the Bridge, Captain Abernethy satisfied himself the scout was a carrier plane and they both now knew *Pecos* was in for it. They could not know that four enemy carriers were just eighty miles away to the east, the same four which had done the dirty work at Pearl Harbor. And of course with them were battleships, heavy cruisers and destroyers. At about 1040 *Pecos* changed course to southwest for half an hour and then came back to approximately due south.

The first attack came at 1145 and it was Val dive bombers. Building up to maximum speed of about 14.5 knots Captain Abernethy did a superb job of twisting and turning and the first bombs were close but missed. The first hit was a 500 lb. bomb at 1203 which hit near the starboard 3-inch anti-aircraft gun knocking a large hole in the deck and killing some of the gun crew. Lieutenant Stone got permission from the captain to reorganize the gun crew and joined in the hot anti-aircraft fire.[47] Wave after wave of dive bombers from each of the carriers continued the attacks. Two more hits were made starting fires and flooding but the damage control parties managed to bring them under control. About 1230 there was lull in the battle but it did not last long.

There was time to bring up more ammunition and every gun possible was in action—5- and 3-inch guns, .50 cal. and .30 cal. machine guns, .30 cal. rifles. The enemy pilots later remarked about the fierce anti-aircraft fire and sometimes had their aim ruined. The relentless

---

[47] D.R. Messimer, *Pawns of War*, Naval Institute Press, Annapolis, 1983. p. 138.

attacks continued and there was another hit in the hole of the first hit. The explosion wounded more of the 3-inch gun crew including Lieutenant Stone who was hit in the face. Then the gun firing mechanism jammed and when he reached under the gun to trip the sear it fired with the recoil knocking him off the gun platform. He climbed back up and resumed the firing. Then someone yelled "abandon ship" and before the false alarm was corrected it was estimated some 100 men went over the side. The ship could not turn around and pick them up and most were lost.

But the sheer volume of the attacks began to take its toll, a hit forward wiped out the 5-inch gun crews. Another hit knocked out a boiler and speed was reduced to 10.5 knots. Radio messages were sent off giving location and possible sinking. Fortunately *Whipple* receipted but nothing was heard from *Edsall*. At 1501 a heavy attack got two near misses but the one off the port bow caved in the hull below the waterline and the flooding could not be controlled. At 1530 Captain Abernethy ordered abandon ship.

The process of abandoning went fairly smoothly considering the swollen number of men on board from the *Langley* sinking. But there was only one undamaged boat left into which two doctors had placed some of the more seriously wounded. Others were throwing anything over the side that would float—rafts, tables, crates, poles, mattresses, lumber, etc. She was going down by the bow with a port list and as the main deck forward became awash most of the men swam away or jumped a few feet to the sea. But a few men aft could not bring themselves to jump. As the bow went under the stern began to rise and soon the ship was almost vertical with the stern 60 ft in the air and some men still hanging on. A few minutes later at 1548 *Pecos* made her final plunge and was gone leaving the sea alive with five or six hundred struggling men. Some of the bastard enemy pilots could not resist taking a few strafing runs on the helpless men in the water. To compound the misery, the sea was rough and covered with an oil slick.

Whipple had received the last message from *Pecos* at 1531 and immediately put about heading southeast at 19 knots towards the position. At about 1800 when it was twilight several of the officers and men heard booms and rumbles to the northeast which was probably gallant *Edsall* meeting her doom. Sound travels great distances in water. Soon it was dark and many men gave up just as help was arriving. At 1910 a man in the boat spotted the *Whipple* as a dark silhouette and immediately flares went up and flashlights tried signaling. For the next two hours and forty three minutes *Whipple* circled and circled picking up men by any means possible—cargo nets, sea ladders, fire hoses, knotted lines or sending swimmers out to get men too weak to climb.

Then occurred the most tragic and heartrending series of events it is possible to imagine. At 2141 sonar on *Whipple* had contact on what was thought to be a submarine, she ceased rescue operations and went after the supposed submarine. *Whipple* dropped two depth charges on the phantom submarine with no apparent result other than tearing the guts out of men in the water closest to the explosions. Immediately "submarine sightings and noises" multiplied and every big black wave was reported as a sub. It is more than likely that the "sightings" were clusters of men around a raft or the boat which was cut adrift and the noises may have been porpoises talking to each other. Every experienced destroyerman on board knew or should have known that seventy-five percent of all sonar contacts prove to be false. Sonar will sometimes echo on many things—a school of porpoises or fish, a floating object or a collection of flotsam and jetsam. There was plenty of this in the area where *Pecos* sank. Sonar will also sometimes get echos from a sharp temperature gradient.

At 2152 *Whipple* resumed rescue of the desperate men in the water for a few minutes—a precious few—when "submarine" propeller noises were heard only 200 yards away. Again *Whipple* broke off and charged off to drop at 2158 two more depth charges on the "submarine" with exactly the same results as before. Then Captain Karpe of the *Whipple* in conference with Commodore Crouch made the most awful decision of his life. At 2205 he decided to break off any further rescue of the men, clear the area because of submarine danger and set course for Fremantle. I write "awful" in the sense that the decision was awesome in terms of life or death for so many of the gallant officers and men of the *Langley* and *Pecos*. It was his decision to make and Commodore Crouch, Captains Abernethy and McConnell supported him. But the decision should never have been made unless there was positive information that it was an enemy submarine. There was too much at stake, too many lives in the balance for such a decision to be based on the chance there was a submarine out there or something as nebulous as "submarine danger." I wonder if the unlikelihood of an enemy submarine being in that part of the Indian Ocean was considered. I wonder if the numbers percentages were considered as a baseball manager plays his team by the numbers, knowing the great majority of so-called "submarine" contacts turn out to be false.

As it was *Whipple* rescued 233 men leaving upwards of 500 to die in the agony of despair and betrayal. As I write this many years later tears flow freely as they always do when I think about this awful tragedy. Some of them were my shipmates on the *Stewart*. The disaster out there south of Christmas Island that night was on a par with the terrible sinking and loss of life of the USS *Indianapolis* in the closing days of the war. It is the nightmare of every seafaring man that he should ever have to make such a decision as Captain Karpe made that night. The captain of HMS *Dorchester* made such a decision in abandoning the rescue of survivors of the German battleship *Bismarck* because of submarine danger. But he was not abandoning his shipmates or comrades-in-arms as was Captain Karpe. I know it must have been agonizing and heartbreaking for him but I would have erred on the side of humanity in taking a chance there was no real submarine present. I unreservedly condemn the decision to abandon the rescue effort.

With heavy hearts, tears and infinite sadness the rescued survivors and the crew of *Whipple* departed the area of the sinking of *Pecos* leaving behind the pitiful cries of struggling men in the water. It was perhaps merciful that the rough seas ended their suffering rather quickly. *Whipple* set course for Fremantle and had to adjust speed for maximum fuel economy in order to make it. It took over three days and towards the last she had to crawl the last miles. During the voyage the captains of *Langley* and *Pecos* tried to figure out their rescued and lost crew members but it was difficult because of lost records and transients that were on board *Pecos*. There were men from *Houston*, *Marblehead*, *Stewart* and possibly other ships.

There were many questions. Lieutenant Stone formerly of *Stewart* was not among the survivors and was last seen at his 3-inch gun, his face bleeding, one ear partially shot off and shaking his fist at the enemy planes. He was awarded the Silver Star Medal posthumously, but clearly he deserves the highest honor the nation can bestow—the Congressional Medal of Honor. Were any messages sent out by *Whipple* asking for assistance in rescuing survivors? Why was there no rescue operation mounted by ships or planes for the survivors? Later it was learned the light cruiser *Phoenix* was in that part of the Indian Ocean that day. Why was she not sent to help? Where was Vice Admiral Glassford and what was he doing when this disaster was taking place?

Whipple arrived at Fremantle on March 4th the same day Commodore Binford and his four destroyers arrived from Surabaya. *Whipple* too had escaped the debacle in Java and the untenable situation of the former Asiatic Fleet in the Far East. Of the thirteen four stack destroyers in the fleet at the start of the war, *Peary* had been sunk in Port Darwin on 19 February. *Stewart* had been abandoned in Surabaya on

22 February. *Pope* had been sunk in the Java Sea on 1st of March, the same day *Edsall* sailed into oblivion in the Indian Ocean. *Alden, Barker, Bulmer, John D. Edwards, John D. Ford* and *Paul Jones* had already arrived at Fremantle. With the arrival of *Whipple* on the 4th of March, that left two unaccounted for—*Parrott* and *Pillsbury*. Where were they?

These two ships, *Parrott* and *Pillsbury*, out of torpedoes and low on ammunition but their crews augmented by men from the abandoned *Stewart*, had arrived in Tjilatjap on 24 February from Surabaya via the Sunda Strait. Since that day the two ships were on anti-submarine patrols off the harbor entrance. Then with defeat of the Allied ships in the Battle of the Java Sea, some thought was given at Naval Headquarters to evacuation of staff personnel and other men using these ships.

The situation worsened rapidly and there were several groups of personnel to be lifted from Java. In addition to staff, there were patients from the *Houston, Marblehead, Stewart* and other ships. There was the *Stewart* demolition party and others who had missed their ships. The big question was how long should *Parrott* and *Pillsbury* wait in Tjilatjap for evacuees who might never show up. At last the two ships were released and sailed on the morning of 1 March for West Australia. They sailed by separate routes.

Chapter 16

Isabel Runs Gauntlet

WHEN we last left USS *Isabel* (Patrol Yacht 10), the ship to which I had been reassigned upon arrival in Tjilatjap on board *Parrott*, she was anchored in the harbor on the morning of 27th February as the tanker *Pecos* got underway on her last ill-fated voyage. That was a momentous day for *Isabel*. We had understood for several days that shortly all U.S. Navy ships would be ordered out of Java ports to head for West Australia or India and Ceylon but that *Pillsbury* would stay behind a few more days to bring out staff people and stragglers. We on *Isabel* were more than anxious to get going and were acutely aware the enemy was closing in.

Then came a "bombshell." There was a change in plans—*Isabel* was designated to stay behind replacing *Pillsbury* which was to depart that afternoon. Soon word came that the head bossman, Commander Naval Forces, Southwest Pacific wanted our captain to come up to Naval Headquarters. So Captain Jack Payne of *Isabel* went up to Naval Headquarters to see Vice Admiral Glassford who directed him to take *Isabel* up the Kali Donan River which flows into the harbor of Tjilatjap, moor alongside the east bank and camouflage the ship with bushes and palm fronds. We wasted no time in getting with this drill because we were very apprehensive about the daily overflights of enemy spy planes.

The crew of *Isabel* went about the task of camouflage with a will and seemed to be enthusiastic about doing something positive for our own protection. There was a return to light-hearted banter and some began to consider the whole idea as a lark. One of the ship's mess attendants wondered out loud whether the ship was getting ready for a ship's party. It was quite a sight, like something one might see in a movie. We were all brought back to reality by word that *Langley* had been sunk not too far offshore south of Tjilatjap. The only bright spot in that picture was that *Edsall* and *Whipple* had picked up most of her crew and the Air Force men embarked who were to fly the P-40 fighters that were sitting on her decks but were now at the bottom of the sea.

The news of the sinking of *Langley* was a grim reminder of the peril we were in and the slim chance we had of escaping Java waters. *Isabel* like other ships did not receive all radio traffic but only on a need to know basis. As I recall word about *Langley* sinking came down by word of mouth from Naval Headquarters which had been relocated to Tjilatjap. Similarly there were rumors of a big showdown battle that afternoon between Allied cruisers and enemy amphibious forces protected by combatant ships in the Java Sea.

There were other rumors coming from Naval Headquarters. One was that Vice Admiral Glassford and staff would embark in *Isabel* for escape to Fremantle when the time came. When *Parrott* and *Pillsbury* got underway that afternoon for anti-submarine patrols off the harbor, some viewed it as the start of U.S. ships exodus from the East Indies. Another rumor was that *Isabel* was waiting for Dr. Wassel to come down to Tjilatjap from Jogjakarta with his patients for evacuation to Australia. Lieutenant Commander Croyden Wassel, Medical Corps, had been detailed by Admiral Hart for care of the officers and men of the *Houston* and *Marblehead* who had been wounded in the Battle of the Flores Sea on 4 February. These included Commander Goggins, executive officer of the *Marblehead*. There was no indication when or if these events might take place. We knew it made sense to substitute *Isabel* for *Pillsbury* as the last U.S. Navy ship to leave Java if Vice Admiral Glassford was coming aboard. *Isabel* had for many years been the alternate flagship of the four star admiral of the Asiatic Fleet and had suitable quarters designed for the purpose. We would welcome him on board but there was doubt it would ever happen.

The next day was Saturday 28 February and nothing changed as we remained camouflaged all day. That evening I made this entry in my journal, "Moored as before, awaiting word. All ships gone. Evacuation going on. British and U.S. people leaving Java. Submarines and planes carrying out staff people. Merchant ships carrying out civilians." We also learned with some relief that *Edsall* and *Whipple* had rescued nearly all the survivors of *Langley*. Of course we knew nothing of the plans of the three groups of ships to try an escape from the Java Sea that night. These were the four destroyers at Surabaya, *Houston* and *Perth* at Batavia, *Exeter, Encounter* and *Pope* also at Surabaya. But we of *Isabel* were livid that there was no word of plans for us to get the hell out of there. Being upriver we did not know *Parrott* and *Pillsbury* returned to port that night from anti-submarine patrol. The next day, Sunday March 1st was much the same in the morning hours. *Parrott* and *Pillsbury* got underway, destination not known to us. Rumors were that

Langley survivors had been successfully transferred by *Edsall* and *Whipple* to *Pecos* which then headed for Australia. During the morning word began to come in that *Houston* and *Perth* had been sunk soon after midnight near Sunda Strait with heavy loss of life. We also began to hear rumors of enemy landings on both ends of the island of *Java*. Then there was word of a transportation hitch with Dr. Wassel and his patients and they would not be coming on board.

Shortly after noon we on *Isabel* were electrified by word that we would be departing that evening. But there was a catch to it— we were required to escort the merchant ship *Sea Witch* then unloading cargo in the harbor and we did not know when she would be ready to sail. Then we heard Vice Admiral Glassford and his staff would not be coming on board after all. *Isabel* fueled and began to take on staff passengers. Captain Payne paid a visit to Naval Headquarters and began looking for a pilot for a night time departure of *Sea Witch*. We hoped it would be soon after dark.

All afternoon bad news kept coming in. We heard that about midday *Exeter*, *Encounter* and *Pope* had been rundown and sunk in the Java Sea. Next was the terrible news that *Pecos* herself had been sunk with all those *Langley* survivors on board. This was softened somewhat by a bad report that most of them were picked up by *Edsall* and *Whipple*. We did not know that *Edsall* herself had been sunk with all hands and just how truly horrible was sinking of *Pecos* with appalling loss of life in this one of the major disasters of the war. Then there was a rumor that an enemy convoy was headed for Tjilatjap. That did it. We were ready to go.

About dark we got an estimated departure time of midnight for *Sea Witch*. But we had one more chore to do—we had to rendezvous with the submarine *Spearfish* to put a new captain on board, Lieutenant Commander J.C. Dempsey. This mission was fraught with danger because enemy submarines had been reported off the harbor entrance for several days and *Isabel* had no sonar gear. We were underway shortly after 2100 and cleared the minefields in about an hour. It was bright moonlight and we felt like a sitting duck out there providing a nice target for enemy submarines. *Isabel* steered zigzag courses off the harbor entrance as the only defensive thing we could do while looking for *Spearfish*. But it was more a case of letting the submarine find us rather than we finding the sub. That is the way it worked out and at about 2330 *Spearfish* surfaced nearby. There were some tense moments until she was identified. Transfer was completed quickly.

Then we waited anxiously for *Sea Witch* to clear the harbor and minefield and join up with us for our dash southward. She was due out at midnight which came and went but was still not in sight. Captain Payne had great difficulty in getting a harbor pilot to bring *Sea Witch* out of the harbor and through the minefield. Readers will remember that *Sea Witch* was the merchant ship attached to the convoy en route from Australia to India which along with *Langley* had P-40 fighter planes on board intended for the defense of Java. The difference was that fighters on *Sea Witch* were still packed in crates. When the Allied Strike Force was soundly defeated in the Battle of the Java Sea, the whole defense picture changed. Java was doomed. But there was the question of what to do about the P-40 fighters in crates on board *Sea Witch*. U.S. Army Air Force men on Java who were to operate the flyable fighters on arrival and assemble those in crates, upon learning of the loss of *Langley*, destroyed their remaining fighters, climbed into a B-17 and left Java on the 28th.

It was too late to divert *Sea Witch* with her valuable cargo to a safer port. *Edsall* which had been directed to deliver some of the Air Force men rescued from *Langley* to Tjilatjap was caught by the enemy on March 1st and was never heard from again. It was now clearly foolhardy to unload the crated fighters which would fall into the hands of the enemy unless destroyed beforehand.

Vice Admiral Helfrich, RNN who had relieved Admiral Hart on February 15 and under whom Vice Admiral Glassford and our ships were operating had by now concluded no further defense of Java was possible and fled the island himself for Ceylon on March 2nd. But that word had not trickled down to the harbor master at Tjilatjap and on the afternoon of March 1st he refused to provide a pilot for *Sea Witch* until those crated P-40 fighter planes were unloaded to lighters brought alongside for the purpose. Enter Commander H.H. Keith who had been captain of the *Peary* when she had been bombed during the devastating attack of Cavite on 10 December, 1941. He had been badly wounded and hospitalized and of course had to give up his command. Some time back he had recovered sufficiently to report for duty and in Tjilatjap he had been acting as sort of a U.S. Navy port captain.

We don't know what Vice Admiral Glassford may have said to Commander Keith but the latter went aboard *Sea Witch* on March 1st and with her captain supervised unloading her cargo onto the lighters. It was Sunday, the Dutch were not working and native stevedores had long since fled when bombing started. Using the ship's crew and some USN men who could be rounded up, they made a big show of offloading *Sea Witch* during daylight. But what they were putting on the lighters was miscellaneous cargo, Army Air Force vehicles, .50 cal. ammunition, not the crated fighters.

Meanwhile Captain Payne of *Isabel* with the help of a taxi driver had found a pilot who agreed to take *Sea Witch* out for three times the normal fee. Sure enough, sometime after dark the Dutch authorities had decided it was not a good idea for the crated fighters to fall into the hands of the enemy and ordered the cargo on the lighters to be dumped into the sea. This Commander Keith was happy to do and was later reported to have been seen grinning from ear to ear. He had saved the valuable cargo of fighter planes. As they say, timing is everything. The pieces were falling into place as to why Vice Admiral Glassford had been so firm that *Isabel* must escort *Sea Witch* to safe waters. In addition to her P-40 fighter cargo she was a new C-3 merchant ship of 10,000 tons and valuable in her own right.

While waiting off the harbor entrance for *Sea Witch* to emerge, she was already overdue when at about half an hour after midnight we were just about frightened out of our wits by shouts of the lookouts that a torpedo wake was sighted to port coming in.

We held our breath. There was no time for evasive action and the damn thing passed under the ship in the bridge area without hitting. It would have blown us to bits. Talk about a guardian angel! The captain wasted no time in turning away from whence it came and sped away as fast as *Isabel* would go on short notice.

With this scare the captain was considering leaving *Sea Witch* to her own devices. She might never come out. Then he remembered how adamant Vice Admiral Glassford was that he get *Sea Witch* to safe waters and decided to wait awhile longer. Finally at about 0130 on the 2nd of March *Sea Witch* stood out of the harbor and joined up as the two of us headed due south at 14 knots with *Isabel* 500 yards ahead. At last we were on our way and all hands breathed a guarded sigh of relief. I am sure many of us lifted a prayer. I don't think anyone on board did not realize the terrible danger we were in. At least we would have a running, if not a fighting chance, to escape death or as POWs. That night I made a notation in my journal, "HAVE HELL OF A GAUNTLET TO RUN."

Soon after setting course due south the weather turned nasty and did not clear up until about noon. For the 2nd of March, 1942 I made this entry in my journal, "Running for our lives and at dawn a bare 75 miles from the coast." Sure enough at 1230 a two engine enemy plane spotted us and circled several times but dropped no bombs. We did not open fire and he shoved off north in half an hour. Have never been so scared in my life. All afternoon we lived in mortal fear and dread of bombers and warships with hardly anything to fight them with. "Oh my Guardian Angel!"

We knew the plane would be calling in air strikes and surface forces. The captain called all hands on the main deck and gave us a little talk. He said we could expect to be attacked at any time and if we were going to be sunk we would go down fighting—throwing spuds at them if nothing else available. If we were desperate and it was possible we would try to ram the enemy. We were to put on our lifejackets and keep them on, get our valuables together such as money, watches, jewelry, photos, and protect them as best we could—to some this meant condoms. Then he said God bless you all and Good Luck! And all of us knew we would need all the luck and blessings we could get.

There followed until darkness the most awful, terror-filled hours of my whole life before or since. Later in the war while serving on a cruiser and an aircraft carrier in combat and under attack with some near misses, there was nothing like that feeling I had on *Isabel* that afternoon. Similarly while serving as captain of a destroyer in the Korean war in combat and under fire of a shore battery which shot holes in our smokestacks, there was nothing like the doom we felt. The difference was that *Isabel* had no effective means of defense. As gunnery officer of *Isabel* I was acutely aware that the puny guns we had would not come close to matching anything we might meet in the Indian Ocean. The tension that afternoon could have been cut with a knife and was close to unbearable. Anyone who shouted, talked loud or attempted a bit of humor was immediately glared at and cursed out of the side of mouths drawn with anxiety. A slammed door was like a cannon shot signaling the start of death throes of *Isabel* and our last minutes of life on this earth. They drew the same glares and curses. I think I know now how a prisoner under death sentence feels as he sits in his cell waiting for guards to come and escort him to the electric chair. Darkness came as a reprieve.

Meanwhile all during the day of the 2nd of March our radiomen kept hearing distress calls from merchant ships broadcasting "Raider, Raider!" and from Allied ships saying they were under attack by cruisers or destroyers. It was impossible to identify which ships and where they were located. Later the crew of a PBY patrol plane which left Tjilatjap on the 2nd for Australia and flew by us reported that just over the horizon about 40 miles to the east was an enemy cruiser and two destroyers. If we had headed southeast on a direct course to Fremantle rather than due south we might have run smack dab into that enemy force. We knew enemy ships were running amuck in the Indian Ocean sinking ships right and left. If we had known the tremendous size of the task forces we would have been even more frightened.

The order for Allied evacuation of Tjilatjap and other ports in Java produced upwards of a hundred merchant and warships and on the 2nd they were scattered all over the Indian Ocean as targets for the enemy. We concluded the enemy was so busy with other targets they never got around to us but knew exactly where we were. The situation was likened to a pack of wolves tearing into a widely scattered flock of sheep killing a lot of them but not getting them all. *Isabel* and *Sea Witch* were lucky that day.

The next day was Tuesday the 3rd of March and we were still fearful of enemy planes. We continued to get official reports of enemy forces and sometimes commercial newscasts on the wardroom radio. Many enemy submarines were reported in the Indian Ocean. An aircraft carrier, cruiser and five destroyers were reported at large. At about 0900 the lookouts sighted a warship hull down off on the starboard beam. She appeared to be a cruiser on a southeast course designed to intercept us.

I was officer of the deck at the time and climbed higher to the searchlight platform on the foremast to get a better look. She looked Japanese, had five turrets, three forward and two aft just like the *Mogami* class enemy cruisers. My heart stopped beating for awhile and one could feel the groans of anguish on board *Isabel*. Oh Lordy, we are in for it now, we thought.

But then I noticed something on the cruiser that looked familiar. It was an airplane crane on the stern which I knew was distinctive for the class of light cruisers on which I had served. During this time she was challenging us by signal light and we observed her gun turrets training out and aiming at us. She turned out to be USS *Phoenix* (CL-46) my old light cruiser home. Quickly I sent over a message to the effect "Don't shoot! This is your old shipmate Wick Alford." It had been less than eighteen months since I had left her after two years on board and I still had many friends over there. On *Isabel* we had no idea that a U.S. cruiser was within ten thousand miles of us out in the middle of the Indian Ocean. What a break! Oh, my Guardian Angel!

Then our captain cooked up a cunning message to *Phoenix* to the effect—"We would like to join up with you. We will screen you," very carefully not mentioning *Isabel* had no sonar and could hardly screen a rowboat. She came back with "How much speed can you make?" We replied 14 knots and her response was "Sorry, Bon voyage!" With that she disappeared over the horizon ahead at 25 knots. Actually *Isabel* was designed for 26 knots but *Sea Witch* could only do 14 and we had to stay with her. Besides *Isabel* could not sustain high speed for any great length of time.

Later we learned *Phoenix* had been the escort for the convoy en route from Australia to India from which *Langley* and *Sea Witch* had broken off for bringing fighter planes to Java. My guess is that *Phoenix* did not know the terrible danger she was in. The massive enemy forces in the Indian Ocean at that time would have sunk her too if they had known and could find her.

My journal entry for March 4th was, "On, on, on to Fremantle. The sea is getting rough making life miserable. *Isabel* is a poor ocean going ship. She takes on waves and leaks them below decks. It is getting cold as we go farther south and most of the men have no winter clothes." But every mile we covered and the drop in temperature was proof we were moving away from danger. There was a noticeable lessening of apprehension. The next day there was growing optimism and my journal entry for 5 March was short—"Arrive Fremantle tomorrow thank goodness. Hope to get some mail." Then on the 6th—"Arrived Fremantle, West Australia." In my cabin I went to my knees in thanks for deliverance.

Chapter 17

"Titivate Ship"[48]

THE arrival of *Isabel* and *Sea Witch* at Fremantle, West Australia was something of a miracle. Indeed the engineer officer of *Isabel* reported that upon anchoring there was just fuel enough for one more hour of steaming. But the greater significance was that we had run the gauntlet of a good portion of the entire Japanese Fleet. A "spit kit" like *Isabel* was no big deal but a valuable C-3 ship and cargo had been saved for the war effort. We believed we got through because we stayed clear of the direct route from Tjilatjap to Fremantle as long as practicable. We suspected the enemy would be along that route looking for us.

Thank goodness the *Parrott* also arrived the same day we did with approximately a third of our former shipmates on *Stewart* including Ensign Brinkley. It is understood that she too stayed well clear of the rhumb line where she suspected the wily enemy would be lurking. Then we were looking for *Pillsbury*, also with a third of our *Stewart* shipmates. Both ships had departed Tjilatjap twelve hours before *Isabel* sailed but had taken separate routes. We hoped she would show up soon as well as other missing ships.

On Saturday 7 March I went over to the *John D. Edwards* to visit with Commodore Binford and my classmate Bruce Garrett. The Commodore told me all about the Battle of the Java Sea and their escape from Surabaya. He also told me that our former captain, Lieutenant Commander H.P. Smith was on his way back to the states and that it was reported Lieutenant Stone had been lost in the sinking of *Pecos*. He had no information on Lieutenant Clark who had been sent back overland from Tjilatjap to Surabaya to demolish *Stewart*. The commodore also related how when *Whipple* arrived at Fremantle with the *Langley* and *Pecos* survivors on the 4th of March and found the *Phoenix*

---

[48] A term frequently used on board Navy ships for straightening things up, stowing away gear, tidying up the decks and making things ship-shape. Here used in the sense of tying up loose ends and accounting for surviving ships of the former Asiatic Fleet and groups of men escaping capture by the enemy in Java.

snugly sitting there in the harbor looking fat, dumb and happy, indignation started to rise.

Asiatic Fleet sailors knew or found out that *Phoenix* had escorted that convoy to India, had reached her destination, turned around and headed back to Fremantle. On her return voyage she had passed reasonably close to where *Langley* and *Pecos* had been attacked and sunk. Questions were being asked, "Where was *Phoenix*, by God, when the ships were being attacked and their shipmates killed in the bombings? Why didn't she come to their aid? And where the hell was *Phoenix* when *Pecos* was sunk and their shipmates by the hundreds were dying and drowning. And why was not a rescue operation mounted?"

It reached a boiling point ashore when liberty parties from the various ships met up with liberty parties from *Phoenix* and a terrific brawl ensued. And it was not just an individual ship thing. It was the Asiatic Fleet versus the Pacific Fleet which had not come to our aid when our ships were being sunk and our sailors dying. The resentment of our men was understandable and seemed to be especially aimed at those damned, sleek, prissy cruisers like *Phoenix* which would not dirty their hands helping the great unwashed, the ships of the Asiatic Fleet. At least that was the perception, rightly or wrongly. Of course *Phoenix* would have helped if she had known of the disasters taking place.

It was undoubtedly a communications breakdown, radio frequencies not guarded or some kind of glitch. Nevertheless there seemed to be an antiseptic quality about the rigid formality of keeping separate the roles, missions and tasks of ships in the different fleets as if we were ships of a different navy from a different country. We had seen this before when *Houston* and *Stewart* met *Pensacola* at Torres Strait. Besides, some of our men felt, *Phoenix* was the same class as *Boise* which was not popular with Asiatic Fleet sailors. No matter whose fault, whether deserved or not, when the chips were down and the shooting started *Boise* was nowhere around.

Phoenix had to cancel liberty on the 5th and with the shore patrol had to take measures to prevent any more brawls. On Sunday 8th I went aboard *Phoenix* and chatted with old friends and shipmates. They seemed not to be aware of the sinkings, tragedies and heartbreak in the Asiatic Fleet. This was the day the Dutch formally surrendered Java to the Japanese. Those of us who had gotten to know some nice Dutch people were very sad about that.

Meanwhile the hospitality of the Australians for our men was outstanding and very heartwarming. Some on liberty who had a little too much Swan beer and went to sleep on a homeowners lawn might wake up with a pillow under his head, a blanket keeping him warm and an invitation to breakfast. The Aussies were very frightened of the Japanese and with good reason. From what I could observe the enemy could have taken West Australia with one division of troops. An Aussie greeting to one of us Yanks might go something like this—"Hello Yank! Welcome! Glad you came to save us. Then we would reply, but we came to be saved. We were running for our lives." One most satisfying aspect of our arrival in Australia was access to fresh milk, ice cream, fresh foods and steak. Also it was nice to see so many beautiful women.

On the 9th I went ashore, found a cable office and sent my lovely wife a cable that I was alive and well. She had not heard from me in about two months. Later I learned that soon after *Stewart* was abandoned on 22 February a news item in papers back home said *Stewart* had been lost. There was nothing as to whether she was sunk, blown up or what. And not a word was said about the crew. She suffered terrible anxiety not knowing if I was alive or lost with the ship. Not being able to ease her anguish until we arrived in Australia was heartbreaking for me as well.

On the 10th, miracle of miracles, Lieutenant Clark with his demolition crew and our former executive officer Lieutenant Smiley arrived from Tjilatjap on board an old Dutch steamer the *Generaal Verspijck* of about 1200 tons. We never thought we would ever see them again. He also brought out three wounded men in addition to Lieutenant Smiley who had been injured by shrapnel in the Battle of Badoeng Strait. On orders from Vice Admiral Glassford of 24 February Lieutenant Clark had proceeded by car from Tjilatjap back to Surabaya on the 25th with orders to prepare for demolition of *Stewart* to be carried out when ordered. With his crew of seven senior enlisted men he proceeded to place demolition charges in strategic places around the ship with appropriate wiring for making the final connection and detonation when ordered. Later he reported that when he arrived at the shipyard, Surabaya on the 25th the position and the condition of *Stewart* was essentially the same as it was when we abandoned her three days before on the 22nd of February. But just about anything that could be moved, unscrewed, unbolted or that was not welded down was gone. Before and after the Battle of the Java Sea, Commodore Binford's five destroyers had about a full day to strip *Stewart* of anything portable. To this day I still get thanks from old sailors for this or that piece of equipment—machine guns, rifles, radios, tools, spare parts, etc. The 4-inch guns were still there and had been offered to the Dutch Navy by

Commander Murphy who was U.S. Navy liaison in Surabaya. He had also directed that preparations for demolition of *Stewart* be kept from the Dutch authorities which hardly seemed necessary since they were preparing to scuttle their own remaining ships in March.

Preparations were completed on 28 February except for the final connections. At 1100 on the 1st of March U.S. Naval Headquarters gave the order to proceed with destruction. However the enemy air raids that morning had heavily hit the shipyard and one or more bombs had hit the floating drydock in which *Stewart* lay partially on her side. The drydock was half sunk and continuing to settle slowly. *Stewart* appeared to have had a direct hit in the forward engine room which was completely flooded as were the boiler rooms and the forecastle was awash. It was feared that some of the wires to the demolition charges might short out in the flooding but the detonations went as planned as far as could be ascertained. However because of the flooding it was not possible to determine by inspection the extent of the damage. An 80 lb. charge was set off in the after handling room and it was hoped this would also explode a small number of depth charges and a few rounds of ammunition in the after magazine. But apparently this did not happen. Nevertheless Lieutenant Clark reported to Vice Admiral William A. Glassford, Commander Naval Forces, Southwest Pacific that he believed *Stewart* was left in such a condition as to be of no value to the enemy.

Upon completion of his task Lieutenant Clark picked up two *Stewart* patients at Central Burger Hospital, Surabaya, and with his crew of picked men proceeded by automobile back to Tjilatjap arriving about 1400 March 2nd. A valiant Dutch lady was of great assistance in acting as guide for the trip. The patients were Lieutenant Clare B. Smiley former executive officer of *Stewart* and Gunners Mate Vernon Fowler. On arrival at Tjilatjap Lieutenant Clark soon learned that the last U.S. Navy ship, *Isabel*, had left the night before. He also learned that the 1200 ton Dutch steamer *Generaal Verspijck* had been turned over to the British for taking out personnel. Commodore J.A. Collins, Australian Navy, senior officer present, very kindly authorized Lieutenant Clark and his party to take passage to Fremantle. By this time his group included one of Dr. Wassel's patients and five U.S. civilians who were stranded in Tjilatjap. During the voyage his group who were not wounded joined in working the steamer, shoveling coal or whatever needed to be done to help them escape from Java. Their arrival in Fremantle was a great surprise and satisfaction for all of us.

Another event must be related in our effort to "titivate ship" and tie up the loose ends of the story of the Asiatic Fleet in the early months of the war. This is the story of Dr. Wassel who had been personally detailed by Admiral Hart to care for the wounded officers and men of the *Houston* and *Marblehead* after the Battle of the Flores Sea. The doctor arrived in Tjilatjap from Jogjakarta by train on 25 February with 40 patients, of whom 30 were ambulatory and ten on stretchers. All but the ten on stretchers were assigned to *Pecos* which was scheduled to sail on the morning of the 27th for India.

Captain Abernethy of the *Pecos* refused to take the stretcher cases and we now know it was a blessing in disguise for them. We have no way of knowing how many, if any, of the 30 ambulatory patients of Dr. Wassel survived the tragic sinking of *Pecos* which also had most of the *Langley* survivors on board. Dr. Wassel then took his stretcher patients back to Jogjakarta and on hearing that the enemy had landed on both ends of Java explored every way possible to get them flown out.

Some U.S. Army Air personnel at a nearby airfield promised to fly out the patients if there was room. But this did not pan out and the only thing Dr. Wassel got was a Ford sedan the Army people abandoned when they left. Desperately the good doctor flagged down a British antiaircraft unit en route to Tjilatjap and persuaded them to make room for six of his patients in their lorries and other vehicles. With Dr. Wassel at the wheel of the Ford sedan and with four of his patients including Commander Goggins, former executive officer of the *Marblehead*, the whole group set out on safari for Tjilatjap. The vehicle convoy stopped for tea at 1700 but Dr. Wassel and his four in the Ford plowed on to Tjilatjap arriving about 2230 on Sunday the 1st of March.

There he learned to his dismay that *Isabel* had left only about an hour earlier. I am sure that Captain Payne of the *Isabel* would have waited for him if he had known he was coming. But we remember that *Isabel* was committed to rendezvous with a submarine off the harbor entrance that night and also to escort *Sea Witch* when she emerged after midnight. We would certainly have welcomed him and his four patients riding in the Ford on board but even if that had worked out I doubt if he personally would have embarked. He would have stayed behind to look after the other six patients in the vehicle convoy expected to arrive the next day. Indeed unknown to Dr. Wassel at the time, one of the six patients in that convoy did get aboard *Isabel* because the British Army officer in charge of the anti-aircraft unit had gone on ahead of the vehicle convoy to make arrangements for his men and had a patient with him. He delivered the patient alongside *Isabel* just as we were taking in our docklines.

Dr. Wassel was then fortunate to find a place to sleep for himself and the four patients who arrived with him in the Ford. The next morning the doctor exhausted every possibility of getting his patients out of Java but without success. There were unsettling reports of ships loaded with refugees being sunk off the harbor entrance. The British vehicle convoy arrived about noon but one of the patients was missing. He had become too ill to travel and was left at a small hospital about 35 miles away.

Dr. Wassel continued his unrelenting search for a ship during the afternoon and with the help of a Dutch liaison official finally found a ship captain who agreed to embark the group. Then Dr. Wassel wasted no time in getting his patients, now down to eight, aboard the small vessel *Janssens* of 300 tons and diesel powered. There were no rooms or bunks available and Dr. Wassel bedded down some of his patients under an awning on the fantail and some in a smoking lounge. The British promised to send out the missing patient later if possible. After dark the little ship departed Tjilatjap and once clear of the mine field she ran into a violent squall which probably protected her from submarines.

On into the night went the little ship overloaded with more than 600 refugees of every stripe and level. There were Dutch naval officers, British seamen, Australian soldiers, diplomats, prominent civilians, women and children plus the intrepid Dr. Wassel and his eight patients. But when dawn broke Commander Goggins who had recovered from his wounds enough to be startled and aghast that the ship had been hugging the coast heading east all night, protested vehemently to the captain of the ship. The captain stated that the Netherlands Navy Admiralty had advised him to go 800 miles to the east before turning south. Despite it being pointed out to him he was heading into a hornets nest of enemy planes on the island of Bali he continued east. Sure enough at about 0930 a large flight of enemy bombers heading west in the direction of Tjilatjap flew over the little ship *Janssens*.

No bombs were dropped but undoubtedly the airfield on Bali was alerted. *Janssens* was now well within fighter range of the airfield and about 1030 here they came. Three fighter planes worked over the little ship strafing with .30 cal. and 20mm machine guns. Dutch sailors got off some .30 cal. machine gunfire and the attack did not last long. But the topsides were shot up badly and eight refugees were wounded. But none of the American patients were hit and fortunately the operation of the ship was unimpaired. However some of the refugees became hysterical and demanded to be put ashore. The captain put into a small harbor and anchored close to shore to be less visible to planes. About 160 people elected to leave the ship and were put ashore.

But most of the refugees chose to stay on board and take their chances on reaching West Australia. After dark the little ship got underway again and by this time the day's events had made a true believer of the captain. He decided he had better get out of range of the enemy fighter planes as soon as possible and headed south as fast as the little ship would go. Unfortunately that was only seven knots. On *Janssens* plodded through the night and at dawn anxious eyes scanned the horizon and the skies for ships and planes. But none were sighted during the day and optimism began to grow. It was too soon to relax however because everyone had been told that enemy battleships, cruisers, destroyers, submarines and aircraft carriers with their planes were all over the Indian Ocean. Days passed and confidence grew.

Meanwhile the refugees regardless of their status pitched in to help with necessary work on the little ship-food service, the engine room, cleaning and maintenance. *Janssen* had left Tjilatjap late on March 2nd but did not leave the Java coast until late on the 3rd. Now after over a week of diesel motoring she was still well short of Fremantle and maintenance problems began to mount. A steering casualty had the ship running in circles for awhile but managed after two hours to get back on course using arduous hand steering. But a week underway at only seven knots covers a lot of miles and on March 11th a U.S. Navy PBY plane was sighted.

The sight of a friendly aircraft excited everyone and optimism began to soar on the little ship. But the next day they had a scare when a submarine surfaced astern. It was only the interaction of the submarine with an Australian bomber aircraft that convinced the refugees the submarine was friendly. Then spirits rose very high and although the next day was Friday the 13th of March there was no evidence anyone felt any foreboding of an unlucky day. Deliverance looked to be at hand.

It was indeed a lucky day for the refugees when *Janssens* anchored in the harbor of Fremantle, West Australia on Friday 13th of March 1942. And they all knew it, especially Dr. Wassel and his patients. The patients had every reason to thank God and Dr. Wassel for getting them out of Java and saving them from death or a living hell as prisoners of war. The story of Dr. Wassel and his patients is one of the great sagas of naval history. A fairly creditable motion picture was made about the story with actor Gary Cooper playing Dr. Wassel. For his devotion to duty, tender care and tireless efforts to save his patients Dr. Wassel was awarded the Navy Cross.

Meanwhile the arrival of *Isabel* and the *Parrott* in Fremantle on 6 March had accounted for all thirteen of the four stack destroyers except one. That one was *Pillsbury* which had departed Java on 1 March the same day as *Parrott* but had taken a separate route. The remaining destroyers in Fremantle as well as other ships of the former Asiatic Fleet then watched anxiously for the arrival of *Pillsbury* and other overdue ships—the gunboat USS *Asheville*, British destroyer *Stronghold* and Australian sloop *Yarra*. There had been rumors, fears and bits of good but inconclusive information that these ships were missing and presumed lost. Still there was hope the ships might show up.

The arrival in Fremantle of Lieutenant Clark and his *Stewart* demolition team on 10 March gave renewed hope the missing ships might arrive. Still later the arrival of Dr. Wassel and his patients on March 13th gave just a flicker of dying hope the missing ships might have survived. But it was not until the 16th of March that an official list of missing ships came out that were presumed lost. We had not known exactly what happened to our cruisers but we did know about when and where they were sunk. We had similar sketchy information on the loss of *Encounter*, *Pope* and *Yarra*. A few of the crew of *Yarra* were picked up by a Dutch submarine on 9 March. But *Asheville*, *Pillsbury* and British destroyer *Stronghold* disappeared without a trace.

They too like the *Edsall* had sailed into oblivion, had vanished in a void and like the legendary "Flying Dutchman" had disappeared into the mists of time, doomed to sail the seven seas forever. It was several years after the war that charts from Japanese sources were found which showed approximate locations of the sinkings of Allied ships in the Indian Ocean in that time period. The charts showed that *Asheville* was sunk on 2 March by ships of the Japanese 4th Destroyer Division fairly close to the direct route between Tjilatjap and Fremantle. This sinking was particularly painful to me because our former *Stewart* shipmate Ensign W.H. Harris was aboard. All hands were lost and I consider it shameful that records available to me do not show a posthumous award or decoration of any kind for her commanding officer Lieutenant Commander Jacob William Britt.

The Japanese charts also show that *Stronghold* was sunk on 2 March, the same date as *Asheville* sinking and not too far away, also with loss of all hands. Curiously the charts do not show what enemy units were involved. But the charts are clear that the *Pillsbury* was sunk on 2 March by the heavy cruisers *Atago* and *Takao* almost due south from Bali Strait. This indicated *Pillsbury* had headed southeast from Tjilatjap towards the northwest coast of Australia when she was caught, run down and smothered under the concentrated 8-inch gunfire of the enemy cruisers. One can imagine the anguish and despair of Captain Pound and his crew as they may have tried to outrun the enemy, elude them in a smoke screen or perhaps in desperation attempted to ram—only to be over-whelmed with an avalanche of shells as the little ship was pounded beneath the waves. And there her gallant, heroic crew to a man died or drowned in a welter of exploding shells, mangled steel, mangled bodies, death and destruction.

The loss of *Pillsbury* and all hands which included 30 of our former *Stewart* shipmates was for me one of the most painful experiences of the war. The thirty included Chief Machinist's Mate Paul R. Seifert who had been highly commended by *Stewart* Captain H.P. Smith for superbly acting as engineer officer during the Battle of Badoeng Strait. Chief Seifert was later awarded the Silver Star posthumously. But I hold it was not enough, that he should have been awarded the highest honor the nation can bestow—the Congressional Medal of Honor.

Concerning Commander Harold Clay Pound, Commanding officer of *Pillsbury*, the only record to which I have access shows he was awarded the Navy Cross. I assume the award was for his superb performance as captain of *Pillsbury* in the Battle of Badoeng Strait. But for that battle and his last battle against overwhelming odds in which fighting his ship to the last, he went down with his ship, I hold that he too deserves the highest honor the nation can bestow—the Congressional Medal of Honor. Finally, on a personal note, I was particularly saddened by the loss of two classmates who went down with the *Pillsbury*, Lieutenants junior grade Edmundo Gandia and Howard P. Fischer. The latter had been my roommate on the passenger liner taking us from San Francisco to Manila in late 1940. God rest their brave souls.

There were some additional escapes from the maelstrom that was the Philippines, Java and the long string of the Netherlands East Indies in the early months of the war. Among these was General MacArthur to Australia, the yacht *Lanikai* under Kemp Tolley (later Rear Admiral) and submarines bringing out selected personnel from Corregidor before it surrendered. There may have been others. Indeed there was high indignation among the former Asiatic Fleet ships in Fremantle when a submarine arrived from Manila and Corregidor with a boatload of nurses.

The anger arose from the assumption that the nurses if left behind would have been able to ply their trade in taking care of the sick and wounded. But they were brought out instead of valuable and experienced officers and men who could have helped fight the war. Instead they were left behind to rot and die in POW camps. But the assumption might have been wrong—the nurses might not have been able to practice their profession. The rumor was that President Franklin Roosevelt had ordered that the nurses be brought out for compassionate reasons.

There was no doubt that the arrival of *Parrott* and *Isabel* at Fremantle on 6 March 1942 marked the end of the former Asiatic Fleet surface ship operations in the Far East. True, submarines continued to operate in the enemy backyard. *Isabel* as the last U.S. Navy ship to escape from *Java* was supposed to close the door and turn out the lights. Then the arrival of Lieutenant Clark's group on the 10th, Dr. Wassel, his patients and other refugees on the 13th had added some sense of finality to the Asiatic Fleet. But it was not until the 16th of March that a final and official list of missing and lost ships came out. The list included cruisers *Exeter, Houston, Perth*, destroyers *Edsall, Encounter, Pillsbury, Pope* and gunboat *Asheville*. What a terrible defeat!

When we add to these our known Allied losses of *Bittern, Canopus, De Ruyter, Electra, Finch, Java, Jupiter, Langley, Peary, Pecos, Perch, Pigeon, Quail, Sealion, Shark, Stewart, Stronghold, S-36, Tanager*, the Dutch destroyers, motor torpedo boats, many PBY aircraft, river gunboats and numerous small craft, it was an unmitigated disaster. The naval losses to the U.S. alone was 22 ships, 1826 men killed and 519 made prisoners of war. When we consider the early loss of the British battleship *Prince of Wales* and the battle cruiser *Repulse*, the fall of Hong Kong, Manila and the Philippines, Singapore and finally the fall of Java, the defeat assumes Homeric proportions. I mean the Japanese beat the hell out of us and our Allies out there. They kicked our butts.

How and why did this happen? There are many reasons and in a way, were it not for the tragic loss of life and ships, we deserved to be taught a lesson. Perhaps the most egregious mistake of the pre-war United States stance or foreign policy in the Far East was our failure to match commitments with the force to back it up. Zounds! This is national security course 101, primer stuff. It was the reverse of Teddy Roosevelt's dictum "Walk softly and carry a big stick." Instead we were treading heavily, making a lot of noise and showing with a few exceptions, a fleet of old, close to worn out ships. There were no fighter planes for protection of the fleet. In no sense could *Langley* be considered a modern aircraft carrier. In no sense could old four-pipe destroyers with 4-inch guns and faulty torpedoes be compared with modern Japanese destroyers twice their size and firepower. It does not seem possible such mismatches were not known.

When nations do that some rogue nation is sure to call the bluff of such self-delusion. But once having made the decision to block further expansion of the Japanese empire and deny them any access to oil, one would think it prudent to identify potential allies, search them out and work out a modus operandi with them if war came. But in Washington it was always a case of we want to do it and we are going to do it but never got around to it. And once war came it would appear imperative to form an allied command immediately with a commander of rank and experience in the area and medium where the war will be waged.

In this situation, it was essentially a sea war and the obvious choice was four star Admiral Thomas C. Hart. Placing a distinguished officer of his caliber and stature as subordinate to a surplus British field marshal was a crime in my book. Attention should have been paid to the long-standing tradition of the British Royal Navy that none of their ships would ever be pushed around by British Army types. A good case could have been made for a Dutch admiral as supreme commander but there were none of the rank, experience and stature available. That President Roosevelt and Prime Minister Churchill agreed to this odd ABDA command structure was a precursor to their betrayal of the eastern European countries behind the iron curtain. How could they have sold out the freedom of those countries when that was precisely the reason Britain went to war in the first place! It raises questions of honor, aside from gullibility about Stalin.

If anyone would be inclined to find fault with Admiral Hart in the Far East, and I am not, he would most likely say the Admiral prewar should have raised holy hell as General MacArthur did to get reinforcements. He should have demanded more ships—cruisers, new destroyers, meaningful air cover and yes, battleships. The British committed cruisers and capital ships, unfortunately without air cover. And yes, he should have made damn sure our torpedoes worked under realistic conditions. After the war started he should still have demanded more ships including aircraft carriers if the United States was serious about playing for time until our country could mobilize, outbuild and defeat the Axis powers. Also Admiral Hart should have resigned rather than accept the ABDA command arrangement.

When the shooting started and the lot of the Asiatic Fleet was thrown in with the fortunes of the gallant Dutch, the indomitable British, and the intrepid Australians, questions began to be raised. How long must the Fleet stay with a lost cause for a no longer meaningful commitment? How long must the Asiatic Fleet stay just to save face? How many more good men must be sacrificed along with their ships? It was felt in the Asiatic Fleet by all units that their most valuable assets were the trained, experienced men. Had anyone noticed that when Britain received the fifty old four stack destroyers from the U.S., she did not pit them against the modern German destroyers? No, they were used for convoys and other secondary tasks. Would the Pacific Fleet have placed four stack destroyers with fast carrier task forces? No, but they were pitted against modern Japanese destroyers twice their size and firepower.

Everyone knew what the outcome in the Far East was going to be. We, the British and the Dutch were going to lose our colonial empires. Why not take the long view of history and not sacrifice any more ships and men for a futile cling to empire? When the fleet departed Manila Bay why not keep going around Australia and rejoin the Pacific Fleet? We didn't because we could not abandon our friends. We fought like hell in a delaying action of three months and maybe we thought we were playing for time for the Pacific Fleet to come to our rescue. But what we were really doing was playing for time for our nation to gear up and turn out the ships, guns and planes necessary for the long haul to victory. There are some who feel the three months delay of the formidable Japanese war machine was crucial and give the Asiatic Fleet credit for it. But not very many. To paraphrase Winston Churchill, "Never was so much owed to so many by so many who never recognized the debt."

Then in mid-March 1942 the Asiatic Fleet was no more and the surviving eight four stackers reverted to convoying and other tasks more suited to their capabilities. In the epilogue we shall tell what happened to ex-*Stewart* lying halfway on her side in a sunken drydock in Surabaya harbor, the final disposition of the eight surviving four-pipers and what the future held for some of the personalities mentioned in the narrative. Thus ends the stirring story of the four stack destroyers of the famous U.S. Asiatic Fleet.

Chapter 18

Born Again—
Under the Rising Sun

LIEUTENANT Commander Shizuo Fukui was perplexed. It was the sunken hulk of the old American destroyer *Stewart* that was wrinkling his brow and giving him indigestion. The hulk had been under water for the better part of a year, nestled firmly in the embrace of the drydock that had sunk under her when it was hit by five or six Japanese bombs during an air raid. Raising the destroyer would be easy. All he had to do was raise the drydock and both would be above water. He also believed that the task of getting the old ship seaworthy again would only need time and labor. All he had to do was recondition her Babcock & Wilcox boilers, her Parsons turbines, straighten her port shaft and the rest would follow. It was an exercise in restoration more than a refit. She was already obsolescent in her power plant and spares would be a problem but he had a whole shipyard of trained workers at his disposal. What he could not scrounge his machinists would make from scratch. No, the real problem was disguising her telltale silhouette so that Japanese planes and ships would not mistake her for an American man of war and fire on her.

Fukui ordered the work to commence in February of 1943, a whole year after she and her drydock were sunk. Now her hull and superstructure swarmed with yard workers. Sparks from countless acetylene torches cascaded down her rusted flanks and the air rang, day and night with the sounds of hammers and drills as she was slowly restored to life under the eyes of one of Japan's best naval architects. The 29-year old lieutenant commander was saddled with an enormous responsibility. In addition to this wreck, he also had several others, lately of the Royal Netherlands Navy to raise and restore to service.

By early June, she was upright and beginning to resemble a warship again. Her new commanding officer Senior Lieutenant Tamotsu Mizutani saw her for the first time that summer. He was joined by Lieutenant junior grade Tsurayuki Okubo who would serve as his executive officer and who would write a book about his days aboard. These two officers were in time joined by Ensign Okada and a skeleton crew of warrant officers and senior chiefs.

Fukui was pleased with the progress she was making and thought he had a solution to altering her silhouette. By removing her forward stack and trunking her boiler uptakes from the forward fireroom into the second stack he gave her a distinctly pregnant appearance. He removed the 12 torpedo tubes as an added measure. Next he stripped her of her main armament—the four 4 inchers and the 3-inch anti-aircraft gun. In their place he substituted some Dutch cannon liberated from the defenders of Surabaya the previous year. They were two 75mm anti-aircraft guns and two 12.7mm machine guns. Since there were no more Allied ships in the area to worry about and few if any Allied planes, she was considered to be adequately armed.

On 15 June she was designated Patrol Boat No. 102. Her silhouette was made a part of all Imperial Japanese Navy recognition books, That late summer and early autumn she finished refitting and more and more of her crew reported to Mizutani for duty and training. The officers were now faced with a truly daunting task. All of the 102 boat's manuals and machinery publications had been burned when she was abandoned. New ones had to be written. Likewise, her gauges and instruments had been stripped from her and had now to be replaced by gauges and instruments her Japanese crew could read. There were no spare parts to speak of. For the rest of her life, as a Japanese vessel she would be plagued by a shortage of parts that would follow her like a Gypsy curse. But, slowly and with a will, these problems were overcome and she began to "shape up" like a real ship. Once more the shrill blast of the bosun whistle ordered her crew. Once more her hull vibrated to the power of her engines.

The time for her sea trials was nearing when Captain Mizutani decided to hold a religious ceremony to ask the blessing of Japan's powerful sea gods for his ship. Lieutenant Okubo wrote to his wife in Osaka and asked her to send an amulet from that city's famous Sumiyoshi Shrine for the ceremony. When it arrived the crew began the ceremony and asked the priests to invoke the protection of the gods Sokotsutsu-no-Ono-mikoto, Nakatsu-no-Ino-mikoto, Uwatsutsu-no-Ono-mikoto and the dead Empress Jingu who, centuries before, had repulsed a huge Korean fleet. These were gods whose intercession fishermen and navigators prayed for. The dead Empress was a favorite of the Imperial Japanese Navy.

On 20 September 1943 she was formally commissioned as Patrol Boat 102 and began sea trials the next day. After a month of sea trials, she was judged fit for combat operations and 18 October 1943 she stood out from Balikpapan with two tankers, the *Kenyo Maru* and the

Nichisi Maru. Her complement of three commissioned officers, seven warrant officers and 108 seamen and petty officers was "light" by U.S. standards. At the time the ex-*Stewart* was abandoned in Surabaya, her complement was seven commissioned officers and 138 enlisted.

Soon after she went back to her old stomping grounds, reports began to filter back that an American destroyer was operating in such places as the Makassar Strait, New Guinea, Palau, Halmahera and the Sulu Archipelago. U.S. Naval Intelligence had known about the resurrection of *Stewart* and even had reconnaissance photos of her standing upright in her drydock in the summer of 1943. Indeed Lieutenant Francis Clark, formerly of *Stewart*, had reported in early March 1942 that the ship had been destroyed to the extent she would be of no use to the Japanese. Then in the summer of 1943 he was himself called in to Navy Headquarters in Brisbane, Australia and shown the recent reconnaissance photos of Surabaya showing ex-*Stewart* still in the same drydock and on an even keel. There is no known public record that he was called on the carpet and reprimanded in any way. But it was still disconcerting to know that the Old China Hand was back on station and working for the other side. It was embarrassing yes, but not surprising. It is likely that even if *Stewart* had been demolished into small pieces, the Japanese would have painstakingly put her back together if only for psychological and propaganda purposes. Indeed ex-*Stewart* had risen from the ashes and debris of her former self like the legendary "Phoenix" bird of mythology and fated to repeat the rebirth forever. Yes, she was "Born Again" but this time hostile to her former friends.

On 20 October 1943 while escorting two tankers, *Genyo Maru* and *Azuma Maru*, the PB102 picked up a submarine contact and commenced laying down depth charges. The attack lasted for two hours and expended 65 depth charges. Captain Mizutani gave no quarter to what he thought was an American submarine operating in the Makassar Strait. His lookouts spotted a large oil slick and floating debris where they thought the submarine should have been. A radio report of the "kill" was made and a seaplane was sent to investigate Mizutani's claim. The kill was "confirmed" and Captain Mizutani received a congratulatory message from fleet headquarters from no less a personage than Admiral Daigo himself.

A few days later while still on patrol in the Makassar Strait, the crew of PB102 was horrified to see the wakes of three torpedoes coming straight at them. She successfully evaded and retired from the area. On 30 October at about 160 miles north of the equator in the Celebes Sea, lookouts spotted a submarine hastily diving. An immediate attack was ordered and after making several runs, the lookouts spotted a huge geyser of black water rise 40 feet into the air while at the same time she was ordered to rejoin the convoy. When PB102 returned to the area 18 hours later, she saw a huge oil slick.

In October 1943 the U.S. Navy lost two submarines in the Pacific. S-44 was sunk by a Japanese destroyer while on patrol somewhere in the vicinity of Paramushiro in the Kurile Islands on the 7th and USS *Wahoo* was thought to have been lost in the Sea of Japan about the 11th. Both sinkings happened far from the locations PB102 made in her reports. However Captain Mizutani really thought he had sunk these submarines and he made a big show of it by congratulating his crew in public on 3 November at Balikpapan during celebrations marking the Emperor's birthday.

To further bolster the crew's morale and refresh them, he granted liberty first to the port watch and later to the starboard watch. But the port including the brothels was jammed with Army troops and the inevitable brawl ensued. The executive officer Okubo went ashore in support of his men and promptly got involved in the melee himself when he almost beaned the base commander. The matter was quietly forgotten and no punishment ensued. But Lieutenant Okubo had earned greater respect from the crew since he had championed their cause ashore.

Back on patrol on 8 November 1943 PB102 was attacked by yet another submarine and despite Captain Mizutani's best effort to evade them, three torpedoes sped right for the ship. Alarm bells and whistles sounded all over the ship as the crew braced themselves for the dreaded shocks which never came. The torpedoes had been set for a deeper draft ship and passed harmlessly under the keel. Not wishing to tempt fate, Captain Mizutani retired at full speed. Three days later on 11 November, they were not so lucky. A lone torpedo hit the port screw but failed to explode. It did however throw a scare into all on board.

Then the constant strain of escort and patrol duty was taking its toll on the power plant. Engines and boilers were too old for this continuous steaming. They began to break down and the crew was ingenious in their repair methods. Somehow they kept up pressure in the boilers and kept the turbines and shafts turning. But they needed a yard period. After escort of two more ships PB102 was ordered back to Surabaya, a treasured liberty port, for a rest and refit. Holland which had been overrun by Hitler two years before had also lost its most prized colony to Japan, Germany's ally. The Dutch who had fled Holland and gone to the Netherlands Indies were now in internment camps, their homes and businesses now in the hands of Japanese bureaucrats and military officers. The world had indeed turned upside down for them.

But for now, the PB102 crew made good use of the port and its facilities to rest and refit. All hands were promoted. And they restored themselves in the time-honored way of sailors all over the world—they got drunk and raised hell. By now they had good reason to. The war was turning against Japan and her Navy had been hard-pressed to keep its commitments. The invincible military machine was being rolled up all over the Pacific.

Suddenly the PB102 overhaul period was curtailed and she was ordered to sea. She left port without the sound detection gear she had so desperately needed. She was seaworthy though just marginally. Her boilers were still acting up but the engineering department still managed feats of improvisation to keep them running. She was even assigned a medical officer, a real doctor.

On 2 January 1944 PB102 stood out to sea from Balikpapan and entered Makassar Strait, her old hunting grounds. Two days later she was guided to a submarine contact by a patrol plane. While Captain Mizutani attacked the contact, the patrol plane circled overhead watching the game of cat and mouse unfolding below. For over five long, grueling hours PB102 pressed the attack and laid back to await the telltale oil slick and cork debris but none came. Nevertheless, Captain Mizutani felt he had killed the American submarine. But *Scorpion* was the only U.S. submarine lost in the Pacific in January 1944, reported overdue and presumed lost in the East China Sea, probably from hitting a mine.

Meanwhile the acute shortage of food on board and ashore was beginning to take its toll on PB102. For the first time beri-beri was seen in the crew. Special efforts were made to secure fresh food and vegetables for the crew at every opportunity. Lieutenant Okubo and the paymaster would go ashore with sake, tobacco and other trading materials and come back with fresh fruit, vegetables and meat. The alternative was meager rations of miso and dried sweet potato vines, hardly a diet for fighting men.

In this way did the crew survive the crippling effects of the U.S. naval offensive. More U.S. submarines were coming into service with better torpedoes and the toll of Japanese shipping was ever higher. Aside from this the crew's days melted into one another, broiled in the equatorial sun creating a misery of rashes, prickly heat and sheer discomfort as the old ship shuttled across the vast oceans. Then the crew had taken to calling PB102 that "gray haired old woman from America" for reasons that could only be guessed at. Day after day she cleft the seas of the Pacific shepherding the helpless from the inevitable.

Her charges were attacked as she was. They were invariably hit, sometimes sunk but never PB102. She always came through unscathed and the crew's faith in the "gray haired old woman from America" assumed mythic proportions. They began to feel invincible; or better yet, unconquerable. But she wasn't. She was slowly disintegrating from age, stress and the ceaseless action of wind and wave. On 19 June 1944 she began an extended period in the naval yard at Cavite on the southern shore of Manila Bay.

Two months later she was judged ready for sea again and left Cavite on 22 August bound for Kaohsiung on Formosa. To escape detection, she hugged the west coast of Luzon. In early August three U.S. submarines departed Fremantle, Australia. Their assigned patrol area was south of Luzon Strait and they were to pay special attention to the traffic moving to and from Subic Bay. It is a seven mile long natural harbor about 35 miles north of Manila Bay and had been a U.S. naval base since 1901. The three U.S. submarines arrived in their area late on 21 August and began attacking enemy shipping immediately with considerable success.

The attacks of the U.S. submarines continued several days with *Haddo* commanded by Chester Nimitz, Jr., *Hake* commanded by Frank Hayler and *Harder* commanded by the legendary Sam Dealey, dubbed the "destroyer killer" for his feat of having sunk six of them. Early on the morning of 24 August *Hake* spotted two ships leaving Dasol Bay, near Subic. They were PB102 and minesweeper Patrol Escort 22 (PE22) which gained sonar contact on *Hake* then trying to get in attack position but had to take evasive action. *Harder* was nearby as verified by visual periscope sighting. *Hake* then observed PB102 returning to Dasol Bay to assist tanker *Niyo Maru* while PE22 remained patrolling outside. PE22 then gained sonar contact and shortly *Hake* heard 15 rapid depth charge explosions. *Harder* was never heard from again and lost with all hands.

PE22 had gotten the intrepid Sam Dealey. But Captain Mizutani of PB102 brazenly told a bald face lie when he reported that it was PE22 which returned to Dasol Bay and that PB102 had attacked and sunk *Harder*. Exhaustive postwar analysis confirmed that PB102 was in the area but took no part in the sinking of *Harder*. All the while the strain of ceaseless patrolling by PB102 was working attrition on the old power plant. At one point engineer officer Ensign Okada got drunk and with his leading chief went to see the captain to demand some help with their problems.

Shortly thereafter PB102 was ordered to Cavite for an overhaul period. Upon completion she set course for Kaohsiung on Formosa, a Japanese possession since 1895. The crew were eager for anything Japanese. While there the port was attacked by U.S. Army Air Force bombers which did great damage but PB102 emerged untouched. While escorting a convoy from Formosa to the Philippines the formation was attacked by U.S. carrier planes. Great damage was done to the transports and several were sunk. But PB102 again emerged unscathed giving rise to the mythic invincibility of the "gray haired old woman from America."

Then in the fall of 1944 as Japan was running out of gas and steam, a great effort was made to repel the U.S. forces landing on Leyte in the Philippines. The effort went into the history books as the largest naval engagement in history. Actually it was four separate battles: Sibuyan Sea—24 October, Surigao Strait—24 and 25 October, Samar—25 October and Cape Engano—26 October. PB102 was judged too old and too slow to take part in the great battle and was given a rescue mission. When the super battleship *Musashi* was attacked and sunk in the Sibuyan Sea by U.S. carrier aircraft, it was PB102 that picked up survivors from the oily sea. She was destined to repeat such missions that autumn.

Respite came in late November when PB102 was ordered to Japanese home waters for the first time for a major refit. She entered the dockyard on Mukai Jima Island near Kure on 19 November 1944. The crew's families were present and greeted their long-lost sons and husbands with great emotion. The crew was jubilant at being home again after such a long and punishing absence. While at the great naval base at Kure, PB102 was greatly improved and her silhouette changed markedly.

Naval architect Fukui pulled off the antiquated armaments he had installed in 1943 at Surabaya and in their place he installed two 80mm anti-aircraft guns, four double mounts of 25mm machine guns and eight 25mm machine guns in single mounts. He also increased her depth charge capacity to 72. He pulled off the old foremast and replaced it with the more familiar light tripod masts seen on Japanese ships. He lowered her three funnels and enlarged her bilge keels. He had surface and air search radar installed and improved crew living areas. However a boiler had to be taken out of service for lack of spare parts and her maximum speed reduced to 25 knots, fully ten knots less than first sea trials in 1920.

Soon renewed, rested and re-supplied, PB102 returned to patrol and escort duty. But this time she was forbidden to stop and rescue survivors of torpedoed ships for fear she would be sunk by U.S. planes and submarines which roamed the seas and skies at will. New Year's day 1945 found her back in Japan for a brief rest but she was soon back in the East China Sea. On 14 January 1945 PB102 was back in Kure for a maintenance check on her boiler tubes. On the 24th of January her executive officer, Lieutenant Okubo was transferred to an 800 ton gunboat for duty.

Thereafter PB102 operated generally in Japanese home waters, the Yellow Sea and the East China Sea for three months seemingly bearing a charmed life. But on 28 April 1945 she was attacked in the Yellow Sea by U.S. Army Air Force bombers and badly damaged. At last the myth of her invincibility was exploded. She lost 38 men in the attack and a grisly comparison is suggested with U.S. casualties of the *Stewart* crew at time of the Battle of Badoeng Strait and later enemy action. One man was killed in the fight on 20 February 1942. Two transferred to *Edsall* and seven to *Pecos* went down with those ships on 1 March. But twenty-eight who were transferred to *Pillsbury* went down with that ship the next day bringing the total to 38. However one officer went down with the *Pecos* and one officer went down with the *Asheville* bringing the grand total to 40 who lost their lives to enemy action. The books almost balanced in this macabre accounting.

Then PB102 was ordered back to the big Kure naval shipyard for repairs. The end of the war came on 14 August 1945 and found her still at Kure, her repairs unfinished and clearly her fighting days were over. The atomic bomb dropped over nearby Hiroshima was too far away to inflict any further damage on PB102. War's end found Lieutenant Okubo in command of 48 midget submarines and ready to do or die for the Emperor. He and Captain Mizutani met for the last time on the 14th of August and heard the Emperor of Japan ask for his warriors to abandon the war lest it bring more bloodshed to their country. Nine days later on 23 August 1945 Lieutenant Commander Tamotsu Mizutani and eleven others knelt on the sidewalk before the Imperial Palace and committed hara-kiri.

When the U.S. Navy occupation forces found their old abandoned ship *Stewart*, she was still riding at anchor at the giant Japanese naval base at Kure. The Imperial Japanese Navy Patrol Boat 102, ex-USS

Stewart, had also been abandoned by her Japanese crew, her captors. As they say, what goes around, comes around.

Chapter 19

Homeward Bound

DURING 1944 and 1945 some American pilots and submarine commanders reported what appeared to be a U.S. flush-deck destroyer deep within Japanese waters. Something looked vaguely familiar about the vessel but her silhouette did not fit any known classes of enemy ships. She could not be positively identified at that time and was classified as one of the mysteries of the war. Although photo reconnaissance of Surabaya harbor back in the summer of 1943 had indicated that the enemy might be trying to raise and repair abandoned *Stewart*, no additional sightings were reported later that year. But when the war ended in August 1945 the mystery was cleared up when U.S. Navy Occupation Forces found my old ship, formerly USS *Stewart* (DD-224). She had been renamed Patrol Boat 102 and was found anchored with some Japanese warships approximately midway between the Kure naval base and what remained of the city of Hiroshima.

The ship was rusty, dirty, rat-infested and quite unseaworthy when found by U.S. personnel who partially described her condition as follows: "Below decks, Japanese characters were painted on the bulkheads and doors. Pin-up pictures of geisha girls lined the crew's living quarters. Rings of ash remained in many compartments where incense had been burned before miniature shrines." As at Surabaya when abandoned on 22 February 1942, she had again been stripped to some extent. At the insistence of U.S. occupation officials she was fumigated, scraped, cleaned, painted and shined from stem to stern by Japanese workers. Then with a Japanese crew and U.S. Navy officers she managed to get up enough steam to sail the 20 miles to Hiro Wan, Honshu where she tied up alongside USS *Compton* (DD-705) and was turned over to the U.S. Navy.

Meanwhile a call had gone out to U.S. fleet ships present in Japanese waters for any personnel who had formerly served on *Stewart* to volunteer to come back on board and help sail her back home. A rosy scenario was presented—the ship would be shoving off soon for the states which would be about a two week voyage and then she would make a triumphant entry under the Golden Gate bridge into San Francisco Bay and take part in the victory celebrations going on all over the country. There were few former *Stewart* men available so the offer was extended to men who had served on any four piper or those with high point scores for return home. This was a system of points based on seniority, performance of duty, time overseas and other factors to determine priority for return to the U.S. Some men jumped at the chance.

On 29 October 1945 the re-commissioning ceremony was held on board. The commissioning orders were read by Vice Admiral Jesse B. Oldendorf, Commander of Battleship Squadron One and Commander Southwestern Japan Force and the ship was restored to the U.S. Navy as USS DD-224. But not as *Stewart* since a new USS *Stewart* (DE-238) had been commissioned in the U.S. Navy on 31 May 1943. The Chief of Naval Operations directed that the recovered ship be referred to as "DD-224 without name." This seemed a bit awkward so the new crew began to refer to the ship as RAMP 224, which stood for Recovered Allied Military Personnel. There was a fever in the U.S. Occupation Forces in Japan to find and free prisoners of war held in the homeland and in outlying territories. The POWs included those of the U.S., our Allies, Australians, British, Dutch and others. Some of them had been POWs for three years under the most appalling conditions of malnutrition, sickness, exposure and brutality. Many had died. It was an emotional thing with our forces. Admirals were sometimes moved to tears when interviewing newly freed POWs. It was a tribute to the humanity of our men that they chose to name the recovered old ship as "RAMP."

The new commanding officer of DD-224 was Lieutenant Commander Harold H. Ellison, Class of 1942 at the Naval Academy. The new executive officer was mustang Lieutenant junior grade Grady T. Burns who had been a Machinist's Mate, First Class on board *Stewart* when she was abandoned in Surabaya on 22 February, 1942. I remember him very well as a very competent first class petty officer. USS DD-224 conducted engine trials in the Inland Sea on 2 November 1945 and reached a speed of 20 knots without any problems. On the 3rd she went alongside the repair ship *Vulcan* for a few days of additional work on her old machinery and pieces of equipment. On the 8th of November 1945, DD-224 departed Hiro Wan, Japan en route to Okinawa as the first leg of her long voyage back to the United States after an absence of over 23 years.

On the very next day occurred the first of the many problems that would plague the ship on her voyage home, when all engines were stopped due to loss of fuel suction. The fuel oil pump was repaired in half an hour and the ship continued confidently on her way. She arrived at Buckner Bay on the east coast of Okinawa on the 10th, refueled and on the following day departed in company with USS *Wesson* (DE-184) en route to Guam. Generally DD-224 was operated the same as when the Japanese ran her. However a section of the crew's quarters was left untouched for possible exhibition purposes. On the 13th of November at 1335 the engines again stopped because of loss of fuel oil suction. The fuel oil pump was repaired and the ship underway in less than two hours.

Later that evening there was a reduction gear casualty which was repaired by 2127. But shortly thereafter fuel oil suction was lost again and restored at 2220. The engines then ran well until shortly after midnight when the fuel oil pump failed again. This time it was determined machine tool work on the pump was required which DD-224 could not do. *Wesson* agreed to try and at dawn the pump valves were sent over, machined and sent back at 1015. Good progress was made for several hours at 15 knots and later about nine hours at 14 knots the morning of the 15th.

But there were six more failures on that day and this was rapidly becoming a nightmare. Fortunately during the night of 15-16 November she had a good twelve hours of steaming. On the 17th of November there was the same casualty and this time no more repairs could be made on board. In the afternoon *Wesson* took DD-224 under tow and with the aid of a tug soon brought her into Apra Harbor, Guam. After extensive repairs she failed engineering tests on 25 November and more work ensued. More mishaps—there was a fire on board and yard craft punched two holes in the portside.

By this time disillusionment had set in and the crew were having second thoughts about having made a bad choice on the quickest way to get back home to their families. On the 10th of December all repairs were completed and engineering tests were successful. At 1310 DD-224 got underway in company with SC-1036 en route to Eniwetok, the Marshall Islands. The engines worked fine for two days until 1530 on the 12th when her same old troubles returned. Over the next two days repeated efforts and tries were made to no avail and on the 14th a request was made to the authorities at Eniwetok for a tow.

On the 16th tug ATR-20 arrived and took DD-224 under tow. This went well at eight knots until about 1100 on the 17th when SC-1036 ran out of gas and also had to be taken in tow astern of DD-224. This sad entourage arrived at Eniwetok lagoon on 20 December. The day after Christmas 1945 thirty men were transferred off the ship and on the 27th two more for onward routing to the U.S. It was soon determined that DD-224 could not be fixed at Eniwetok and on 4 January 1946 she once more found herself on the end of a string from ATR-35 en route to Pearl Harbor. The destination was changed to Kwajalein where she arrived on 8 January. Then six more men were transferred.

After that the situation went from bad to worse. Setting out on the 27th of January under tow of ATR-86 assisted by ATR-64 the weather soon worsened and began parting tow lines. They had to return to Kwajalein arriving back on 1 February. The next day with better weather the group set out again and on the 11th were near Johnston Island. On the 18th the group reached Pearl Harbor. This time no effort was made to repair the main propulsion plant.

Just three days later DD-224 was again on the end of a tow line from ATF-148 en route to San Francisco at a speed of about eight knots. It was just as if she was an embarrassment to the great Pacific Fleet headquarters at Pearl Harbor and was being given the bums rush. The voyage went well for the next four days and speed was increased to 10 knots. On the 26th the gas generator expired and could not be repaired. Once again the ship had no power, was dark and cold iron. On the 2nd of March with land almost in sight, the tow cable parted again about 2 p.m. A new tow was passed and at 1725 the two were underway again but now at only five knots. On the afternoon of the 4th a pilot came aboard the tug and the ships entered the channel to San Francisco Bay. But just as the voyage appeared to have been completed, the tow line parted again and DD-224 anchored off the California coast at 1930 about five miles west of the Golden Gate bridge. It was as if she was ashamed to return to the U.S. on the end of a string.

Meanwhile the quartermasters and signalmen had been preparing a "Homeward Bound" pennant using such scraps of bunting as could be found regardless of the color. It was a tradition as old as the Navy and all hands entered into the spirit of the effort. The rules for making such a pennant were rather loose but usually one foot was added to the pennant for each month the ship was overseas. If this formula had been used for DD-224 her pennant would have been over 280 feet long and dragging in the water aft.

Early on the morning of 5 March tug ATR-23 took DD-224 under tow and proceeded up the channel. Passing under the Golden Gate bridge, members of the press came on board at 0930. Photographs of the ship entering the harbor show her "Homeward Bound" pennant appearing to be about 24 feet long streaming from the top of the foremast. The pennant probably had one foot for each year she was overseas. At about 1000 on Tuesday 5 March, 1946 DD-224 (ex-USS *Stewart*) moored at a berth on the San Francisco waterfront. DD-224 had finally completed her around the world voyage she had started almost 24 years before. The ship had returned home.

The voyage from Japan to San Francisco would normally take about two weeks for a ship in good condition, but it required almost four months, towing by a destroyer escort, six tugs, numerous engine repairs, two emergency generators and about a dozen tow lines. This is not to mention sleepless nights, working in darkness in desperate efforts to keep her going, and plenty of choice curse words. Now DD-224 had completed her triumphant voyage home but where were the cheering throngs? Where were the brass bands and patriotic speeches? The victory celebrations were gone.

The arrival of DD-224 was anti-climactic. Questions were being asked. Why was she brought halfway around the world at great expense, trouble and agony of soul? Whose idea was this in the first place? What do we do with DD-224? Obviously as a warship DD-224 was completely worthless. At one time she might have had patriotic, morale and celebratory value at the end of the war. But now the whole episode would have to be placed in the file entitled "It seemed like a good idea at the time." On the 26th of March the ship was moved by tugs across the bay to Oakland.

Towards the end of April a caretaker crew took over DD-224 and her skipper sent to other duty. Pending a decision as to her ultimate disposition, DD-224 remained at Oakland until 23 May, 1946 when she was decommissioned. Later that day she was towed into the Pacific off the coast of California. On the morning of 24 May 1946 she lay still and silent in the fog, like an apparition floating upon the sea. Now, no ship's boats swung from graceful davits. The gulls that had perched upon her rusting superstructure were the first to see the swift planes coming at wave top level and rose, wheeling in screeching protest.

The Corsairs and Hellcats climbed in a sinuous arc to mast top height and loosed salvo after salvo of deadly rockets, then curved away as the explosions whipsawed her brittle hull and opened her seams to the sea. She absorbed these rude blows as she had absorbed others during her long life. She began to tire noticeably and then settled in the sea like an old steamer down on her marks. She favored her port side and as she rolled further in that direction, her funnels touched the sea which flooded into her boilers and engine spaces. She lay on her side briefly as if to gain a second wind. But none came.

Then she rolled over on her back releasing geysers of trapped air through her ruined hull. A cry, half scream, half groan escaped her as boilers and engines, stressed now beyond reason, tore loose from their beds and crashed through her upper decks to the sea below taking her with them to a decent and honorable resting place in the deep blue sea of her home waters.

One moment she was there and the next she was gone leaving just a swirl on the surface of the sea and the fond memories of generations of Asiatic Fleet sailors who remembered their beloved "*Stew Maru*." She also left one of the gripping sea stories of the great Second World War of the Twentieth Century.

Chapter 20

Remaining Destroyers and Other Ships

THE remaining eight 4-pipe destroyers which had escaped from Java and arrived in Fremantle the first week in March 1942 needed repairs, rest and medical attention desperately. But the tender *Black Hawk* could only handle the emergency jobs necessary to make ships ready for sea. After about ten days the destroyers started convoy escort duties, first between Fremantle and Melbourne, then extending to Sydney, Brisbane and sometimes reversing those routes. Then increasingly they were convoy escorts to New Caledonia, the Fiji Islands, other outlying places.

Eventually they all reached Pearl Harbor. Like everyone else who saw the spectacle for the first time, the men of the four stackers were bug-eyed at the devastation along battleship row. But then they remembered the disasters which the Japanese had so recently inflicted on the Asiatic Fleet. Soon there were convoys back to continental U.S. and mercifully some naval shipyard availabilities for the tired, overworked, run down and broken down old World War I destroyers of the former Asiatic Fleet.

Some of the old ships wound up in the Mare Island, California Naval Shipyard as early as June 1942. But there were no brass bands, no cheering throngs, no welcoming committees. At Mare Island they never heard of the Asiatic Fleet. They didn't know about the terrible loss of ships sunk and the tragic loss of life. Such bad news coming so soon after the Pearl Harbor disaster was more than some officials in Washington thought the people of the country could bear. A postwar perusal of the New York Times and other leading newspapers of the day reveals a miasma of lies, propaganda, suppression of facts or downplaying of losses. It was always—we are winning but we have lost the Philippines—we are winning but we have lost most of our ships—we are winning but we have fallen back to Australia.

Granted that the men of the former Asiatic Fleet were back stateside after several years in the Far East and this was heady stuff for them. There was a natural tendency to relax and unwind after a grueling life or death struggle with the enemy in the early months of the war in the Dutch East Indies. Some of them may have been a bit wild to the extent of catching the attention of the local gendarmes. Sometimes there were "all points bulletins" to local police to watch out for those "bearded and weird Asiatic Fleet sailors." It was a tough readjustment time. It was also a reservoir of tough, trained and well-experienced men to form cadres of personnel for new construction ships.

At the U.S. naval shipyards four of the ships were converted to AGs—fleet auxiliary ships—*Whipple*, *Bulmer*, *John D. Ford* and *Paul Jones*. For the remainder of the war all the ships continued convoy escort and general auxiliary assignments. Suffice it to say, none of them were ever again committed to frontline combat roles and none ever again had contact with the enemy. At least one, *Parrott* operated for a time on the east coast. But in May 1944 she was rammed by a merchant ship in Norfolk, Virginia and had to be beached to avoid sinking. She was damaged beyond repair and was later sold for scrap.

Immediately after the war ended, *Alden*, *Barker* and *John D. Edwards* were stricken from the Navy Register and sold for scrap. The other four—those converted to AGs—were held on a while longer and later stricken from the Navy Register—*Bulmer* on 25 September, *John D. Ford* and *Paul Jones* on 16 and 25 November and *Whipple* on 5 December 1945. All were sold for scrap. Let it be said with pride that DD-224 ex-*Stewart* was the last and only one of the four stackers to find a decent resting place at sea off California.

The light cruiser *Phoenix* (CL-46) on which I had served the first two years of my commissioned service, did not tarry long in Fremantle after arriving in early March 1942. While she was cordially welcomed by the Australians, her presence was not at all appreciated by the surviving remnants of the Asiatic Fleet. Questions were being asked why she had not helped defend our ships being sunk up near Java and why she had not gone to rescue the hundreds of struggling men left to die in the rough water when *Pecos* was sunk. It is safe to write that it was not the fault of the ship but that of the staffs of the two different fleets under which the ships were operating.

After rejoining the Pacific Fleet *Phoenix* participated creditably in all the major campaigns of the war and earned numerous engagement stars. When war ended *Phoenix* was sold to Argentina, renamed *General Belgrano* and for a time was the pride of their Navy. But alas, during the Falklands War with Great Britain in 1982, *General Belgrano* was torpedoed by a Royal Navy nuclear-powered submarine and sunk with heavy loss of life.

USS *Gold Star* (AG-12)—In Fremantle in March 1942 when sailors and officers from the surviving ships went ashore and began to relax over a soothing libation, the talk inevitably turned to that old question "What ever happened to that cargo of good San Miguel beer and whiskey the supply ship *Gold Star* had in her holds?" To this day, some 60 plus years later, the same question is being asked when old Asiatic Fleet veterans have a reunion.

The most ingenious explanation is that the precious cargo was offloaded to a lighter-barge in Port Darwin which was then sunk and destroyed in the great enemy air raid of 19 February 1942. Others are skeptical and say that would be a perfect cover for a nefarious scheme to make off with the booze and set up a saloon somewhere. Some stoutly claim the San Miguel beer began appearing in a Port Darwin pub later that year. Others claim the whiskey started appearing in a Brisbane officers club that year. One thing is clear, the speculation will never cease and it will always be a good enough reason to order another round of drinks.

USS *Isabel* (PY-10)—Upon arrival of *Isabel* in the harbor of Fremantle, West Australia on 6 March 1942, the ship was allowed about two weeks for rest and repairs. Thereafter her job was escorting into the harbor U.S. submarines returning from war patrols. This was done at night. The reason—if they approached in the daytime they would always be attacked by the Australian Air Force. This pattern continued to war's end. Then she came home by short legs, hops and jumps to Mare Island shipyard where she was decommissioned. *Isabel* was scrapped in March 1946.

Appendix 1

Personae

LIEUTENANT Commander Harold Page Smith, commanding officer of USS *Stewart* (DD-224) during my time of service on board and at the time she was abandoned in Surabaya on 22 February 1942, was returned to the U.S. immediately afterwards. Upon return he was awarded the Navy Cross and required to join some other naval heroes in traipsing around the country appearing at recruiting rallies, sales of war bonds and other patriotic events. At that time the morale of the country was low so soon after Pearl Harbor, the sinking of the *Houston* and other losses. The nation needed some heroes. But he hated the assignment with a passion and thought it was foolish in the extreme. Later he related to me how he had pulled every string in the book to get out of that duty and finally did. I saw him again in late 1943 in Pearl Harbor as he was on his way back to the fighting as a destroyer squadron commander. In the late 1940's he was commanding officer of the battleship *Missouri* (BB-63) and left her just a few weeks before she grounded off Old Point Comfort, Virginia, to the embarrassment of the entire Navy. He had to go back on board and take command back from the new captain whose career was over.

Promoted to flag rank, he served as Chief of Naval Personnel and was proud that he had abolished the practice of officers allowed to retire at the next higher rank—resulting in a surfeit of "tombstone admirals." He went on to four star rank of admiral in his last assignment as Commander-in-Chief, Naval Forces Europe, Commander-in-Chief, Atlantic Fleet and Supreme Allied Commander Atlantic. Upon his retirement on 1 May 1965 he was requested to appear at the Pentagon to be awarded the Distinguished Service Medal by the Secretary of Defense Robert McNamara. He declined the honor and requested the medal be mailed to him. Later he was summoned to the White House and the medal was pinned on him by President Lyndon B. Johnson.

I last saw him in the summer of 1989 when he attended a reunion of the four-stack destroyers held in Virginia Beach, Virginia. He was as gracious and courteous as ever to everyone regardless of rank or rate. He was truly a great naval officer, a scholar and a gentleman. He was quite the finest officer I have ever known. He died on 4 January 1993 while tending the roses in his flower garden at his home in Virginia Beach. He was just short of his 89th birthday.

Commodore, then Commander Thomas Howell Binford, Commander of Destroyer Division 58, returned to the U.S. shortly after his escape from Java with four destroyers and arrival at Fremantle in early March 1942. He too was awarded the Navy Cross. I was never able to follow his career the remainder of the war and in postwar years. He retired in August 1954 in the rank of vice admiral and died in August 1973.

Lieutenant Clare B. Smiley, executive officer of the *Stewart* in the Battle of Badoeng Strait during which he was wounded, was returned to the U.S. as a patient soon after he was brought out of Java by Lieutenant Francis Clark, engineering officer of *Stewart*. Lt. Smiley was awarded the Bronze Star but I was not able to follow his career before he retired in May 1953 in the rank of rear admiral. He died in 1983.

Lieutenant Archibald Stone, Jr. was torpedo/communications officer of *Stewart* during Battle of Badoeng Strait and at her abandonment on 22 February 1942. He escaped from Surabaya on board *Parrott* and was later transferred to *Pecos*. He went down with that ship when she was attacked by enemy planes and sunk on 1 March 1942. He was awarded the Silver Star, posthumously.

Lieutenant Francis Edward Clark, was engineer officer of *Stewart* at time of her abandonment. A few days later made a valiant effort to destroy the ship but with limited success. He then escaped to West Australia with his demolition crew on board a tramp steamer bringing out with him some patients and stragglers. He remained in the Southwest Pacific during the war after which I lost track. He retired in July 1960 in the rank of commander, earlier than his class of 1937 would normally hang up their suits. He then went into the merchant marine for several years. I saw him just once since March 1942 and that was at the 1989 four stacker reunion in Virginia Beach. I often wondered if he had been called on the carpet and disciplined in some way when it was found the enemy had raised, repaired and put ex-*Stewart* in their service as Patrol Boat 102. But somehow I never thought it politic to ask. He died in 1996.

Ensign John Thomas Brinkley, with whom I shared a stateroom on board *Stewart*, escaped from Java on the *Parrott* and is believed to have transferred to a submarine at Fremantle. He was reported to have ended the war as a lieutenant commander on board USS *Billfish*. Since then efforts to find him have failed.

Master Chief Signalman William E. Kale, general quarters helmsman on *Stewart*, is retired and living in Ohio. His journal kept during the early months of the war is a magnificent testament to the spirit, morale and competence of the men below decks. In recent years he completed the monumental task of accounting for all men of *Stewart*—whether killed on board, transferred to other ships and killed and those who survived the war. Since 1990 he has kept track of those still living and their whereabouts. He was a worthy shipmate.

Lieutenant Commander Floyd Bruce Garrett, classmate at the Naval Academy with whom I had traveled to the Far East in the fall of 1940 and assigned to the four stack destroyer *John D. Edwards*, eventually returned to the U.S. on board that ship in the summer of 1942. On his promotion to two and a half stripes he was assigned to his first command as captain of the *Farragut* class destroyer USS *Monaghan* (DD-354). Scarcely a week had passed when he went down with his ship as she capsized in a monstrous typhoon while operating with the Third Fleet. There were only six survivors. It was a strange turn of events and circumstances that he had survived the onslaught of the Japanese in the Dutch East Indies only to perish in unmerciful wind and waves of a typhoon. Our classmate Captain Charles Raymond Calhoun has written a gripping account of the loss of *Monaghan* and two other destroyers in his scholarly book: *Typhoon: The Other Enemy*.

Crewman Lloyd Charles McKenzie, who wrote interesting letters home while he was serving on board *Stewart*, was returned to the U.S. before the war when he had completed his time in the Far East. Subsequently he went into submarines and during the war served on board USS *Triton* (SS-201) for five successful war patrols. On the sixth war patrol *Triton* went down with the loss of all hands on 15 March 1943 southwest of Rabaul when depth-charged by three Japanese destroyers. Torpedoman First Class Lloyd C. McKenzie left a grieving widow with two little daughters and grieving parents. He was truly one of the finest type of Americans ever to have served in the United States Navy.

Lieutenant John Walker Payne, Jr. who was captain of the *Isabel* on which I escaped from Java to Australia in March 1942, was returned to the U.S. soon after arrival in Fremantle. Subsequently he took command of the presidential yacht *Potomac*. He retired in June 1950 in the rank of commander and was killed on 30 June 1956 when the plane on which he was a passenger crashed into the Grand Canyon, Arizona.

Lieutenant Marion Hugo Buaas, classmate and executive officer of *Isabel* during my time on board, returned to the U.S. in 1943 and went into aviation (lighter-than-air). Subsequently he returned to surface ships and had a distinguished career in destroyers. Retiring on 1 July 1968 as a captain, he worked for several years in defense industries. Captain Buaas died in 1999.

Lieutenant Harold S. Hamlin, classmate who was turret one officer on board *Houston* during the Battle of the Java Sea and the Battle of Sunda Strait in which the ship was overwhelmed and sunk with heavy loss of life including Captain A.H. Rooks. Hal Hamlin survived and spent the rest of the war as a POW building railroads on the island of Taiwan/Formosa. At war's end he returned to active duty and retired in 1961 in the rank of captain. Awarded the Bronze Star for his magnificent performance of duty in combat on board *Houston*. We spent many hours discussing our time in the Asiatic Fleet. He died in 1978.

Lieutenant William O. Spears, classmate and torpedo officer of *Pope* during the Battle of Balikpapan, the Battle of Badoeng Strait and the second day of the Battle of the Java Sea, in which *Pope* was sunk. He survived and spent the rest of the war as POW on the island of Celebes. At war's end he too returned to active duty and retired in 1968 in the rank of captain. He was awarded several Bronze Stars for his performance in combat on board *Pope*. We also spent many hours talking about our experiences in four stack destroyers of the Asiatic Fleet. Bill Spears died 1995.

The author returned from the Far East in January 1943. Next was service on USS *Mobile* (CL-63) in Gilberts/Tarawa, Marshalls and the Solomons Campaigns. Then came service on USS *Bennington* (CV-20) in the Iwo Jima and Okinawa Campaigns. Postwar service was primarily in destroyers including command of USS *Renshaw* (DDE-499) during the Korean War. Retirement was in 1967 in the rank of captain. Thrice awarded the Bronze Star Medal with combat "V" device authorized for service in *Stewart*, *Isabel*, *Bennington* and *Renshaw*. Commendation Medal with Combat V for service in *Mobile*.

Appendix 2

Recognitions, Decorations and Awards

ONE of the more disturbing aspects of the rapid and resounding defeat of the Asiatic Fleet in the first three months of the war in the Far East, was the number of officers and men whose courage, devotion to duty and sacrifices were sometimes not recognized. Or if they were recognized the awards were inadequate and not commensurate with awards made in other theaters and sometimes with those made in the Asiatic Fleet. Up to that time there does not seem to have been a clear understanding of guidelines, standards or criteria for the various levels of awards and decorations. As the war progressed criteria were developed and standards evolved. This was particularly true in the submarine service. And whether it was true or not, there was the perception in the Navy that the U.S. Army Air Force was handing out decorations like popcorn.

In all the wars of the United States there emerged in the Asiatic Fleet in the early months of World War II a naval hero of such stature, courage, devotion to duty and sacrifice that his performance has not and never will be surpassed.

That was Captain A. H. Rooks of the *Houston*, who went down with his ship fighting to the last, and was awarded posthumously the Congressional Medal of Honor. But Captain John M. Bermingham of the *Peary*, who went down with his ship fighting to the last, was not so honored. *Peary* was sunk on 19 February and *Houston* on the night of 28 February. The two ships had been operating together. The Naval Academy Register shows Lieutenant Commander Bermingham was awarded the Navy Cross but it is understood this was for bringing his ship out of Manila Bay to Port Darwin under very hazardous conditions. Clearly his death in mortal combat lifts his heroism, courage and devotion to the Medal of Honor category.

Lieutenant Archibald Stone, formerly of *Stewart*, was reassigned to *Pecos* and went down to his death in that ship. He is shown in the Alumni Register as having been awarded the Silver Star. But it is understood he was recommended for that award by Captain Smith of *Stewart* for his performance of duty during the Battle of Badoeng Strait and for disposition of classified material when *Stewart* had to be abandoned. On the *Pecos*, he was assigned to an anti-aircraft gun crew and kept his gun firing as the ship sank. He was last seen at his gun, wounded, face bleeding, one ear partially shot off and shaking his fist at the enemy planes. Clearly his death in mortal combat lifts him to a Medal of Honor.

Chief Machinist's Mate Paul R. Seifert, who was acting engineer officer of *Stewart* during the Battle of Badoeng Strait, was awarded the Silver Star for his performance in the battle. But upon abandonment of the *Stewart* he was reassigned to the USS *Pillsbury* and went down to his death on that ship when she was lost with all hands on 2 March 1942. Clearly his courage, heroism and sacrifice unto death lifts him to Medal of Honor category.

I have written letter after letter to the Secretary of Defense, the Secretary of the Navy, The Chief of Naval Operations and the Vice Chief of Naval Operations to take action for correction of these inequities. Invariably these gentlemen have delegated their authority to subordinates, who however well-meaning, just do not seem to understand what is at stake here. Follow-up letters have been stonewalled or unanswered. Meanwhile records of black soldiers in World War II have been re-examined and several Medals of Honor awarded, no doubt well-deserved. But not more so than those mentioned above.

I have also written the Secretary of Defense and the Secretary of the Navy to consider the Congressional Medal of Honor for the captains of the *Asheville*, *Edsall* and *Pillsbury*, all three of which went down to their deaths in their ships sunk in the Indian Ocean with loss of all hands. Indeed, the Alumni Register does not show an award of any kind for Lieutenant Commander J.W. Britt, captain of the *Asheville*. If this is true, it is an outrage and should be corrected.

These inequities have rankled with me for over fifty-five years and I hope that readers will join me in urging that amends be made to the surviving families of these naval heroes.

Appendix 3

Ship's Company Personnel of USS *Stewart* (DD-224) at Time of Battle of Badoeng Strait, 20 February, and Abandonment, 22 February 1942

Officers

BINFORD, Thomas H., Commander, ComDesDiv 58, survived the war.
SMITH, Harold P., Lieutenant Commander, Captain, survived the war.
SMILEY, Clare B., Lieutenant, executive officer, survived the war.
STONE, Archibald, Lieutenant, torpedo officer, transferred to *Pecos*, killed in action.
CLARK, Francis E., Lieutenant, engineer officer, survived the war.
   ALFORD, Lodwick H., Lieutenant (jg), gunnery officer, survived the war.
BRINKLEY, John T., Ensign, First Lieutenant, survived the war.
   HARRIS, William H., Asst. Comm. officer, transferred to *Asheville*, killed in action.

Enlisted Personnel

ALLISON, Frederick, CFC, survived the war.
ARNOLD, Max, EM2/c, transferred to *Pillsbury*, killed in action.
BARWICK, John, CCS, survived sinking of *Pecos*.
BAUTISTA, Rafael, CCK, survived the war.
BECKEL, Henry, TM2/c, survived the war.
BENNETT, James, BM2/c, survived the war.
BERRY, Frank, TM1/C, transferred to *Pillsbury*, killed in action.
BITOON, Bernardo, OK1/c, survived the war.
BRODIE, James, CMM(PA), survived the war.
BURNS, Grady, MM1/c, survived the war.

CATU, Francisco, OSt, survived the war.
COSGROVE, Thomas, RM2/c, survived the war.
GOTTEN, Gerod, MM2/c, transferred to *Pillsbury*, killed in action.
CRIST, Clark, TM2/c, survived the war.
CUSHMAN, Lawrence, SM1/c, transferred to *Pillsbury*, killed in action.
DIERKENS, Herman, S1/c, survived the war.
DISPO, Isabelo, St2/c, survived the war.
DOVE, Frank, S1/c, survived sinking of *Pecos*.
DOWLING, John, WT1/c, survived sinking of *Pecos*.
DROY, Peter, BM1/c, transferred to *Pillsbury*, killed in action.
ELLSWORTH, Marion, RM1/c, survived the war.
ELLZEY, Luther, QM3/c, transferred to *Pillsbury*, killed in action.
FALLUCCA, Joseph, S2/c, survived sinking of *Pope*, survived as POW.
FETERLY, Allen, S1/c, survived the war.
FISHER, Thomas, S1/c, survived the war.
FRANKOFF, Walter, CCS, survived the war.
FOWLER, Vernon, GM3/c, survived the war.
FLYNN, Carl, WT2/c, transferred to *Pecos*, killed in action.
FRONDORF, Victor, CRM, survived the war.
GABEL, Andrew, WT1/c, survived the war.
GIBSON, Alvin, MM1/c, survived the war.
GILCHRIST, Charles, CGM, survived the war.
GOOSBY, Malcolm, COX, survived sinking of *Pecos*.
GRINSTEAD, Ray, F1/c, transferred to *Pecos*, killed in action.
GROTHE, Henry, GM1/c, survived the war.
GUND, Paul, F1/c, transferred to *Pecos*, killed in action.
HANSON, Harlan, BM2/c, survived the war.
HAPTONSTALL, Basil, BM2/c, survived sinking of *Pecos*.
HARPER, Arthur, SM3/c, survived the war.
HAWKINS, James, QM1/c, survived the war.
HAZEN, William, S1/c, transferred to *Pillsbury*, killed in action.
HEBERT, Michael, SCK, survived the war.
HENDERSON, Howard, GM3/c, transferred to *Pillsbury*, killed in action.
HENDRY, Malone, CWT, survived the war.
HENRY, Herman, COX, survived the war.
HESTER, William, CMM, survived the war.
HIATT, William, S1/c, transferred to *Pillsbury*, killed in action.
HILLHOUSE, William, CMM, survived the war.

HIXON, Guy, Y3/c, survived the war.
HORNE, George, CMM, survived the war.
HOWARD, Bennie, RM1/c, survived the war.
HOWARD, Donald, SC1/c, survived the war.
JONES, Thomas, GM1/c, transferred to *Pillsbury*, killed in action.
KALE, William E., SM2/c, survived the war.
KAUFFMAN, Carlton, WT2/c, survived the war.
KAUSING, Primo, CMM, survived sinking of *Pecos*.
KINSELLA, John, CTM, survived the war.
KOLB, Harmon, CMM, survived sinking of *Pecos*.
KUSACK, Joseph, CSM, survived the war.
LAURIDSEN, Wilbur, PM3/c, transferred to *Pillsbury*, killed in action.
LAYL, Ralph, CBM, survived the war.
LEE, Wilson, MM1/c, transferred to *Pillsbury*, killed in action.
LEWIS, Ellis, WT2/c, survived the war.
LINDLY, James, CGM, survived the war.
LITTLE, Lewis, F1/c, survived the war.
MAHAN, Talmadge, RM3/c, survived the war.
MANION, John, S2/c, transferred to *Pillsbury*, killed in action.
MARCANTEL, Herschel, CMM, survived sinking of *Pecos*.
MARSH, Charlie, MM1/c, survived the war.
MARSHALL, Robert, TM3/c, transferred to *Pillsbury*, killed in action.
MARTIN, Richard, CMM, survived the war.
McCLUNE, Donald, CPHM, survived the war.
McDONALD, Clyde, CWT, survived the war.
MITCHELL, Paul, S1/c, transferred to *Pillsbury*, killed in action.
NELSON, Oscar, CWT(PA), survived the war.
NEUFFER, Howard, CCM, survived the war.
ORMILLA, Emiliano, OS3/c, transferred to *Pillsbury*, killed in action.
PAPA, Anello, F1/c, transferred to *Pillsbury*, killed in action.
PARKIN, John, CWT, survived the war.
PEPPERS, Robert, SM2/c, survived the war.
PIENCIAK, John, F1/c, transferred to *Pillsbury*, killed in action.
PIERCE, Edward, BM1/c, transferred to *Pecos*, killed in action.
PIERCE, Jack, WT2/c, survived the war.
POLZKILL, Bernard, WT2/c, survived the war.
QUAGLIATO, Frank, MM2/c, survived the war.
RAICHEL, Walter, SF1/c, survived the war.
RATHBUN, Robert, BM2/c, survived the war.

RAYNER, John, QM3/c, transferred to *Edsall*, killed in action.
RICE, Harold, RM3/c, died in Dutch hospital, Surabaya.
RICE, Vernon S1/c, transferred to *Pillsbury*, killed in action.
REIDELER, Burley, WT1/c, survived sinking of *Pecos*.
RICHARDSON, Donald, F1/c, survived the war.
RICKS, Troy, CWT, survived the war.
ROBBINS, William, CEM, survived sinking of *Pecos*.
ROSE, Clarence, CY, survived the war.
RUGGLES, Carl, WT2/c, survived sinking of *Pecos*.
RUTHOSKY, Charles, F2/c, survived the war.
RYAN, David, CTM, transferred to *Edsall*, killed in action.
SALES, Pershing, GM1/c, survived the war.
SATTERFIELD, Richard, F2/c, transfer to *Pillsbury*, killed in action.
SCHEEL, William, CRM, survived the war.
SCHUMANN, John, CCM, survived the war.
SEIFERT, Paul, CMM(PA), transferred to *Pillsbury*, killed in action.
SETTEM, John, CMM, survived the war.
SHAW, Jack, SK2/c, survived the war.
SHOWS, J.B., WT1/c, survived the war.
SHOWS, W.H., GM2/c, survived the war.
SIMS, Norman, SC2/c, transferred to *Pillsbury*, killed in action.
SMITH, Gilbert, Y1/c, survived the war.
SMITH, Leroy, CMM, survived sinking of *Pecos*.
SMITH, Robert, MM2/c, survived the war.
SNAPP, William, SM3/c, transferred to *Pillsbury*, killed in action.
SNIDER, George, CBM, survived the war.
SNOW, Irvine, SF2/c, transferred to *Pillsbury*, killed in action.
SOKACZ, John, CMM, transferred to *Pillsbury*, killed in action.
STANGE, Robert, GM1/c, survived the war.
STANLEY, Eugene, S2/c, killed in action on *Stewart*, 20 February 1942.
STARUSKTA, Jerry, S1/c, survived the war.
STETTLER, Robert, S2/c, transferred to *Pillsbury*, killed in action.
STEWART, John, GM1/c, survived the war.
STOUT, Daryl, WT1/c, survived the war.
SULLIVAN, Michael, BM2/c, survived the war.
SWETT, Robert, CMM, survived sinking of *Pecos*.
SWENSON, Carl, BM2/c, survived sinking of *Pecos*.
SWORDS, Richard, MM1/c, survived the war.
TAYLOR, Hugh, S2/c, transferred to *Pecos*, killed in action.

THOMAS, Charley, S1/c, survived sinking of *Houston*, survived as POW.
THORSON, Harold, MM1/c, transferred to *Pecos*, killed in action.
TIMBROOK, Kenneth, GM2/c, survived sinking of *Pecos*.
TUNIS, Glen, GM3/c, transferred to *Pillsbury*, killed in action.
VON HOLDT, George, Baker2/c, survived the war.
WEAVER, Herbert, WT1/c, transferred to *Pecos*, killed in action.
WESTFALL, Ellsworth, CTM, survived the war.
WHITEHEAD, Frederick, EM3/c, survived the war.
WILSON, Woodrow, COX, survived the war.
WOOD, Harry, MM1/c, transferred to *Pillsbury*, killed in action.
WRIGHT, Edsel, S1/c, survived the war.

Bibliography

PRIMARY SOURCES

Official U.S. Navy Reports

Bermingham, J.M. Lieutenant Commander, Commanding Officer, USS *Peary* (DD-226). "Engagements with the Enemy."

Catlett, W.J., Lieutenant, Survivor USS *Peary* (DD-226). "Sinking of the USS *Peary*."

Clark, F.E., Lieutenant. "Report of Destruction of USS *Stewart*, 12 March 1942."

Coley, L.E., Lieutenant Commander, Commanding Officer, USS *Alden* (DD-211). "Battle of the Java Sea, 27 February 1942."

Eccles, H.E., Lieutenant Commander, Commanding Officer, USS *John D. Edwards* (DD-216). "Java Sea Battle, 27 February 1942."

Navy Department Publication to Surviving Crew Members of USS *Stewart* (DD-224), 15 March 1946.

Official Log Books

USS *Stewart* (DD-224), 12/1/41 to 2/22/42.

Parker, E.N., Lieutenant Commander, ComDesDiv 59. "Action Between ABDA and Japanese Forces on 27 February 1942."

Payne, J.W., Lieutenant, Commanding Officer, USS *Isabel* (PY-10). "Activities of USS *Isabel*, 3 December 1941 to 7 March 1942."

Smith, H.P., Lieutenant Commander, Commanding Officer, USS *Stewart* (DD-224). "Report of Naval Engagement between DesDiv 58 and Japanese Forces in Badoeng Strait, 20 February 1942."

—. "Report of Drydocking Casualty and Final Abandonment of USS *Stewart* (DD-224), 23 February 1942."

Unofficial Articles, Diaries, Journals, Logs

Alford, L.H., Lieutenant (jg), Gunnery Officer, USS *Stewart* (DD-224). Journal 1/1/42 to 3/16/42.

Buaas, M.H., Lieutenant (jg), Executive Officer, USS *Isabel* (PY-10). "Personal Diary, Period 29 November 1941 to 7 March 1942."

Clark, F.E., Lieutenant, Engineer Officer, USS *Stewart* (DD-224). "Personal Diary between 9 December 1941 and 8 January 1942."
Kale, W.E., Signalman 2/c, USS *Stewart* (DD-224). "Personal Log Between 8 December 1941 and 23 February 1942."
Klar, J.W. "Operational History of USS *Stewart* (DD-224)." *Warship International*, 1989 No. 2.
—. "USS DD-224 (ex-*Stewart*): The Voyage Home." *Warship International*, 1990, No. l.
Layl, R., Seaman 1/c, USS *Stewart* (DD-224). Letter 17 March 1999.
Platt, R.F. "Calendar Log" (Daily Locations, Asiatic Fleet ships).
Saqqal, G. "An Embarrassing About-Face: U.S. Destroyer in Imperial Japanese Navy."

Interviews

Bermingham, J.M., Lieutenant Commander, Commanding Officer, USS *Peary* (DD-226). 6 January 1942.
Binford, T.H., Commander, ComDesDiv 58, USS *Stewart* (DD-224). Daily until 22 February 1942. Last time 7 March 1942.
Buaas, M.H., Lieutenant (jg), Executive Officer, USS *Isabel* (PY-10). Daily, 25 February to 18 August 1942. Frequently for 57 years.
Clark, F.E., Lieutenant, Engineer Officer, USS *Stewart* (DD-224). Daily to 22 February 1942. Last time, 1989.
Fischer, H.P., Lieutenant (jg), Engineer Officer, USS *Pillsbury* (DD-227). 22 February 1942.
Garrett, F.B., Lieutenant (jg), First Lieutenant, USS *John D. Edwards* (DD-216). 7 March 1942.
Hamlin, H.S., Lieutenant (jg), Turret 1 Officer, USS *Houston* (CA-30). 2 January 1942. Postwar to 1961.
Parker, E.N., Vice Admiral (former ComDesDiv 59). 1989 interview.
Rockwell, F.W., Vice Admiral (former Commandant 16th Naval District). Postwar until 1979.
Smith, H.P., Admiral (former CINCEUR and CINCLANTFLT). To 1989.
Spears, W.O., Lieutenant (jg), Torpedo Officer, USS *Pope* (DD-225). 22 February 1942 and frequently until death in 1995.

SECONDARY SOURCES

Books

Alden, J.D. *Flush Decks and Four Pipes*. Annapolis: Naval Institute Press, 1965.

Naval History Division. *Dictionary of American Naval Fighting Ships*. Washington, D.C.: Department of the Navy, 1968.

Dull, P.S. *A Battle History of the Imperial Japanese Navy, 1941-45*.

Layton, E.T. *And I Was There*. New York: Quill, 1985

Leutze, J. *A Different Kind of Victory*. Annapolis: Naval Institute Press, 1981.

Messimer, D.R. *Pawns of War*. Annapolis: Naval Institute Press, 1983.

—. *In the Hands of Fate*. Annapolis: Naval Institute Press, 1985.

Morison, S.E. *History of U.S. Naval Operations in World War II*.

Mullin, J.D. *Another Six Hundred*. Privately published.

Van Oosten, F.C. *The Battle of the Java Sea*. Annapolis: Naval Institute Press, 1976.

Rohwer, J. and G. Hummelchen. *Chronology of the War at Sea, 1939-45*. New York: Arco Publishing Company.

Roscoe, T. *U.S. Destroyer Operations in World War II*. Annapolis: Naval Institute Press, 1953.

Stinnett, Robert B. *Day of Deceit: The Truth About FDR and Pearl Harbor*. New York: The Free Press, 1999.

Winslow, W.G. *The Fleet the Gods Forgot*. Annapolis: Naval Institute Press, 1982.

—. *The Ghost That Died at Sunda Strait*. Annapolis: Naval Institute Press, 1984.

Brief Biography of Lodwick H. Alford

ENTERED the Navy from Georgia in 1932 and graduated from the U.S. Naval Academy with the class of 1938. Served in battleships, cruisers, aircraft carriers and auxiliary craft. Early in career specialized in gunnery, later in personnel management and command of U.S. Navy ships. With the Asiatic Fleet early in the great war and remainder of the conflict in a cruiser and aircraft carrier of Pacific Fleet.

In senior ranks commanded a Fletcher class destroyer in the Korean War, a division of four destroyers in the Atlantic Fleet, a squadron of eight destroyers in the Sixth Fleet and 18,000-ton destroyer tender in the Atlantic Fleet. Thrice awarded the Bronze Star Medal and Commendation Medal all for service in combat. Retired 1967 in the rank of captain with 35 years service.

Numerous articles published in quarterlies, monthly and weekly publications, naval, historical, genealogical, alumni and church magazines. Published 300 page family history. BS, U.S. Naval Academy MA, George Washington University Diploma, American University—Masters Equivalent Diploma, U.S. Naval War College Diploma, U.S. National War College.

Made in the USA
San Bernardino, CA
24 November 2013